THE COMPLETE GUIDE TO
JAPANESE DRINKS

SAKE, SHOCHU, JAPANESE WHISKY, BEER, WINE, COCKTAILS AND OTHER BEVERAGES

STEPHEN LYMAN and CHRIS BUNTING

TUTTLE Publishing

Tokyo | Rutland, Vermont | Singapore

Contents

Preface

by Chris Bunting

Why are an Englishman and an American writing a book about Japanese alcohol traditions? Probably for the same reason that Lafcadio Hearn (aka Koizumi Yakumo), an Irishman born in Greece who lived in Chicago, was first to write down the oral traditions of Japanese fables. Westerners have been curious about Japan since we first encountered this inscrutable island whose fully formed civil society had developed completely without Western influences.

My previous book, *Drinking Japan,* was written on the premise that Japan is the best place to drink alcohol in the world; I spent nearly 300 pages making that case, complete with bar recommendations. *Drinking Japan* was published just 30 days after the Tohoku earthquake, tsunami and nuclear disaster had taken nearly 20,000 lives on the eastern coast of Honshu, Japan's main island, and we donated a portion of the proceeds from the book to disaster relief. The disaster hurt the nation badly: international tourism to Japan declined by nearly 30 percent that year.

Drinking Japan gained a worldwide readership. I started to receive Twitter messages and emails from one Stephen Lyman, a New Yorker who was fast becoming one of the foremost Western experts on traditional Japanese shochu and Okinawan awamori. He was pestering me for an update to the guide, and while I agreed that one was needed, the world had changed. And I had, as well: shortly after the publication of *Drinking Japan*, I found myself back in the UK with my family, no longer a denizen of Tokyo's drinking districts. Not easily dissuaded, Stephen continued to correspond with me periodically for several years before we hit on the idea of doing a new drinks guide together. This entire collaboration has occurred online—we met in person just once, for about 24 hours in the spring of 2018, when Stephen visited me in the north of England for food, drink and conversation.

In creating this book, we decided that, rather than guide readers through drinking establishments in Japan, we'd guide them through Japanese alcohol traditions and leave it to them where they'd like to drink. As such, the premise of the volume you hold in your hands is, "You don't need to go to Japan to enjoy Japan's incredible drinking culture." *Japanese Drinks* is the result. We hope you enjoy this book as much as we enjoyed writing it.

Kanpai!
Chris Bunting
Ilkley, United Kingdom

Front endpaper Hibiya Bar Whisky-S, Tokyo, see page 143. **Page 1** Woodblock print of woman drinking sake, by Kitagawa Utamaro, c. 1802. **Page 2** Customer and bartender in Tokyo sake bar Akaboshi to Kumagai, see page 134. **Pages 4–5** Bottles of Awamori from Okinawa. Note the prominent use of "soju" on the label. This misnomer causes no shortage of confusion among American drinkers (see page 51). **Left** A shochu brewer at work.

JAPAN'S RICH DRINKING CULTURE

In nearly every major city in the world you can now find some of the finest examples of Japanese sake, whisky, beer, umeshu plum liqueur, shochu and awamori; occasionally you'll even stumble upon some surprisingly good Japanese wine. You're also very likely to find a cocktail bar staffed by talented Japanese bartenders serving cocktails that have been very much influenced by Japan's emergence as one of the finest cocktail cultures in the world.

Since the average Japanese restaurant overseas may carry only a few kinds of sake, one or two brands of shochu or umeshu, and some mass-produced Japanese beer, it may be hard to conceive that there are more than 2,000 active breweries and distilleries producing more than 20,000 unique products in a country whose land area is roughly equivalent to Germany in the European Union, or Montana in the United States. Since even most Americans don't know how big Montana is, Japan is equivalent to roughly 4 percent of the US inland area and 40 percent in population (its population is just 25 percent of the EU's). It's also difficult to imagine that Japan's alcohol traditions go back more than 2,000 years. Around that time in the world's history, Confucius was philosophizing in China, Buddhism was growing in India, Pythagoras was working on a theorem, Athens and Sparta were fighting, written language was emerging in ancient American civilizations, and London consisted of a few huts surrounded by a mud wall along the banks of a river that would one day be called the Thames.

To say that alcohol traditions in Japan are deep and broad would be an exercise in understatement. While this book roughly divides Japanese alcohol traditions into *washu* (Japanese alcohols) and *yoshu* (Japanese interpretations of foreign alcohol), the simple fact is that all Japanese alcohol could correctly be classified as yoshu. Whether Japan has made the tradition completely its own or whether it's still considered borrowed is just a matter of recency. Fermented rice-based alcohol existed in China and India for as long as 2,000 years before it arrived in Japan. Distilled spirits in China and Thailand predate Japanese distilling traditions by at least hundreds of years; the earliest verified uses of distillation for producing drinking spirits date back to the 10th century in northern Italy. Yet Japanese shochu and Okinawan awamori are so distinct from their Thai, Korean and Chinese spirit cousins as to be unrecognizable in their heritage. On the other hand, the production of whisky, beer and wine in Japan all follow the opening of the country after Commodore Matthew Perry sailed his black ships into Tokyo Bay on July 8, 1853.

History of Alcohol in Japan

The history of alcohol in Japan is inseparable from the history of Japan. The Japanese seem to have been enthusiastic about their alcohol from the earliest times. Rice cultivation in Japan is now believed to have begun more than 3,000 years ago in Kyushu, the island closest to China, where wetland rice cultivation was first developed. Sake-brewing, albeit in a very rustic form, began shortly thereafter. The first written record of Japanese drinking is actually found in China. *The History of the Kingdom of Wei*, written in 297 AD,

of one notoriously penniless drunkard ask, "How much did you drink?" he replies, "Half a pound."

In the countryside, peasants were more proactive. The *Zohyo Monogatari*, a sort of management manual for samurai officers published in the mid to late 1600s, advises against giving too much food to the lowest rank of soldiers drawn from the peasantry. "You can give rice enough for three or four days, but no more than five days. If you give ten days' worth of rice they will put eight or nine days' worth into making sake. If you let that happen, they will starve and die," the guide advises. "With three or four days' worth of rice, they will still make their unrefined sake but they will not starve."

reported that the Japanese were fond of their alcohol. At funerals, the Chinese observer wrote, "The head mourners wail and lament, while friends sing, dance and drink liquor."

In the oldest Japanese chronicles, the *Kojiki* (712 AD) and the *Nihon shoki* (720 AD), there are drinking songs, stories of intoxicated emperors ("'I am drunk with the soothing liquor, with the smiling liquor,' he sang") and several bloodthirsty tales of getting the better of opponents with alcohol. In fact, if the chronicles are to be believed, serving sake to unsuspecting foes and then skewering them was a very popular ruse. The emperor's men get a group of enemies drunk only to crack their heads with mallets; the imperial commander sings as his warriors bludgeon the tipsy renegades. In another tale, an eight-headed serpent meets his end after getting plastered on eight buckets of sake.

Ordinary Japanese people also seemed to have acquired their taste for alcohol early, even though officially sanctioned sake was far too expensive for ordinary people to drink, and home brewing was largely prohibited. Despite this, there is plenty of evidence of a popular drinking culture especially in urban centers. Some working-class consumption in these towns hung on the coattails of the sake industry. Poor housewives would offer to wash the bags used in sake-making so they could squeeze a weak brew for their families. A genre of jokes from the Edo period (1603–1868) centers on eating alcoholic sake lees (leftover solids)—when the friends

In the villages themselves, a cat-and-mouse game with the authorities over the production and use of rice for illicit purposes led to the rise of regional dialects throughout Japan. These allowed locals to speak freely of their hidden rice and home brewing without fear of being caught by Kyoto or Edo tax collectors who might overhear their conversations. This illegal activity continued well into the 20th century. One old woman interviewed in *Noka ga oshieru doburoku no tsukurikata* (Farmers teach how to make unrefined sake), a wonderful little book published in 2007 about the Japanese home-brewing scene, said she still brewed late at night because of memories of police raids from her childhood. The Japanese sake writer Hisao Nagayama recalled that, in his own village in the 1950s, farmers would ring bells, blow conchs, and clang pots if any official-looking stranger came into the area. At that time some 40,000 people were being arrested for illegal brewing every year. Nagayama's parents kept their home brew in the ceiling above the toilet because the latrine's stench disguised the smell of alcohol from prying noses.

If there is a theme running through Japanese alcohol history, it is the people's endless inventiveness when it comes to obtaining drink. The established view is that Japanese alcohol culture begins and ends with the fermented rice drink called sake, but the rural brewers interviewed by the

Facing page Woodblock print by Toyohara Chikanobu (1838–1912) shows legendary 8-headed serpent Yamata-no-Orochi facing his demise at the hands of Shinto storm god Susanoo, who lured the serpent with sake (notice the head bottom center still drinking). **Above** Warm sake is served to a passing laborer in a bygone era. **Right** A foreigner is plied with sake after Japan opens to overseas trade.

authors of *Noka ga oshieru doburoku no tsukurikata* reveal recipes using just about any ingredient that came to hand. In fact, more obscure ingredients may have been easier to use than the heavily taxed and regulated rice. One 91-year-old, for instance, recalled a recipe for making wine brewed from wild mountain grapes. Other villages used other fruits, millet, corn or sweet potatoes.

Despite its popularity—or perhaps because of it—there were innumerable attempts to suppress alcohol consumption in Japan. Buddhism, one of Japan's two main religions, takes a far less enthusiastic view of liquor than Catholicism and many other religions. There were imperial decrees against alcohol in 722, 732, 737, 758 and 770 AD, and similar proclamations occurred regularly throughout the succeeding centuries. Still, normal Japanese people consistently ignored or side-stepped these regulations, tending more toward a philosophy of life encapsulated by the eighth-century poet Otomo no Tabito: "Rather be a pot of sake than a human being."

The last concerted effort to rein in the Japanese penchant for drinking occurred at the height of the Prohibition era in the United States. A few voices in Japan hesitantly suggested that their country should impose a similar ban. Japan had

been assiduously copying its neighbor across the Pacific since the Meiji reforms of the late 19th century. Perhaps the next enlightened thing to do was to follow America in outlawing alcohol?

The opposition was immediate and vociferous. The *Japan Chronicle*, a leading English-language newspaper at the time, reported people driving around cities throwing pro-alcohol leaflets onto the streets. The propagandists claimed that there was no example of an advanced civilization that had not embraced alcohol. Booze was essential for progress! Of course, the claim was false, but it is a measure of alcohol's place in Japanese culture that its proponents were considered mainstream while the prohibitionists were widely dismissed as extremists. The idea of a ban never really got off the ground. A law was introduced in 1922 forbidding children from drinking, and 17 villages nationwide went "dry," but the rest of Japan spent the Prohibition era picking the bones of America's alcohol industry, shipping over secondhand equipment from defunct US firms to help build its fledgling beer and wine industries.

This pervasive view of alcohol as beneficial is perhaps best reflected by the Japanese Shinto religion, in which alcohol

Left The father of Japanese bartending, Tatsuro Yamazaki (1920–2016), trained hundreds of bartenders during his career and almost single-handedly professionalized the bar industry after World War II.
Below Young women preparing to visit a shrine in traditional dress in front of sake barrels donated to the gods.
Facing page, top The Japanese celebrate cherry blossom season with enthusiastic drinking.
Facing page, bottom *Toso* (herbed sake) is served at a rural Buddhist temple in Oita prefecture at New Year's.

autumn, full-moon viewing parties are alcohol-soaked; the New Year celebrations are incomplete in many families without *toso*, a herb-infused sake thought to guarantee health in the coming year. In fact, even today in rural Japan it is fairly common for a family to drive (with a designated driver, of course) around to local shrines and temples to ring in the new year, giving thanks to the gods and then sampling the offered hot sake and toso late into the night before returning home for mochi rice cakes and soba noodles—traditional New Year's foods thought to bring long life and wellness (they also happen to be a nice way to soak up the evening's accumulated alcohol).

The details of these traditions vary widely from region to region, but a common feature is that the consumption of alcohol often seems to be as important as the excuse for it. The American scholars Robert Smith and Ella Wiswell, in their book *The Women of Suye Mura*, describing 1930s rural society in Suye village, Kumamoto prefecture, quoted a Mrs. Toyama, who organized a cherry-blossom viewing party: "It is called *hanami* (flower viewing), but, since the cherry blossoms are gone, we'll look at the violets in the fields instead."

Smith and Wiswell were astonished by the Bacchanalian energy of the Japanese farmers they studied. "The people of Suye were always ready for a party, and one cannot but be impressed by their seemingly limitless capacity to find occasions for them. Most parties, whether attended by both women and men, or by men or women only, involved

consumption is incorporated at almost every turn. The most sacred part of a Shinto wedding is the *san-san-ku-do*, in which the couple ceremonially drinks alcohol to bind themselves in matrimony. The Girls' Festival in March is toasted with sweet, low-alcohol *amazake*. (In the days when arrests were still common, March was a prime time for home brewing, because the booze could always be excused as amazake gone bad.) The coming of the cherry blossoms brings *hanami* picnics celebrating spring with enthusiastic drinking during the day, an otherwise taboo behavior. In

dancing, singing, eating and heavy drinking, and almost invariably considerable sexual joking and play. There were parties given to mark the naming of a new baby, returning from a visit to a shrine or temple, celebrating a variety of festivals and holidays, sending off conscripts and welcoming them back, dedicating new buildings, marking the end of rice planting and harvest, completing the silk producing cycle and every other enterprise involving more than two or three people."

On one occasion, Wiswell attended vaccination day at a school. "Mothers came from all directions, and the school room looked like a nursery with babies crawling all over the place. When I left, all the older children had received their vaccinations and the doctor was well through the babies. On my way down the stairs I met the custodian with a barrel of shochu and bottles of beer. 'The drinking has started,' he said. It had not occurred to me, even after all these months, that even a vaccination clinic calls for drinking afterwards."

This all comes from a description of peasant life in southern Kyushu in the 1930s. Middle-class city dwellers and farmers in other parts of Japan may have had quite different norms. Wiswell does quote a school principal's wife from a neighboring village, finding the antics of the village women "quite surprising." There were, and still are, all sorts of drinking cultures in the country. Today, if you look at a map of Japan's alcohol consumption, you will find the people of

POURING FOR OTHERS

When drinking in a group in Japan, it is customary to pour other people's drinks, and it is polite to wait for others in the group to pour yours. This may sound overly formal to the uninitiated, but can be a great way to interact and make friends. This custom can also be used to strike up a conversation with people in adjoining groups. If you want to be really polite, pour while holding the bottle with two hands and hold your glass in two hands when receiving. If possible, try to accept drinks offered by people in the group who have not poured for you and swiftly pick up the bottle and pour for them (in many cases, people are pouring because they want their glass refilled). A further nuance, if you want to be really polite, is to pour for older guests before pouring for younger ones.

Kyushu drink nearly twice as much shochu per person per year as the rest of Japan and four times more than parts of the Kansai region (where Osaka and Kyoto are located). The heartland of sake is the center and north of Honshu, the main island. In Niigata prefecture in northwestern Honshu they drink about 17 quarts (16 liters) of sake per year per person, while in Okinawa and Kagoshima they drink only about a quart (a liter) per person. Yamanashi likes its wine. Two prefectures, Tokyo and Hokkaido, drink just about everything to excess. Perhaps the only generalization that it's possible to make is that wherever you travel in Japan you will find yourself in the midst of a complex and deeply rooted drinking culture. This shows through in the products that are made and the way Japanese people enjoy drinking them.

Alcohol as Social Elixir

As you likely know if you've ever interacted with Japanese people, they can be intensely private and resistant to social interactions with strangers. This is true whether you're a

foreigner or not. Culturally, Japanese people are suspicious of strangers due to millennia of an agrarian mindset in which your grandparent's neighbors were your neighbor's grandparents. Generations of families lived together in tight-knit communities with very little need to interact with strangers. The samurai and later merchant class were responsible for trade and the transport of goods, so peasants rarely traveled more than a few miles from their birthplace. In fact, the appearance of strangers was seen as a sign of trouble, as can be seen in a robust genre of Japanese cinema depicting the samurai era. Perhaps the most famous of these is *The Seven Samurai*, in which peasants hire *ronin* (masterless samurai) to protect their village against marauders. The peasants distrust the samurai, hiding their daughters and their meager

Above Customers enjoy an al fresco izakaya experience, a rare sight in Japan. **Facing page** The *aka-chochin*, meaning "red lantern," is such a common symbol of an izakaya that many older Japanese simply refer to izakaya as "aka-chochin."

valuables. In the film it's revealed that the villagers have a history of murdering wandering samurai like their protectors, and are only relying on them now that an existential threat appears. The film ends with the peasants going on as before, planting rice next to the graves of their saviors. While modernization has upended such social norms everywhere except in the most rural villages, the social reticence remains.

The Meiji Restoration (1868) modernized Japan in a hurry. The rush toward modernization destroyed many traditions, including the long-standing "castle towns," which were urban hubs centered around protecting the interests of the shogun or the local feudal lord. In their place, government was centralized and trade encouraged. Almost overnight, cottage industries, long the purview of local communities, became professionalized. Guilds arose and cities began to grow as industry took root. It's estimated that less than 15 percent of the Japanese population consisted of city dwellers at the time of the Meiji Restoration and that these numbers stayed relatively stable through 1920, but between 1920 and 2000 the numbers essentially flipped. In fact, today less than 10 percent of Japan's population is rural. All of those strangers crammed together in rapidly growing cities has resulted in enormous social upheaval.

Enter alcohol as a social elixir. In modern Japanese life, the *nomikai* (drinking party) is a near necessity to socialize, succeed academically, get ahead in business and even marry. People make new friends by attending drinking parties organized by their existing friends. Professors drink with their students. Students drink with their classmates. Bosses drink with their employees. Employees drink with their coworkers. Meanwhile, an entire matchmaking industry has grown up based around bringing strangers together to meet members of the opposite sex in a social environment revolving around drinking. All in all, Japanese social activities are highly alcohol focused.

The pressures of modern urban life are the same wherever you are from. For the Japanese, given their intensely hierarchical society, along with a desire to maintain harmony and avoid conflict (vital in an agrarian community), there are few outlets for this stress. Many turn to social drinking after work to take the edge off. Professor Kouichi "Raku" Sakaguchi of Kyushu University considers the *izakaya* (see below) the "safe space" between the stresses of work and the stresses of home. By washing away the tribulations of work with a glass or two before heading home to face a cranky child or a spouse who has had a bad day, harmony can be maintained more easily.

A "SIT DOWN SAKE-SHOP": THE IZAKAYA

It might be easiest to characterize the *izakaya* as a "gastropub," or perhaps as a "Japanese tapas bar"; that is, a place to share some dishes while enjoying drinks with friends. However, the name literally means "sit-sake-shop." Prior to this innovation, Japanese would visit their favorite sake maker, refill their storage pot with their favorite brew, and return home to enjoy the drink. Someone, somewhere, decided to start serving food at their sake shop and inviting their customers to drink on premises. Thus the izakaya was born. Today the izakaya is as varied as the drinking culture of Japan, ranging from a six-seat dining bar with a single chef whipping up the day's menu served with her favorite drinks, to massive chains with iPads for menus and hundreds of food and drink options. Another layer to this uniquely Japanese dining style is that guests often make a night of it. An izakaya meal can begin after work and end when the kitchen closes—in fact, it's not uncommon when making a reservation at a popular izakaya to have them warn that reservations are only for two hours, or two and a half if they're feeling generous. More traditional places would never dream of inconveniencing their customers like this, but economic realities sometimes win out. Alternatively, you may find a group of revelers on an izakaya crawl, popping in to place after place until it's time to call it a night.

The izakaya can help ease these pressures in other ways as well. When the boss invites his employees out to drink, the nomikai or *bureiko* (lit. "putting aside rank") party represents a place where underlings can express their feelings freely without fear of reprisal. Such parties, which date back to the 14th century, are intended to allow everyone to relax and act and talk freely; any indiscretions are completely forgotten in the morning. They can get quite boisterous, with neckties sometimes ending up tied like traditional *hachimaki* festival headbands around the heads of normally staid salarymen once the alcohol starts flowing.

The pervasiveness of bureiko has led to a backlash among some younger employees who do not always appreciate or understand the rituals. These parties are especially difficult for people with alcohol sensitivity (approximately one third of Japanese suffer from an inability to safely metabolize alcohol). Bosses expect their employees to match them drink for drink, or at least to pretend to. Furthermore, hazing can happen if things get out of hand. There's a recent trend away from these parties being "part of the job," and it's much more acceptable now to decline than it was in the past.

While Japan is certainly a male-dominated society even today, alcohol is part of life for most adults, perhaps except

Left An open door allows a peek inside an izakaya.

Below Standing bars, called *tachinomi* in Japanese, are casual spots with cheap drinks and snacks. Items are usually paid for as they are delivered allowing customers to leave whenever they are ready rather than wait for a check They also allow for the breakdown of social barriers as its easier to talk to a stranger when you're not seated at a table.

Facing page This casual izakaya has large windows. More traditional izakaya allow for no view to the interior to protect the privacy of their customers.

for women with small children, for obvious reasons. The sight of women drinking is not necessarily a new phenomenon, though. Ella Wiswell tells the story of a "baby-naming party" in Kumamoto in the 1930s. "Everybody got very drunk. The old grandmother became very playful with Masakichi, and Ichiro's father was pawing one of his sisters-in-law. Mrs. Wauchi was very far gone, and the two of us must have made a funny sight coming home huddled under her shawl, as I was without a coat. We stumbled along, talking loudly, and she kept telling me how good it felt to be drunk. Later, Mrs. Hayashi stopped by completely drunk, saying how sorry she was that she had not left the party when we did. Her husband will be angry at her for being kept waiting, she said, but she does love to drink, and just could not tear herself away sooner. She was sure her husband will divorce her, she laughed, for coming home late and drunk again. Today the women were discussing the Kawaze women's escapade of the night before [which we don't learn more of] and how drunk they were when they finally went for their after-party."

It was certainly perfectly normal for respectable women in postwar Japan to largely abstain from drinking; in fact there is currently a moral panic gripping Japan about the problem of younger women who like to drink. However, a large part of the increasing popularity of Japanese sake, shochu and wine has been driven by drinking trends among young women, especially those in urban areas who have chosen to have careers rather than families, or who perhaps have postponed marriage and family for their careers.

More recently, alcohol consumption has been declining in Japan as the population ages and many young people abstain due to cost or other interests. To further complicate matters for Japanese alcohol producers, a recent United Nations report predicts that Japan's population will shrink by 34 percent by the turn of the next century if current birth and death rates continue. These circumstances mean there is a dire need for Japanese alcohol products to become a robust export commodity. Otherwise, many—perhaps most—of those 2,000-plus breweries and distilleries will simply cease to exist, and an incredibly rich drinking tradition will be in danger of disappearing.

PART ONE

NATIVE JAPANESE ALCOHOL TRADITIONS

和酒 *Washu*

The chapters in this section will cover sake, shochu, awamori and the fruit-based liqueurs called *kajitsu-shu*; in other words, alcohol traditions that originate in Japan. Along with the history, brands and trends related to these drinks, we'll explore the brewing and production processes.

清酒

Sake

The Soul of Japan

THE HISTORY OF SAKE

To begin with, sake is not rice wine. That unfortunate mistranslation was a clumsy attempt by sake importers in the 1970s to make sake accessible to Westerners. The earliest evidence of winemaking was around 7,000 BC, but beer and sake didn't appear for another 3,000 years. The reason for this was simple—that is, it's simple to make wine, but not to make beer or sake. To make wine you only need grapes and feet: wine was traditionally made by stomping on grapes to break their skins; the natural yeasts from the feet would efficiently convert the sugars in the grapes to alcohol. Getting from the first stomp to the finished product might take 10 days to two weeks, with virtually no human intervention between the stepping and the pressing. If you step on rice, however, all you'll have is dirty rice. Grapes have large quantities of sugar that yeast can efficiently convert to alcohol, while rice is rich in starch, which needs to be broken into simple sugars before yeast can do its job.

The first sake-making appears to have been just as unsettlingly unsanitary as the image of dirty feet stepping on grapes, if not more so. Rice-based alcohol was first made in China, but Japan did not have access to it until the arrival of rice cultivation from the continent sometime around 1,000 BC. The earliest sake believed to have been made in Japan was *kuchikamizake* ("mouth-chewed sake"). Villagers—usually those too young or too old to participate in hunting, gathering or agriculture—would diligently chew steamed rice and spit it into a communal jar. By the end of the work day,

Left Coworkers play a sake- drinking game on a company outing to a hot-spring resort in Aichi prefecture in 1961.

Facing page Print by Kuniyoshi Utagawa (1798–1861) depicts sake being served to young warrior Soga Sukenari (1172–1193), who avenged his father's death with his brother Soga Tokimune before they both committed ritual suicide.

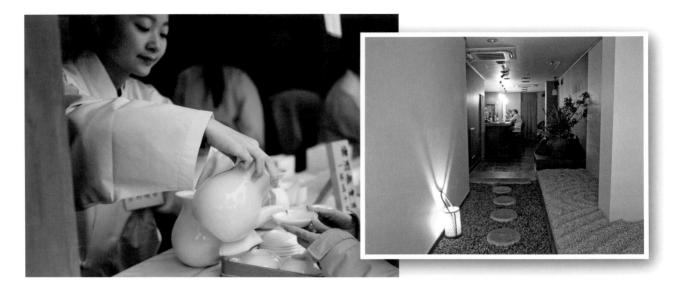

the chewing and enzymes in the saliva would have converted the starches into sugars, and the yeast could begin making alcohol. The weak brew could be consumed in the evening. If the villagers were more patient, a beer-strength beverage would be available in about a week.

It is believed that sake was regarded as a gift from the gods due to the way it changed how people felt. As such, it became associated with the Shinto religion, and the making of kuchikamizake was elevated to a religious experience by Shinto priests, who recruited virginal young girls to do the chewing and spitting. This is vividly portrayed in the 2016 animated movie *Your Name* (*Kimi no na wa*) in which the protagonist, a teenage girl whose family runs the local shrine, is embarrassed to make kuchikamizake at the town festival with her classmates looking on. The spiritual relevance of this traditional drink is revealed later in the film. Lest you think this is a long-dead custom, kuchikamizake festivals continued in Okinawa until the 1930s; middle-aged Okinawans claim it was still being served at temples into the 1970s. If you'd like to try it at home, it's very simple. Steam some rice, chew each bite for four minutes, spit the liquefied rice into a container and leave it covered with a cloth for one week. You'll have a cloudy 5 percent brew that's quite a bit sweeter and more acidic than modern sake. You may enjoy it, but expect family and friends to be less enthusiastic.

Fortunately for hygiene, sake production evolved as more advanced techniques than chewing and saliva were discovered to convert the starches in the rice into alcohol. By the sixth century, koji mold (see page 30) imported from the continent offered a more sanitary way of breaking down the starches than peasant spit. Around a century later, sake was being made in a filtered style and sold as a commodity, as evidenced by the word *seishu* (清酒, clear sake) discovered on a wooden tablet dating from about 700 AD in the remains of a warehouse in the city of Nara.

Nara Sake

The above should be regarded as the prehistory of sake. The brew made at that time was nearly unrecognizable—a sour, pungent, often cloudy alcohol delivery vehicle. Clearly, advancements had been made, as it could be consumed warm and was good enough to sell. However, modern sake production methods were developed in Nara, which became the capital of Japan for a brief time during the Nara period (710–794). During the subsequent Heian period (795–1185), when the capital moved to Kyoto, the Nara Buddhist temples were still politically powerful, but the economic realities of their loss of centrality required them to get creative. That creativity led to the development of modern sake-making techniques—many of which are still used, albeit in modified form, today.

Virtually all stages of sake production were developed or improved upon by the Nara brewer-priests: rice polishing, making the yeast starter, building the main fermentation, filtration and pasteurization. Filtration—separating the solids from the liquids—made clarified sake possible. This process is so linked to Nara that pickles made in sake lees (leftover solids) are still called *narazuke* (Nara pickles).

Pasteurization was first documented by a Nara sake maker in 1568 (296 years before Louis Pasteur, working in the wine industry, "discovered" that heating wine or beer killed the active organisms). We'll learn more about making sake later, but for now it's enough to understand that the basic foundations were all developed or refined by the artisan priests of Nara. Until some of these modern methods were developed, it was impossible to produce more than approximately 130 gallons (500 liters) of sake per batch. Records indicate that once those technologies were established, much larger volumes of sake were being produced. In fact, official accounts report that on January 3, 1582, in a Nara sake brewery, a young woman drowned in a 48,000-gallon (1800-liter) wooden fermentation vat.

The privatization of sake production is also believed to have started in Nara toward the end of the Heian period. The exact date is unknown, but somewhere about 900 years ago the oldest continuously operated sake brewery, Imanishi Shuzo, was established. It claims its brand, Mimurosugi, is the longest-living brand in sake history. The Kenbishi Shuzo brewery in Hyogo, however, also claims the oldest branded sake. We will likely never know which is older. Other private sake breweries may have predated Imanishi and Kenbishi, but they are lost to history.

Some of this alcohol was apparently quite sophisticated: we know that aristocrats were warming sake in the early 900s, and the tipple would have had to have been highly filtered to taste good enough to heat. Some of the ruling class became very fond of their sake. In 995, when the nobleman Michitaka Fujiwara was on his deathbed, his priests told him to turn his face toward heaven and chant a sacred prayer. He flatly refused, replying, "What's the point

of going to heaven when there's no one to drink with?" A lack of drinking buddies in the afterlife was not the biggest worry for poorer drinkers who got a taste for the cripplingly expensive temple sake. A ghost story from the 9th century tells of a man who bought 8 gallons (37 liters) of alcohol from a temple on credit but was unable to pay his debt. He was reincarnated as an ox and had to return to the temple to work off his bill.

The Koji Riot

Certainly, by the year 1200, sake was being sold as a commodity to commoners in the cities, and over the next three or four centuries this growing market transformed the industry. The grip of religious institutions on sake-making loosened slowly; over time, it became commercialized, and merchant-run businesses began to dominate. The transition was never more dramatically illustrated than in the Kyoto koji riot of 1444.

At that time, Kitano Shrine held a legal monopoly on Kyoto's production of koji, the mold used in sake-making to convert starches into sugar (see page 30). For many years, however, the some 340 sake makers in the city had been complaining that the supply provided by the shrine's guild was not meeting booming demand, and that the prices were grossly inflated. They started building their own illicit facilities to make up the shortfall, but these were periodically broken up by soldiers sent to enforce the monopoly throughout the 1420s and '30s. In 1443, the situation came to

Right Sake being served at a religious ceremony. Sake has long had religious associations in Japan.

a head when the sake makers simply stopped buying the shrine's koji.

The shrine petitioned the shogunate, and its koji makers locked themselves in their sacred precincts to place added pressure on the authorities while they deliberated. Initially, the shogunate seemed likely to back the status quo, but popular protests in the city and the lobbying power of the sake makers (who were among the city's wealthiest citizens and the main money lenders) brought a dramatic change of policy. Soldiers were sent not to break up the brewers' koji rooms, but to root the koji guild out of the shrine. The scene quickly turned ugly. Forty people were killed, Kitano Shrine and other buildings in the area were torched, and the priests' domination of sake-brewing was smashed forever.

When the smoke cleared, the foundations of the modern sake industry could be seen. It took centuries to complete the transfer of power, but the trend was toward secular commerce. During the Muromachi period (1392–1573) there came about increasing differentiation between sake makers,

distributors and shops selling to the public. Brands started to emerge, as did, of course, the fitful, often silly government regulation prohibiting alcohol which seems to be a feature of any mature drink market. At one stage, the shogunate even tried to legislate what commoners could eat at a party: they could either have three different food dishes and one soup or one soup, two dishes, and three glasses of sake. Needless to say, no one seems to have taken much notice.

Edo Sake

In September 1699, the low-ranked samurai Bunzaemon Asahi confided to his personal journal: "I got back at night. I had drunk so much that I puked a lot." Bunzaemon's diary, the *Omu rochuki (*Diary of a Caged Parrot), has left us a wonderfully vivid, vomit-stained picture of the Genroku era (1699–1704), a time of relative peace and prosperity when it seems the life of a warrior was largely about downing vast quantities of sake and suffering the inevitable consequences.

Bunzaemon and his friends were allowed to drink on their

Facing page Sake barrels donated to shrines are meant to bring the sake makers good fortune while also letting the locals know that the breweries support the shrine.

This page Shingen Takada, one of the greatest samurai generals, captured here in a ukiyoe print by Kuniyoshi Utagawa, is famous for plying his troops with sake to warm them up during a cold January battle.

night shifts, and they liked to get properly drunk on their days off. Since only one out of every nine days was spent on guard duty at the castle (the euphemism for the other days was "training at home"), they had plenty of time to carouse. "Around two o'clock in the afternoon, Shinzo came around," Bunzaemon writes. "We drank together and then went out. Then to 'Jinsa.' Had sake and warm tofu. Got back home at dawn." Another entry: "I got so badly drunk and puked so much, I was almost beside myself. Choked and took a big breath. How stupid!"

In the 17th and 18th centuries, the population of the city of Edo (now Tokyo) grew from about 400,000 people to more than a million. Bunzaemon Asahi, the vomiting samurai, was typical: a man from the provinces living on his own in the big city with money burning a hole in his pocket (there were 1.5 times as many men as women). At the peak of Edo's drinking years at the start of the 19th century, one barrel of sake a year was consumed for every man, woman and child in the city, amounting to about 7 fluid ounces (200 milliliters) per person per day. Much of this was cheap unrefined sake called *doburoku*, which was consumed cold. There were more than 1,800 doburoku makers in the city in 1837. But more prosperous tipplers were drinking warmed sake made from much more refined brews imported in huge quantities from the Kansai region of western Japan: the Nada district in Hyogo and the Fushimi district in Kyoto. You will sometimes still hear modern Japanese call an object of poor quality *kudaranai*. The word, which means "did not come down," refers to the Edo view that if goods had not "come down" from these prestigious production centers in Kansai, they weren't worth buying. The view was particularly strong among drinkers, and Kansai sake overwhelmingly dominated Edo's sake market, accounting for about 80 percent of the refined sake consumed in the city.

It was a formidably sophisticated industry. When condescending Westerners arrived in Japan during the Meiji era to "teach the natives" about modern science, they were astounded to learn that Kansai brewers had been heating their sake to destroy microbes nearly 300 years before Louis

Pasteur. Charcoal filtering was also common practice. The original story went that in the early 1600s, a disgruntled worker at an Osaka brewery had dumped ash from a stove into a batch of sake. The brewery owner made a fortune when he discovered that the alcohol rescued from the barrel was unusually clear. This is likely apocryphal; still, someone somewhere in Japan made the discovery that charcoal filtration clarified sake.

MODERN SAKE

The taste, appearance and ways of serving sake have been in constant flux throughout its history. Much as the American economist George Taylor famously theorized that women's hemlines rose and fell with stock prices (miniskirts in the boom times, ankle lengths when the crashes come), the Japanese food historian Osamu Shinoda suggested that sake's sweetness varied with war and peace—dry during peace, sweet when at war. Indeed, records do seem to give the theory at least superficial credibility. In the relatively peaceful

1870s, the typical sake seems to have been quite dry by modern standards. In the war years between 1915 and 1920, and again from the 1930s to the 1940s, sake became very sweet. We currently seem to be headed in the opposite direction—away from the obsession with the super-dry sake of the peaceful 1990s. Today's sake is increasingly flowery and sweet. Given the Japanese government's recent overtures toward changing their constitution to allow war, perhaps the theory will continue to hold?

The most significant change over the past hundred years has been a dramatic shift in the geography of sake. In the 19th century, the dominance of brewers from the Kansai region of western Japan seemed unassailable. Not only did they sell more than anybody else, but their sake was acknowledged to be of a higher quality. They swept the board at the first national sake-tasting competition in 1907. *Rakugo* performers, Japan's traditional sit-down comedians, used to tell jokes about the poor quality of *jizake* ("local sake") from local breweries. But, in 1913, the New Sake Tasting Competition (Shinshu Kanpyokai) dealt a stunning blow to these preconceptions: provincial sake from Akita, Okayama, Ehime and Hiroshima shared the top prizes with Kansai's famous Fushimi and Nada districts. Worse, the results revealed that only 60 percent of the sake from Nada and Fushimi had earned top medals, while Hiroshima boasted an 80 percent success rate and Okayama 70 percent. The country hicks kept winning big prizes, and by 1919, the Nada

makers had become so angry that they refused to take part.

While these competitive reversals had little immediate impact on Kansai's dominance in the real market, the coming of war in the 1930s and 1940s brought long-term changes that affect sake production to this day. A government push to reduce rice use hurt the jizake makers in the short term. Half of the smaller breweries closed, and those that were left were given strictly limited rations of rice, making expansion virtually impossible. The bigger makers who had invested in mass-production machinery made the majority of the cheap adulterated sake that characterized wartime production. Disgruntled drinkers complained about "goldfish sake" that had so much water added that fish were reputed to be able to live in it. After that was regulated out of existence, a more potent but equally specious innovation called *zojoshu* hit the shelves, which contained so much distilled alcohol and sugar that the rice content was cut by more than two thirds.

Zojoshu tended to give its consumers wicked hangovers,

and similarly, its production affected the industry long after the end of the rice shortages. Many of the big breweries were no longer focused on making the highest-quality sake in Japan, as they had been in the Edo and Meiji periods, but on the cheap mass production of plonk, using distilled alcohol and other additives solely to increase the yield. For many years, the Japanese tax code favored these cheap brews, leaving a legacy that still marks the industry. "*Nihonshu* [another word for sake] was dealt a very, very raw hand by the big makers," says Kyoto sake-bar owner Yoram Ofer. "Today everybody from the industry is carrying on about falling sales, but they have only themselves to blame for their terrible image. It's foreigners and young Japanese who are most enthusiastic about sake now, because they weren't around in the days when the big makers were producing that truly foul stuff."

Fortunately, the postwar period also saw the rise of jizake of unprecedented quality. It would be wrong to claim that Nada and Fushimi do not make good alcohol. Many makers in these areas never compromised their principles, and the mass-market makers still have very good products at the top of their ranges. However, the stark reality is that "Kansai sake" is no longer synonymous with quality the way it was a hundred years ago. Regions like Niigata and Akita have gained powerful reputations since jizake started to assert itself in the late 1970s but great drinks are now coming from all over Japan. Indeed, just about every prefecture can claim to be producing good sake.

MAKING SAKE

Fortunately for the sake industry's profits, enjoying sake does not require a detailed understanding of how it is made. After all, most drinkers only have the vaguest of notions of how wine and beer are brewed. Sake production is quite a bit more complicated than winemaking, and much more labor intensive than beer-brewing, at least as traditionally made. The sake brewery is known as the *kura* or *sakagura*. The word "kura" can be translated as "workshop," "warehouse" or "cellar," but "sakagura" means "place where alcohol is made," so shochu distilleries, beer breweries and wineries can also rightly be called sakagura in Japanese.

In its most basic form, sake is made from just four ingredients: rice, water, koji and yeast. Koji and yeast are microorganisms that do the heavy lifting: koji converts starch to sugar and yeast converts sugar to alcohol. While there's much more to it, this is the essential principle, as we will see.

Water

Westerners usually think of water as being tasteless—a clear, inert liquid that can taste bad if chemically treated or polluted, but that otherwise usually disappears into the background. Not so for sake and other Japanese alcohol traditions: most sake breweries are situated near an ideal water source. In fact, breweries have been known to move if their local water source becomes compromised. The water used in sake production is very soft. London tap water is more than twice as hard as the hardest water used in sake production. New York City tap water is considered to be very soft by US standards, yet the water used for sake production in Shizuoka is nearly half as soft again. Water hardness is only one measure, but it does affect the mouthfeel of the sake. Water that is favorable for sake will generally be high in phosphorous and potassium (which are food for koji and yeast) and very low in iron and manganese (which can adversely affect the flavor and color) with an appropriate balance of calcium and magnesium.

Rice

All sake production starts with rice; the rice used in sake production is called *sakamai*. Rice used exclusively for sake production is known as *shuzo kotekimai* (brewing rice). These varieties of rice, which have been cultivated over hundreds of years to be optimized for sake production, have larger grains and a higher starch content than rice intended for the table. Sake-rice plants also tend to be quite tall, often exceeding a man's height, and are notoriously vulnerable to storm damage, which is problematic in the typhoon-prone Japanese archipelago.

More than 100 varieties of sake rice are cultivated in Japan, but the Yamada Nishiki variety is by far the most famous. Although particularly difficult to cultivate, it is still a favorite with many breweries because of its versatility and the complexity of its flavors. According to the sake writer John Gauntner (whose books are a must for anyone learning about sake), Yamada Nishiki tends to produce drinks with fruity, lively and layered flavors; it's "a biggie in terms of enhanced sake flavor and fragrance profiles." Created in 1923 in Hyogo, Yamada Nishiki is the king of premium sake rice.

The similarly named Miyama Nishiki was discovered in 1978 in Nagano, when another sake rice (Takane Nishiki) was exposed to gamma radiation. The mutation resulted in a very high starch content in the center of the grain, a highly sought-after characteristic known as *shinpaku* (white heart).

HOT OR COLD SAKE?

Hot sake was very much the norm in Japan until 1992, when a sake-grading system, based on *seimaibuai* (polishing ratio), was introduced. As premium sake became popular in Japan, the shift was toward chilled sake, which is where many premium *ginjo* and *daiginjo*-grade sakes (see page 37) made from highly polished rice really shine. Suddenly drinking sake warm was associated with low-quality sake and even bad manners. The manga writer Akira Oze tells a story about a sake-brewery owner he knew who asked for his own sake served *kan* (warmed) at an izakaya. The proprietor, not knowing who he was dealing with, refused, saying that to heat that particular sake was heresy. The brewery owner ordered the sake cold alongside hot tofu stew. When his meal arrived, he plonked the sake *tokkuri* (ceramic carafe) in the stew, drawing horrified looks from other patrons and a derisive snort from the proprietor.

Today trends have shifted back toward warming sake, particularly *junmai* and *honjozo* grades (see page 36), which often have lush flavors that open up with a little heat. But don't heat it too much. Alcohol boils at about 173°F (78°C)—a lower temperature than the water used to make a cup of tea. If you want to warm up your sake at home, there are two good ways of doing so: heat a pan of water to the appropriate temperature and then put a tokuri into the pan (it's harder to overheat the sake this way), or place the tokkuri in a pan of cool water and then very gently heat it. Jamie Graves, a New York–based expert who has worked in Michelin-starred Japanese restaurants, says even microwaving sake can warm it nicely, so long as the process is done with great care. Each method has its adherents, and they bicker with each other like English tea drinkers do over the age-old question, "Milk first, or last?"

This new variety became Miyama Nishiki (*miyama* means "beautiful peaks"; the shinpaku was reminiscent of Nagano's famous white-capped mountains). It's usually grown at altitude, so it's a hardy grain; it's also one of the first crops of sake rice to be harvested each year.

Another popular variety is Gohyakumangoku, created in 1983 in Niigata, which tends to be light and dry flavored. Sake makers describe it as being "shy" since it doesn't stand out from the brew. Dewasansan, a more recent strain developed by the Yamagata prefecture agricultural laboratory in the mid 1990s, is a play on the name of the three sacred mountains of the Dewa domain (modern Yamagata prefecture). This variety has led to a steep rise in the quality of Yamagata sake due to its larger shinpaku and softness, which results in a more distinctive flavor.

While most popular modern sake rice varieties were developed at by agricultural scientists in various prefectures, one variety, Omachi, was discovered the old-fashioned way.

Top A rice paddy in Saga prefecture.
Above Different species of sake rice grow to different heights. Taller rice is more susceptible to storm damage.

In 1859, a man called Jinzo Kishimoto was traveling from Tottori prefecture back to his home town of Omachi in Okayama prefecture, when he came across some rice plants in the wild. He carefully picked two plants and cultivated the rice when he got home. It caught on, and Omachi rice is now used to make rich, earthy premium sake.

There are more than 100 varieties of sake rice, but the above-mentioned are some of the best known.

Milling, or polishing, raw rice grains so that the outer portions are removed is the first stage of sake production. The resulting rice is classified by the percentage of weight remaining after polishing (*seimaibuai*). White "table" rice is also polished rice, with the outer bran, proteins, fats, acids and other impurities removed through polishing. Table rice is usually polished to about 90 percent (that is, 10 percent is removed), while premium sake rice is almost always polished to at least 70 percent. More expensive sake generally contains rice that has been polished more, and the polishing rate is

almost always displayed on bottles of premium sake. A lower percentage generally means a more refined sake. Sake rice is specifically cultivated to have a high starch content at the center of the grain. As the rice is polished more finely, this results in a higher ratio of starch to other components. There is a trade-off, however: the more you polish, the more the rice grain is prone to fracturing and the more the rice-polishing mill heats up, so the polishing process is slowed to keep the mill cool and to protect the increasingly delicate rice grains. For perspective, it takes about 2 hours to mill table rice to 90 percent. It takes 48 hours to mill the same quantity of sake rice to a 40 percent seimaibuai (that is, with 60 percent of the kernel removed). In October 2017 it was announced that a 1 percent seimaibuai had been achieved at Tatenokawa Brewery using Dewasansan sake rice. Reportedly it took 1,800 hours of milling and yielded only 150 bottles, which sold for ¥108,000 ($970, £738, €826) each.

Once the rice is polished, it's left to rest for up to 30 days.

This process, known as *karashi* (drying out), allows the moisture content of the polished rice to balance out. If the rice is steamed too soon after polishing, variation in the moisture levels of the grains result in some grains being too hard and others too soft for optimal sake production. Once the rice has been properly dried, the real labor of sake production begins.

Preparing the Rice

In order to begin the process of making koji (the mold that converts starches into sugar) polished rice is washed, soaked, steamed and then cooled. Each of these steps is carefully managed by the master brewer, or *toji*. Washing highly polished rice is very delicate business, so for premium sake the rice is usually hand washed in cold water in very small batches of just a few pounds at a time to remove the residual polishing dust and any other contaminants. The rice is then soaked for a precise amount of time to ensure that it takes on enough water to steam efficiently, but not so much that it become mushy after steaming. The goal is *gaikonainan*—firm on the outside, tender on the inside. For premium sake, the toji will often stand over the soaking rice with a stopwatch and order his assistants to drain the rice at the exact moment he decides. Less polished rice requires more soaking time—perhaps a few minutes—while highly polished sake rice might be soaked for just a few dozen seconds. The soaked rice is often left overnight to again harmonize its moisture balance before steaming the next morning. Traditionally, steaming took 40 minutes in a large vat called a *koshiki*, but today many

methods of steaming exist. It may take from 20 minutes to more than an hour depending on the brewery and the technology used.

Once the rice is steamed, it is divided into portions depending on what stage various batches of sake are at on that given day. Some will go to koji production, some will be used to build a *shubo* (yeast mother), and some will be added to the *moromi* (main fermentation) at different stages of completion, as explained below. What remains consistent at this point is that the steamed rice is cooled to around body temperature or a little higher before being added to the different stages of production.

Koji Production

Rice koji is essentially moldy rice. This is rice that has been inoculated with koji spores (*tane-koji*) of the koji mold (*koji-kin*). Koji is the general term used for mold from the *Aspergillus* genus of molds, specifically *A. oryzae*, which is used for almost all sake production. The sake-friendly species of koji-kin is known colloquially as *ki-koji* (黄麹 yellow koji) for the greenish-yellow color of the mold once it has gone to

Above Steam rises from a rice steamer. Sake breweries are chilly places in the winter except around these steamers and in the koji room.

Left Steamed rice is inoculated with koji mold spores and mixed by hand to cool the rice and propagate the spores to create rice koji.

spore. Rice koji—koji from here on—is the fundamental building block of sake production. In fact, koji is fundamental to much traditional Japanese fermentation such as soy sauce, miso, rice vinegar, shochu, awamori, and pickles. The portion of the steamed rice to be used for koji production is moved into the *koji muro* (麹室 koji room), a cedar-lined room with precise temperature and humidity control to maximize the efficiency of the koji propagation. The steamed rice is spread flat on a large table and the koji-kin is sprinkled onto the steamed rice with what looks like a large salt shaker, which has holes small enough to prevent the kojified rice grains from coming out, but large enough to let the fine dust of koji spores exit and settle on the steamed rice. This elegant process is, again, precisely controlled by the toji. It's been said the goal is to have 12 to 13 spores per grain of steamed rice—a ridiculously precise goal, but a goal nonetheless. Once an appropriate amount of koji mold has been spread on the rice, the rice is turned by hand to mix the koji spores more evenly onto the surface of the steamed rice grains.

At this point the rice is put into a large pile in the center of the table, wrapped in blankets and left to rest overnight. After 12 hours, it will have dried out and begun sticking together. These clumps are broken up into individual grains, and then wrapped up once more. All the while the koji hyphae are growing onto and into the rice grains and have begun emitting enzymes that convert starches into sugars. This generates heat as well—if left to its own devices, the koji would burn itself out. So about 12 hours later, the rice is broken up once again and moved to small koji boxes where temperature can be much more closely monitored. Every few hours over the next day or so, the rice in each small box is hand sifted and the boxes are reorganized to maximize the koji propagation. When the toji decides the process is finished, *dekoji* occurs. This is when the rice is moved out of the koji room and left to cool in ambient temperatures, which arrests the koji propagation. This entire process takes about 48 hours and requires constant monitoring. Toji and their assistants get little sleep when koji is being made.

Foreign organisms that would contaminate the brew are deterred by acid. Yellow koji does not create much, so sake makers must find other ways to create acid in the fermentation. They often need to ferment at lower temperatures to suppress the growth of other organisms. Now let's take a step back into the past to see how brewers created acid naturally to allow the koji and yeast to do their jobs in making sake without being disrupted by invasive organisms.

Above Rice koji–making is aided by wooden boxes, which are used to help aerate the aerobic koji mold and more easily maintain temperature.

PRODUCTION METHODS

The *shubo* (also called the *moto*) is the yeast mother—the foundation on which every great sake is built. (We use the term "shubo" rather than "moto" throughout, but the meanings are identical.) As we survey production methods, we'll move from the most traditional to the most modern.

The Bodaimoto Production Method

The oldest documentation of private sake production is the *Goshuno-nikki* (Diary of Honored Sake) from Bodaisan Shoryakuji temple in Nara prefecture, written sometime between the 14th and 16th centuries. As mentioned previously, Nara was the birthplace of modern sake production techniques. The diary describes a style of production known as *bodaimoto*, in which raw rice and a small amount of steamed rice was added to water from the Bodaisan Shoryakuji temple, which is situated high up on a hillside overlooking Nara. This mixture was left to sit, allowing natural lactic acid bacteria and wild yeasts to propagate in the slurry. Nobody knew it at the time, but it turns out that the water from Bodaisan Shoryakuji temple is teeming with natural lactic acid bacteria. When added to raw rice with a little bit of steamed rice, the lactic acid in the water begins saccharifying the raw rice, creating an environment in which other microorganisms cannot easily survive.

wooden paddles, then separated into smaller wooden barrels for the *yamaoroshi* (also known as *motosuri*) process in which workers diligently mash the steamed rice and koji rice into a paste. This can take hours. This paste is then returned to the original barrel and mixed once again. Natural lactic acid bacteria will begin to propagate in the paste and the koji will continue to break down the rice. After approximately one week, yeast will be added to the kimoto; the shubo will be completed in about three weeks. A handful of sake breweries still diligently make kimoto-style sake, but the dearth of young workers able to provide the muscle for the arduous yamaoroshi process makes this a very uncommon and rather expensive style of sake.

After three days, the rice was strained and steamed. The steamed rice and the soaking water, rich in lactic acid and yeast, were then added back into a new tank along with koji rice to create the shubo. In this acid- and sugar-rich environment, the yeasts that propagated naturally would begin creating sake very quickly. Meanwhile, the koji would begin its task of breaking down the starches in the steamed rice to make sugar for the yeasts to feast on.

The bodaimoto method was lost to history until the 1990s, when the temple, the local sake breweries and some scientists decided to try to revive it. Now, once a year, a bodaimoto starter is made at the temple and transported to each of the Nara sake breweries, who then make bodaimoto sake reflecting their own unique styles. Were it not for the lactic acid bacteria in the water of the temple, however, this style would have remained lost to history.

The Kimoto Production Method

Before the rediscovery of bodaimoto, *kimoto* was thought to be the oldest type of modern sake-brewing. It's now known that bodaimoto was prevalent in Japan as long as 500 years ago, while kimoto only dates to the late 1600s. Kimoto uses a different production method to create natural lactic acid. Steamed rice and koji rice are mixed with water in an open cedar barrel that is wide and short in shape, almost like an oversized soup bowl. These ingredients are mixed well with

The Yamahai Production Method

With the advent of higher polishing rates, someone in the early 1900s realized that lactic acid propagation would occur with more highly polished rice even without the yamaoroshi paste-making process. *Yamahai* is a shortening of the term *YAMAoroshi-HAIshi-moto*, the "stop yamaoroshi process." A yamahai shubo also takes around three weeks to make, but without the backbreaking mashing step the labor isn't nearly as intense. Yamahai and kimoto sake both tend to have high acidity and a rawness that is absent from more modern styles; this is due to the introduction of natural lactic acid bacteria (and often natural yeasts that also join the party during the open-tank fermentation process).

The Sokujomoto Production Method

Approximately 90 percent of modern premium sake is made using the *sokujomoto* method. The remaining 10 percent is made using the yamahai, kimoto and—very rarely—bodaimoto methods. The reason for this is simple. Rather than needing a week or more to propagate natural lactic acid bacteria to protect the fermentation process, commercially produced lactic acid is added to the shubo on the first day. Water, lactic acid, *koji*, yeast and rice are all combined in the fermentation tank on day one. The shubo itself is completed in about two weeks rather than three, and the *toji* is not at the mercy of the natural lactic acid bacteria to help create the acidic environment that supports the propagation of yeast and koji and discourages other organisms. A sokujomoto is a much more stable and controllable environment for production of very high quality sake in large quantities. A further "cheat" is to perform the sokujomoto at a higher temperature using the *kouontouka* method. Here, water, lactic acid, rice and koji are combined in a high-temperature fermentation to allow for very rapid saccharification of the rice and koji rice, after which yeast can be introduced to commence its propagation. A kouontouka sokujomoto shubo can be completed in just one week using this accelerated method. The trade-off is usually a compromise of elegant flavor and aroma, which cannot be as closely managed in a high-temperature fermentation.

The yeast itself is extremely important. While traditional styles often use natural yeasts that live in the breweries, creating a unique style specific to that particular brewery, sokujomoto sake uses pure commercially available yeast strains. A great deal of research has gone into developing yeasts that will create specific aroma and flavor profiles. Some yeast strains have become so famous that the type of yeast is now prominently displayed on the label (or may even be part of the brand name). The current trend is toward yeasts that produce more glucose, making for a sweeter taste than the dry style that previously dominated premium sake types. This sake also tends to have a shorter shelf life, and so is designed to be consumed shortly after production.

Facing page Steamed rice is prepared for sake production at the Terada Honke Brewery. Some of the rice will be inoculated with koji spores, the rest will be used for other stages of the fermentation process.

Below Management of sake fermentations is critical to the quality of production. This is done through temperature regulation of the tanks themselves, but also through daily mixing to aerate the aerobic koji and to agitate the anaerobic yeast.

The Main Fermentation

Once the shubo is ready, the *moromi* is built. The moromi would be called the mash, or main fermentation, in Western alcohol traditions, although in sake-making most of the heavy lifting has been completed by the time the moromi is made. In modern sake-brewing this is usually accomplished by the three-step method (*sandan-jikomi*), in which steamed rice, koji rice and water are added to the yeasty shubo in three stages over four days. These ingredients are added on days 1, 3 and 4 in progressively larger volumes so that nearly half the volume of the entire moromi is added on day 4. On day 2, known as *odori* (dance), the yeast is given a chance to catch up with the sudden influx of sugars available for its consumption.

This moromi is then left to ferment for two to five weeks. Philip Harper (see page 41), the first foreigner ever to earn the title of *toji* (master brewer) describes what happens next in a wonderfully lyrical passage in his *Insider's Guide to Sake*:

> The tank appears to contain a great swollen heap of very thick porridge. After a couple of days, the moist surface begins to crack in places, and a thin foam appears there. The mash begins to bubble . . . The first fine, watery foam changes into a much thicker, creamier layer of bubbles. At

its peak, this foam rises well over a meter above the surface of the mash . . . This recedes a few days after reaching its peak . . . the mix is much lighter and more obviously liquid by now, and it bubbles and seethes frantically for several days. Gradually, the activity subsides.

The toji will closely monitor this foam progression; by sight and smell alone, he can tell how active the koji and yeast remain in the mash. The toji needs to end the fermentation at the precise moment when the alcohol yield has been maximized, but before the sake is subjected to the off flavors that can occur when yeast begins to die off. At this point, a very small amount of brewer's alcohol may be added to the mash. This was originally done to act as a preservative at a time when pasteurization was not as refined as it is today. Today, with premium sake, this is not intended to increase the alcohol level or to function as a preservative, but rather to capture some aroma components that would be lost in the subsequent stages of production. The brewer's alcohol binds to these volatile compounds and holds them in liquid form to keep those aromas in the sake.

Pressing

By the time it is finished, the moromi can reach up to 20 percent alcohol—the highest percentage in the world for

Far left The master brewer at Kitaya Brewery in Yame, Fukuoka, carefully oversees the addition of brewer's alcohol to his competition-grade daiginjo sake.

Center Cloth bags are filled with moromi (the main fermentation) to prepare for the *shizuku shibori* pressing method. It takes three people to fill each bag and three more to hang each one. Extra care is taken at this stage, because any loss could be catastrophic to a sake's chances at competition.

Below The *shizuku shibori* pressing method uses the weight of the moromi to softly press the sake from the cloth bags.

fermented alcohol. Wine usually reaches 12 to 14 percent, and most beers are far less than 10 percent. This alcohol is retrieved from the moromi through pressing. As with seemingly every other aspect of sake-making, there are various options for pressing sake. One traditional—although costly—method is to hang cloth sacks of moromi from a wooden beam and allow the raw sake to drip from the bags into a container that has been placed beneath. This *shizuku shibori* (also known as *shizukudori* or *fukurozuri*) method is usually reserved for only very premium sake, as it's slow, but results in a finer mouthfeel. In another traditional method that is slightly more efficient, the sacks of moromi are laid flat on top of one another inside of a container called a *fune*. As the sacks are being stacked, some of the sake is pressed out naturally under their weight. Known as *arabashiri*, this can sometimes be found bottled separately as a premium product. Ultimately, an actual weight is placed on top of the bags to press out the liquids, leaving behind the sake *kasu* (solid lees).

A modern method uses an automatic pressing machine that looks like a giant accordion. The moromi is pumped into thin cloth partitions in between the ribs of the accordion, and air bladders between the partitions are inflated to press out the sake. While this is by far the most efficient method, it can still take hours to press an entire batch of moromi.

Post-Fermentation Processes

Once the sake is pressed, a number of additional steps may or may not be taken depending upon the style of sake being made. Once pressed, sake is almost always placed in a holding tank, which allows any remaining sediment to settle. As the sake rests in the tank for one to two weeks, the sediment will collect on the bottom. Careful removal of the sake from a spout above the sediment results in a clearer, more stable product. The sake is then usually filtered using a microfiltration process, which removes any remaining sediment as well as some compounds that could cause off flavors. Filtration may be done with or without carbon or activated carbon. Each step up in filtration results in a more stable sake, but may also remove desirable flavors or aromas. These decisions, like all others, are left to the master brewer.

Pasteurization kills off any remaining yeast, koji, and lactic acid bacteria (or other invasive microorganisms), which again results in a more stable sake. Sake is usually pasteurized twice: once after filtration and once before or after

bottling. However, it may be done at only one of these times or not at all. After filtration and pasteurization sake is usually aged in tanks for three to six months, though sometimes up to a year or even much longer. When the sake is deemed ready to bottle it may be diluted down to 15 to 16 percent alcohol (or whatever the *toji* believes is the best dilution). This increases yield, but also makes for a more food-friendly beverage. Finally, after all of these additional procedures have been completed (or not), the sake is bottled and prepared for delivery to customers.

SAKE STYLES

Although the word "sake" is in such wide use among foreigners that it is impossible to avoid using, it is not a precise term. It is actually the general word in Japanese for any alcohol, including beer, whisky, wine and so on. *Nihonshu* is usually the term used if you want to refer specifically to the brewed rice sake. However, some shochu makers don't like that name because the *"Nihon"* part of the word, meaning "Japan" implies that sake is the national drink; in fact in 2012, both sake and shochu were named *kokushu* (national liquors) of Japan. A more technical term for what we know as sake is *seishu* (清酒). These two characters are useful because they are printed on the labels of all refined sakes. To the uninitiated, sake and shochu bottles

can look quite similar, but shochu always has 焼酎 printed somewhere on the label. Seishu, which means "clear sake," came into use to differentiate charcoal-filtered sake from the unfiltered kind, but now the term is used more generally for all sake. You are going to have to know a bit more than that if you want a product that suits your needs, however. As Kyoto sake-bar owner Yoram Ofer bluntly put it, there is "a lot of garbage and a lot of heaven" in the sake world. Let's begin with the garbage.

Zojoshu (増醸酒)

Zojoshu, the cheapest "sake," is a close friend of technicolor hangovers. Hundreds of liters of distilled alcohol can be added for every ton of white rice used in making this stuff. Other additives such as glucose are also often used to make it remotely palatable. From 2006, these products could no longer be called seishu, and are instead classified simply as"liquor," but zojoshu still appears on the sake shelves. Our advice regarding zojoshu: don't bother.

Futsushu (普通酒)

The *vin ordinaire* of the sake world, this category accounts for the majority of sake sales. It contains much less added alcohol than zojoshu. Like table wine, the *futsushu* category encompasses tedious mass-market bottlings as well as some quite interesting brews. It really depends on who is making it and for what reason. Feel free to explore judiciously.

Now for the heaven:

Honjozo or Honjozoshu (本醸造 or 本醸造酒)

This is premium sake made with polished rice but with a small amount of alcohol added to the moromi (mash). The polishing rate must reach at least 70 percent, and less than 31 gallons (117 liters) of distilled alcohol per ton of rice may be added at the end of the fermentation process for sake to qualify for the honjozo classification. Unlike cheap zojoshu, the alcohol is not added for economy's sake; it helps the brewers create light but aromatic sakes with a pleasant mouthfeel. Fragrant components in the moromi dissolve in the alcohol so they are present in the final sake rather than being left behind in the lees.

Junmai or Junmaishu (純米 or 純米酒)

Junmaishu is pure rice sake: only rice, koji, water, yeast and perhaps a little lactic acid are used in production. Not all

Daiginjo or Daiginjoshu (大吟醸 or 大吟醸酒)

This is the more polished sibling of ginjo. The polishing rate is less than 50 percent, and in some extreme cases can go much lower. Small amounts of alcohol are sometimes added. Though this is the most premium and refined sake on the market, it is more difficult to pair with food due to its highly floral and aromatic qualities. Have fun experimenting!

Sake Variations

If sake could be reduced to only the six levels of purity and refinement listed above, the world would be a dull place. In fact, there is a seemingly endless variety in the methods of making and storing sake. Here are some interesting variations to explore:

Tokubetsu (特別)

This is a frustratingly vague yet usually delicious designation. Tokubetsu simply means "special," but the only specific rule around it is that junmai or honjozo grade sake must be polished to 60 percent or less to qualify as tokubetsu. Beyond that, however, tokubetsu can refer to any appreciable deviation from the sake brewer's normal operations. For example, fermenting at a lower (or higher) temperature, using natural rather than commercial yeasts, using rice from a single town or even a single farmer, or pressing or filtering in a traditional manner could all conceivably qualify as tokubetsu in spirit, if not in point of fact. The rule of thumb here is that it's usually going to taste a bit different and cost a bit more than a similar grade from the same producer.

junmaishu uses rice polished to premium *ginjo* or *daiginjo* standards (see the following category), but this does not mean it is necessarily of inferior quality. In fact, there has been a recent trend toward favoring the robust tastes often associated with relatively unpolished junmaishu. Unlike the honjozo designation, there is no minimum required polishing rate for the junmai category; some 80 percent or even 90 percent junmaishu can be quite compelling.

Ginjo or Ginjoshu (吟醸 or 吟醸酒)

Sake made of very finely milled or polished rice. Polishing must reach at least 60 percent to achieve the ginjo classification. A lot of ginjo is junmai-ginjo made of pure rice, but some ginjo have a small amount of added alcohol, as honjozo does. They are not usually labeled as honjozo-ginjo, however. You have to look at the ingredient list to see if alcohol (アルコール) has been added. If the label doesn't say "junmai," there's a good chance it has been.

Bodaimoto (菩提酛), **Kimoto** (生酛), **Yamahai** (山廃)

These traditional methods of lactic acid production (see page 32) garner their own categories. You'd better believe the brewer is going to let you know about all of that extra labor and time to justify a higher price! These sake varieties are usually more highly acidic and can carry unexpected flavors and aromas. Brewers with the time and labor available have been playing more and more with these traditional styles to explore the complex, untamed tastes that the old natural methods tended to promote. Bodaimoto is the rarest of these styles, so if you happen to find one, drink it!

Genshu (原酒)

Sake is called *genshu* if it is bottled at full strength, straight out of the press. It's usually around 17 to 18 percent alcohol, but may range up to 20 percent in some cases. This designation tends to be more expensive, with a much bigger punch than most sake varieties. Genshu goes well with really rich foods, but tends to overpower more delicate dishes.

Namazake (生酒)

This is unpasteurized sake in its purest form. *Nama* (生) means "raw," and *namazake* usually still has active organisms in the bottle. It can smell and taste quite different from

your average dry sake: boisterous nutty, fruity, herbal and even spicy tastes can be brought out by the extra life that skipping pasteurization allows. You are usually cautioned to make sure your namazake is carefully refrigerated so all that microscopic partying doesn't get out of hand. However, Kyoto sake-bar owner Yoram Ofer is fond of serving namazake that he keeps at room temperature, often for years, and it may offer a wonderfully mild and honeyed taste. "The industry will tend not to want to do that because it's too risky. Sometimes bottles can go off, but it's not true that it always goes bad," he says. There are also two half-measures to namazake: *namazume* (生詰め), which is only pasteurized after filtering (before storage), and *namachozo* (生貯蔵), which is only pasteurized at bottling. In truth, virtually all exported namazake is in one of the latter categories, as the shelf stability of true namazake is too uncertain in today's global sake market.

Suroka (素濾過), **Muroka** (無濾過), **Orizake** (おり酒)

Most sake is charcoal filtered. If it's filtered without charcoal, it's called *suroka*. If filtering is skipped altogether, it is called *muroka*; if the sediment removal process is also skipped, it's *orizake* (*ori* means "sediment"). These all have increasing

Above A unpasteurized *namazake* is best consumed shortly after bottling as its brightness will fade over time.

Right A slightly cloudy *orizake* (left) and a milky *nigori sake* (right) side by side in a Niigata izakaya.

Facing page A selection of sakes at Hi-Collar sake lounge in New York (see page 136).

levels of flavor and coloring. A sake filtered with activated charcoal will be virtually clear, while a muroka sake may be yellowish; orizake will have some faintly visible white specks floating in it or settled at the bottom of the bottle.

Nigorizake (濁り酒)**, Kasseishu** (活性酒)**, Doburoku** (濁酒)
Nigorizake takes the unfiltered thing a step further. Rather than pressing the sake out of the moromi (main fermentation) through a fine filter, nigori is made using only a mesh filter or, alternatively, filtering the sake clear and then reintroducing some lees from the moromi afterwards. Either way, some of the solids from the moromi are present in the final alcohol; as a result, nigorizake ranges in appearance from slightly cloudy to milky. The tastes vary considerably, too, but there is often a strong sweetness. *Kasseishu*, which is unpasteurized nigorizake, can sometimes have a slight fizz to it. At the extreme end of the spectrum, *doburoku* is not filtered or pressed at all. It looks like porridge and can be quite hard to appreciate. This is what most home brew was like in the olden days if you want a taste of what the peasants were making and hiding from the samurai. Doburoku cannot legally be labeled as seishu since it has not been filtered, but it is the progenitor of all of these variations.

Koshu (古酒) or Jukuseishu (熟成酒)

The rediscovery of long-neglected traditions of maturing sake is one of the most exciting developments in the contemporary sake scene. There are diaries and letters showing that aged sake, or *koshu*, was valued highly as early as the 13th century, and Edo-period shop records tell us that three- to nine-year-old sake was two or three times more expensive than *shinshu* (new sake). The *Honcho Shokkan*, a food encyclopedia published in 1697, states, "After three to five years, the taste is rich and the smell is wonderful, and that is the best. From six to ten years, the taste becomes thinner and yet richer. The color darkens and there is a strange aroma. Better than the best!"

When pioneering makers tried to resurrect koshu in the 1970s and 1980s, however, they were sometimes met with outright hostility. The traditions of aging had died out so completely and had been replaced so thoroughly by the modern interest in young sake that koshu was seen as a gimmick at best, and at worst a worrying subversion of "proper" sake values. The *ko* in koshu means "old," suggesting "forgotten" or "neglected," so the appellation "jukuseishu" has been introduced to allay fears, since *jukusei* implies

intentional aging. While there are no official rules for how long a sake must be aged to qualify as a koshu, the Association for Aged Sake has set a voluntary standard of a minimum of three years, which most breweries now follow.

Why did koshu almost disappear in the first place? The growing popularity of wooden barrels for storing sake in the Edo period may have been partly to blame. These barrels allowed much more exposure to air than the pottery vessels they replaced and therefore increased the risk of spoiling. They also imparted woody flavors that may have become overpowering after long aging. More lethal to the tradition, however, were tax laws introduced in the early Meiji era (1868–1912) which forced sake makers to pay taxes on their sake as soon as it was made. Cash-strapped breweries needed a return on their investment as soon as possible. This factor, plus faster distribution networks and wartime shortages, discouraged the aging of sake to such an extent that it became almost unknown.

Fans of the modern koshu scene are rediscovering the complex tastes, fragrances and colors that aging adds to sake. Koshu can be classified into two broad types: air-temperature-aged and refrigerator-aged. Koshu aged by air temperature is often dark in color, with maple-syrup browns or blood reds quite common (the color usually comes from reactions between sugars and amino acids in the liquid rather than from the barrels or pots used for storage). This type has a very wide range of tastes, including some reminiscent of sherry or Chinese Xiaoxing wine. Refrigerator aging, on the other hand, often produces koshu that is lighter in color, ranging from almost transparent to golds and greeny yellows. The taste is usually much closer to the roundness of ginjo sake, along with biscuity and nutty flavors often added by maturation. The sector is such a hive of innovation that strict classification is impossible: makers are playing with combinations of cold and warm storage temperatures, as well as all sorts of storage containers (steel, glass-lined or enamel-lined tanks; bottles; barrels; jars made of earthenware or ceramic) and a seemingly endless variety of brewing techniques (namazake, fortified sake and even sake made with wine yeasts). Hakkaisan, a famous brewery in snowy Niigata, recently released a three-year snow-aged junmai ginjo koshu. It's stored at such a low temperature that the average sake drinker may not even be able to tell the difference between it and a much newer brew.

Other Sake Styles

Even though sake makers have become adventurous with koshu, that's just one small prism in the kaleidoscope of innovation. Brewers are experimenting with wooden fermentation vessels or storage tanks. In the past, wood was used throughout sake production, but it fell out of favor due to the aromas and flavors it imparts during production or aging. Nevertheless, some makers have continued or revived these

styles of *taruzake* (wood-barrel sake), and have begun trying out different kinds of wood such as oak or Japanese cedar.

Brewers are also playing around with sparkling sake. This usually has a lower alcohol content than standard sake, because making the fizz requires halting the tank fermentation earlier than usual. The bubbles are created by secondary fermentation in the bottle. These brews are usually filtered, but significant amounts of sugar and yeast must be allowed into the bottles for the secondary fermentation to take place, so they're usually cloudy and quite sweet. Always innovating, the Hakkaisan brewery in Niigata prefecture has now begun making sparkling sake in a champagne style.

Something to consider as you explore the world of sake is that the styles and variations described above are not separated or delineated. Take for example, the Tamagawa White Label Yamahai Junmai Muroka Nama Genshu from Philip Harper's Kinoshita Brewery (see facing page). The yeast starter for this pure rice sake is created with natural lactic acid bacteria; the drink is bottled unfiltered, unpasteurized and undiluted. It smells and tastes a bit of cheese—absolutely delicious.

Left Hakkaisan's bottle-fermented Awa sake is made in a champagne style.

Below Hakkaisan is produced in the northern prefecture of Niigata which has some of the highest snowfall in Japan. As a result the sake tends to be light and clean with very low temperature fermentations and storage.

SAKE MASTER PHILIP HARPER

Philip Harper first came to Japan in 1988 as a teacher for the Japan Exchange and Teaching (JET) program. He soon fell in with a couple of Japanese guys who were extremely passionate about sake. They drank sake, talked sake, studied sake, visited breweries—and drank more sake. After one of his friends quit his job to work in a brewery, Philip followed suit. By 1991 he was working as a *kurabito* (member of brewery staff) at Ume no Yado Brewery in Nara, the birthplace of sake production.

The work was exhausting—so much so that one evening he fell asleep on his evening bike ride to the brewery and woke up shoeless in a freezing cold stream. He still can't remember how he made it over the guardrail or back up the steep embankment with his bike. When he arrived at the brewery his fellow kurabito were horrified to see that he was covered in blood. Undaunted despite the exhaustion and injuries, he continued at Ume no Yado for 10 years. In 2001 Harper became the first foreigner to be admitted to the Nanbu Brewers' Guild as a *toji* (master brewer). He spent the next six years working at breweries in Ibaraki and Osaka before being hired to take over as the master brewer at Kinoshita Brewery in Kyoto.

Though Harper is a foreigner, he's taken a completely Japanese attitude toward sake production. He learned to make "indestructible" sake at Ume no Yado, and has carried that tradition on at Kinoshita. He hasn't followed the current trend toward making the light, floral, fragile sake that's designed to be consumed shortly after production. Rather, about half of the brewery's production consists of the traditional *yamahai* or *kimoto* styles, which are made with house yeasts rather than pure commercial yeasts, giving them robust flavor and aroma profiles.

Harper is currently working with eight different rice varieties polished to between 88 and 40 percent, depending on what he's making. He's also developed an extensive portfolio of sake that is suitable for aging. In fact, Kinoshita Brewery currently has three or four times more sake aging in warehouses than other breweries its size. Several of these are not bottled until three to six years after production; the brewers are also conducting experiments in their new aging warehouse, which does not have climate control (sake ages faster in higher temperatures). The formula seems to be working: Kinoshita is producing about 3.5 times more sake today than it was when Harper took over.

HOW TO DRINK SAKE

Yusuke Shimoki, the proprietor of the magical Washu Bar Engawa in rural Ishikawa prefecture (page 135), likes to walk his interested customers through a lesson on serving temperature and service vessel. He serves his warmed sake in five-degree increments, monitoring their warming very closely. He is just as meticulous about his serving ware, which includes roughened pottery, porcelain, glass, wood, tin and lacquerware of all different shapes. When he serves you the same sake in different vessels at the same temperature, or at different temperatures in the same type of vessel, it's hard to believe it's the same sake in each cup.

Toji Philip Harper, always a bit of a renegade, recently released a summer sake called Icebreaker. He didn't want sake enthusiasts to geek out over a new summer release from Philip Harper, so he stunned people by recommending it be served on the rocks. He's caught some flak for it, but speaking from experience, it's a lovely drink over ice. Lest the name seem odd, Icebreaker refers to sake as a social lubricant, which will be ably demonstrated if you ever order Icebreaker on the rocks at a standing bar in Japan.

You too can have great fun playing with sake's temperature. Unlike beer and wine, many sakes are tasty at a wide range of temperatures. Finding out what temperature you think best suits a particular sake is part of the enjoyment of drinking. It is worth saying—though this is a matter of personal taste—that many sakes are served either too cold or too hot in restaurants in the West. The serving vessel also matters. A light, floral sake may go best in a stemmed wine glass while some of the more traditional styles are likely to taste better in more traditional service ware such as lacquer, porcelain, or pottery.

For home drinking, always store your sake in the refrigerator. However, you'll want to let it rest at room temperature for a few minutes before serving when it's chilled (see page 28 for tips on serving hot sake). New York City sake expert Jamie Graves finds that sake is often better on the second day after the bottle is opened, but also recommends that it be finished within one to two weeks of opening.

Regardless of how you enjoy your sake, it's a fascinating alcohol category to explore with a dizzying array of styles. Just don't call it "rice wine."

焼酎
Shochu

Japan's Best-kept Secret

JAPAN'S OLDEST DISTILLING TRADITION

There are various theories about exactly how distillation arrived in Japan. Some scholars, pointing to records of liquor carried on boats to Japan from Okinawa in the early 1500s, say it came from those islands. Others argue for a Korean route because of similarities in distilling techniques. What almost everyone agrees is that spirits arrived through the robust China Sea trade in the late 1400s or early 1500s. Further reflection suggests the Korean route is more likely, as black koji, one of the main ingredients in the production of Okinawan spirits, were not introduced to Japan until after shochu production had been established. Furthermore, the Korean Peninsula is very close to Kyushu, shochu's birthplace, across the Strait of Japan.

Many of the world's distilling traditions have a similar origin story. There is some evidence of early distilled spirits in ancient India, China and the Middle East, but the types of liquor we drink now all originated in a wildfire spread of technology that came from the growth of international trade beginning around 1200 AD. Distilled alcohols, unlike brewed wines and beers, do not spoil, so they are well suited to surviving long ocean voyages. In fact, the word "proof," used to denote an alcohol's potency, is actually a maritime term referring to the ability of gunpowder to still ignite if soaked in the alcohol (this was "proof" of the tipple's strength). Gunpowder soaked in alcohol above 57 percent alcohol by volume (ABV) will still ignite, so it was preferred on British Navy ships, which might need gunpowder at a moment's notice. Spilled beer or wine could spoil the gunpowder, but "Navy Strength" rum or gin, which was above proof, would not prevent the cannon from being fired.

Top right Original designs for pot stills were extremely rudimentary. This still, powered by wood fire, was used by the Sengetsu distillery in Kumamoto until the early 20th century.

Bottom left Shochu was traditionally a blue-collar drink from southern Japan. It is often found in 1.8 liter (2 quart) bottles with colorful labels.

The art of distillation seems to have arrived in many regions in the same way as it arrived in Japan—first as an expensive imported commodity; then as a bright idea: "Why are we buying this when we could make it ourselves?" The origin dates for many of the world's distilling traditions are astonishingly close. The first written record of spirits in Korea (1488), Scotch whisky (1494), Okinawan awamori (1534), Japanese shochu (1546) and French calvados (1554) are all within 70 years of each other. The word "shochu," which means "burned alcohol," also has echoes in distilling traditions around the world: brandy (from the German *branntwein* or "burned wine") has a similar root, as does the Spanish *aguardiente* (from the Latin *aqua ardens* or "fire water"), Korean *soju*, and the southern Chinese *shiao-chiu*.

Still, while drinks such as brandy, whisky, vodka and rum (the latter a relative latecomer in the 17th century) have established international reputations, shochu remains relatively obscure outside Japan. To understand the scale, more than three times as much shochu is produced in Japan every year as tequila in Mexico, yet nearly all of it is also consumed in Japan. The reason for this has nothing to do with quality. From the 1630s, Japan largely shut itself off

THE EARLIEST REFERENCE TO SHOCHU

In 1559, frustrated carpenters working on the Koriyama Hachiman Shrine in the Satsuma domain on the island of Kyushu in southern Japan scrawled five lines of graffiti on one of the building's timbers: "The head priest is such a tightwad! He didn't give us shochu even once. What a nuisance!" They even signed and dated their desecration: "2nd year of Eiroku. Sakujiro and Suketaro Tsuruta." It is unknown whether they had better luck on their next job, but their gibe is the earliest known reference to Japanese shochu, Japan's homegrown spirit. It is worth noting that both sake and Okinawan awamori were first mentioned by Chinese dignitaries, while shochu was introduced by graffiti—staying true to its southern blue-collar roots.

A slightly earlier report of hard liquor in the area was written 13 years before the graffiti. The Portuguese merchant captain Jorge Alvares, who later brought Francis Xavier to Kyushu to try to convert the Japanese to Christianity, said he had seen the people of Yamagawa drinking "arrack made from rice." Arrack was a term for distilled alcohol common in Southeast Asia, where Alvares was based; he was likely referring to shochu.

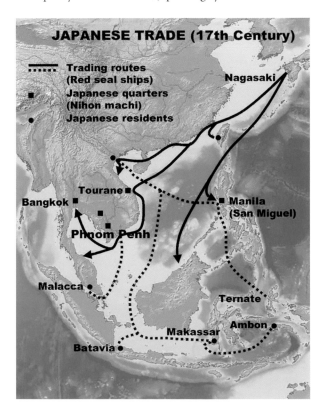

Left During the Tokugawa Shogunate Japan traded extensively with its neighbors, officially through armed merchant sailing ships, known as "red seal" ships, as they were authorized with red-sealed patent letters from the shogun. Other channels were less official, for example when Japanese fishermen would "accidentally" drift too far out to sea and end up on outlying islands where they would trade with fisherman from Korea, China, or the Ryukyu Kingdom (modern day Okinawa).

from the international trade that brought distillation to the country and that would spread the reputations of other distilling traditions. Japan did not become a major trading nation in its own right until the 20th century, nor was it ever a colony of a trading empire; shochu thus stayed local. To this day, it is enjoyed overwhelmingly by domestic consumers. Until the 1970s, it was even more localized, considered a regional blue-collar drink in southern Japan. Kyushu and the surrounding islands, where more than 90 percent of shochu is produced, also consumed virtually all of it.

Not everything came easy. Shochu was not very good at first. The early production process led to a lot of variation in quality, as most shochu was produced by farmers and other home distillers who sold it to neighbors. It was only during the Meiji Restoration that shochu makers were required to formalize their business interests and apply for distilling licenses. The advent of professional shochu makers also led to the rise of the traveling *toji*, master brewers or distillers who moved from region to region following the harvests to make shochu from fresh ingredients. These professionals taught their apprentices, and shochu was gradually elevated from sloppy moonshine to artisanal craft spirits.

A Critical Distinction

There are two types of shochu: *honkaku* shochu (本格焼酎 authentic shochu), and *korui* shochu (甲類焼酎 multiply

distilled shochu). Korui shochu has been around for a little over 100 years, while honkaku shochu has a more than 500-year tradition. This chapter will focus on the latter.

Korui shochu is definitely the cheapest way to buy alcohol in Japan—a 5-quart (5-liter) plastic jug that is 25 percent alcohol by volume (ABV) runs about ¥1,600 (US $14, £11, €12). Unfortunately, it's also completely uninteresting. It is a modern innovation made possible with the introduction of the patent still in the late 19th century. This method strips virtually all flavor from the main ingredients, resulting in nearly pure ethanol that is then diluted back down to a survivable alcohol percentage. Its nearest relative is mass-produced Korean *soju*, which is often bottled at 20 percent ABV or less with sweeteners, citric acid and other flavors added to the distillate. Unfortunately, many Westerners try korui shochu once and conclude that shochu in general is a cheap vodka substitute. They could not be more wrong.

Honkaku shochu is the interesting stuff. Sometimes called *otsu* (乙) or *otsurui* (乙類), referring to "single-distilled" shochu, it traces its single-distillation pot-still method back

Below, left Korui shochu (left) is the cheapest form of alcohol in Japan, but is also completely uninteresting to drink. Honkaku shochu (right), with a 500-year tradition, is often full of individual character.
Below, right The imposing Sakurajima volcano is across Kagoshima Bay from what was once the Satsuma domain. The volcano erupts almost daily and enriches the local soil with ash, which sweet potatoes love.

Top left The Manzen distillery is nestled into a mountain valley along a stream in the foothills of the Kirishima range. This distillery produces only traditional handmade shochu in very small quantities.

Bottom left Toshihiro Manzen tinkers with his traditional cedar pot still, a finicky piece of equipment that yields distinct flavors and aromas for the shochu he produces.

to the origins of distillation. It is often full of individual character, and some of it is quite superb. The price can reflect its premium status, reaching more than ¥30,000 (US $265, £200, €228) for a bottle in some Tokyo liquor stores. There is, however, also some very reasonably priced honkaku shochu, which represents some of the best value of any premium Japanese alcohol.

MAKING HONKAKU SHOCHU

On the northern rim of Kagoshima Bay sits Kirishima, a modest city of about 100,000 people, whose most famous export is *kurozu*, a black rice vinegar made by aging unfiltered sake and vinegar mother in clay pots in the sun for years. Looking south across the bay you'll see Sakurajima, one of the most active volcanoes on earth. To the north above the town is the Kirishima mountain range, a popular resort area famous for hot springs and hiking. There are a

handful of active shochu distilleries in the city of Kirishima, but our destination is in the foothills of the Kirishima mountains.

An access road off the main route into the mountains winds further up into the hills, eventually turning from pavement to gravel. The road winds up along a steep embankment and splits, and we take a left, or a right. Without pause, our driver knows which direction to take at every Y, each leading to another unknown place—a home, a mountain pass, a farm. Finally we reach a gravel road that seems in somewhat better repair, but a bit more grooved than the others. We take it and eventually find ourselves hugging the bank of the Tekogawa river. As we dip into a shallow valley we catch glimpses of a building through the trees.

The two-story wooden distillery stands on the riverbank, dwarfing the neighboring cabin where the small staff spends their idle time and where the *toji*, Toshihiro Manzen, sleeps during the production season. The sound of the river gives everything a calm, zen-like quality. The staff will sometimes fish off the wooden deck of the toji cabin to pass the time.

It's a special place with a sad history. The original company was set up in 1922, but Manzen's father died suddenly in 1969, at the age of 39. Manzen was only 10 years old at the time, so the distillery was shuttered and the family survived on sales from their small liquor shop in Kirishima. Manzen had been too young to learn from his father, so he had to train at neighboring distilleries to learn how to make shochu before reopening the distillery. He wasn't able to do this until he himself was 39, the age at which his father had died.

Manzen's resolutely traditional methods have served him well in the years since the rebirth of his distillery. He has earned a formidable reputation among connoisseurs across

Japan for his rich, aromatic spirits. Most of the tiny production is bought up within days of release, but he has no plans to increase output. "The people who decide to go for big manufacturing have a problem when demand falls. People like me, who have a family perspective, who are making a business for our children and distill the same amount every year, we just keep on going." Evidence of this is abundant across Kyushu, as some large facilities lie partly idle with production capacity that far outstrips demand, which is easily met by skeleton crews.

Manzen and his sons and a small crew make all of the koji by hand. He still uses an old-style cedar still with a "thumper" to catch any overflow from overheating. He tuts at the mere idea of using modern temperature control in his koji room or cooling equipment in his fermentation vats. In contrast, about 25 miles (40 kilometers) away in Miyazaki prefecture is the Kirishima distillery, maker of the bestselling Kuro Kirishima (黒霧島) brand. This facility, as large as any modern factory, uses computer monitoring, robots and all sorts of technology to make more shochu in a day than Manzen makes in a year. Regardless of scale, all honkaku shochu follows roughly the same production process.

The Harvest

Shochu-making is often seasonal, because the freshness of the ingredients is extremely important. In fact, in the case of sweet-potato (*imo*) shochu, which is all Manzen makes, there's no choice. As Tekkan Wakamatsu, *toji* of the Yamato-zakura distillery, a traditional sweet-potato shochu maker even smaller than Manzen, explains, one reason sweet potatoes came to be used for shochu-making was their propensity to rot. "Sweet potatoes begin to rot as soon as they're harvested. Our goal is to have them fermenting within 48 hours of harvest." So the sweet-potato shochu production season begins as soon as the harvest does—usually in late August, depending on the rain and temperatures of the summer months.

Sweet-potato shochu is mainly produced in Kagoshima and Miyazaki prefectures in southern Kyushu. While distilleries in other prefectures do make sweet-potato shochu, many still source their potatoes from southern Kyushu. This is because Sakurajima and other volcanoes active in the region layer the topsoil with mineral-rich ash that the sweet potatoes thrive on.

There are more than 50 varieties of sweet potato used for shochu production, but by far the most popular is Kogane Sengan (黄金千貫), favored for its high starch content (resulting in higher yields) and rich flavors and aromas. Recently red and purple varieties have begun to gain popularity due to their sweet aromas and wine-like tannins. Small distillers work with local farmers to source fresh potatoes daily during the season. Larger producers manage their supply chain by growing their own potatoes for at least part of their yield. Consistency in these relationships can lend additional terroir to these brands. Large distilleries like Kirishima, however, steam, mash and then freeze sweet potatoes during the harvest season to ensure they have enough to distill all year round.

Below The sweet-potato harvest in southern Kyushu runs from about August through December and most potatoes need to be into the fermentation within 48 hours of harvesting, to guarantee freshness. Most potatoes are still grown by small family farms.

Shochu derived from other crops has different seasons (sugarcane in January, barley in May), and some distilleries produce more than one style during the year. Staple crops like rice and barley can also be stored to be used whenever the facility is not busy with seasonal production.

Making the Koji

Koji is fundamental to traditional Japanese alcohol making. Koji is not a yeast, but a mold. Its job is to break down starches in the main ingredient into sugars, which can be turned into alcohol by the yeast. Koji mold needs a medium such as steamed rice, barley, sweet potato or buckwheat for propagation. Koji spores are usually acquired commercially from koji makers, who allow koji-inoculated rice to go to spore, then package this for use by food and alcohol producers. In traditional shochu production at Manzen's distillery, nearly all koji propagation uses rice. After the rice is steamed, it's cooled to a survivable temperature (koji is a living organism; too much heat will kill it); the koji spores are sprinkled onto the steamed rice and mixed in by hand. Unlike sake-making, when a shaker is used to separate the spores from the koji-molded grains of rice, the koji-molded rice itself is sprinkled rather than the spores alone. Once the koji-inoculated rice has been properly aerated (koji mold loves oxygen) and cooled to about body temperature, it is left to rest in the koji room for 40 to 48 hours. As koji mold feeds on the starch, it creates enzymes that convert starch to sugar and it also produces heat, so the koji rice is hand-mixed periodically during this time to further aerate, and manage the temperature.

In larger distilleries this process is done by machine. There are drum-style koji machines that hold a few hundred pounds of rice at a time; the rice is steamed, then the koji propagation process is assisted by slowly turning the drum to keep the koji-inoculated rice aerated and at a proper temperature. Larger koji machines are up to two stories tall and can produce several tons of koji at a time.

There are three main types of koji mold; each affects the taste and aroma of the end product differently. Originally all shochu was produced with yellow koji (*kikoji*, or *A. oryzae*), the same mold used in sake production. However, yellow koji does not generate sufficient acid to fight off other organisms when propagating in the heat of southern Japan. As a result, ferments were often corrupted with unwanted organisms, which gave shochu a bad reputation. Using modern temperature control and hygiene, yellow koji can now produce fresh, elegantly aromatic shochu. At some point—no one is sure when—black koji (*kurokoji*, or *A. awamori*) was introduced to Japan from Okinawa. Black koji produces tremendous amounts of acid during propagation, which makes for a very sour sake, but a rich and earthy shochu. This allowed makers to keep their fermentations free of unwanted organisms and slowly repaired shochu's reputation. Finally, a happy accident led to the discovery of white koji (*shirokoji*, or *A. kawachi*) when Professor Genichiro Kawachi discovered some of his black koji had mutated to white koji (Dr. Kawachi also developed the drum koji machine; until then all koji was mixed by hand). White koji provides light, sweet flavors and aromas. Today most shochu is produced using white koji due to its more balanced nature. Distillers prefer it because black koji grows on everything; drinkers prefer it as the lighter flavors allow the character of the base ingredients to come through more clearly.

First Fermentation

The first fermentation is known as the *ichijishikomi* (or *ichijimoromi*). In this stage the newly propagated koji is mixed with water and yeast and left to ferment, often for a week or more. At Manzen and other traditional shochu distilleries throughout Japan, this is done using the traditional *kametsubo jikomi* (or simply *kamejikomi*) method, using 105–158 gallon (400–600 liter) *kame* clay pots buried nearly to the neck in the distillery floor. This strategy serves a dual purpose: the surrounding earth helps maintain a more constant fermentation temperature, and the low rim height allows the workers to efficiently perform *kai-ire*, the process of mixing the fermentation with a *kaibo*, a bamboo shaft with a wooden mallet attached. This process helps keep the temperature down and aerates the fermentation. Since koji loves oxygen and yeast does not, this process both invigorates the koji and agitates the yeast, creating desirable flavors and aromas that would be missing if this step was skipped. Kai-ire is performed several times a day during the first fermentation, as it is vital to keep the koji active—its work is only beginning.

In larger modern distilleries, large steel vats of up to 10,566 gallons (40,000 liters) are rigorously temperature

controlled using computerized cooling systems. Kai-ire is usually still performed by hand to aid the koji and yeast in their work, but some distilleries employ automated mixing systems as well. The fermentation is usually kept below 86°F (30°C), but this is a decision made by the toji, depending on the flavors and aromas he wants to come through.

Second Fermentation

The second fermentation is known as the *nijishikomi* or *nijimoromi*. On the morning it is to start, the main ingredient (sweet potato, rice, barley, etc.) is washed and steamed (or, occasionally, roasted). Once prepared, this is added to a second fermentation tank along with more water, more yeast and the contents of the first fermentation. The ratio of main ingredient to first fermentation varies by producer, but generally ranges from 2:1 to 8:1.

In traditional distilleries, a single clay pot of first fermentation will be split among four to six clay pots dedicated to the second fermentation. These are then left to ferment for one

This page At the Yamatozakura distillery, koji production begins with steaming the rice and then mixing the koji mold into the freshly steamed rice. After about two days the rice has dried out and the mold has taken hold.

Facing page At the Shirokane distillery, after the koji mold has been propagated it is mixed in by hand before being left to rest. Once the ferment is completed it is moved into the first fermentation.

to two weeks. Depending upon the toji's preference, these pots are either left to their own devices or are mixed using kai-ire as in the first fermentation, although less frequently, since the temperatures are not as volatile as when the koji is most active. In modern distilleries this process utilizes automated temperature controls and mixing mechanisms, as with the first fermentation.

By the end of this process, the fermentation is between 15 and 18 percent alcohol, which is much higher than ferments of other spirits (whiskies are about 5 percent and rum about 10 percent). The fermentation process is also longer than others, which allows a variety of flavors and aromas to arise.

Distillation

There are almost as many shapes and designs of stills as there are shochu makers in Japan. Those used in traditional shochu production, however, share one characteristic: they are all pot stills. Honkaku shochu, by law, can only be distilled once, in a pot still. Column, or patent, continuous distillation stills are prohibited (they make korui shochu), and if you put the distillate back into the pot still to re-distill, it can no longer be sold as authentic shochu, with the accompanying tax breaks for making a traditional alcohol.

Stills are usually made of stainless steel, though some makers have recently been investing in copper stills. The traditional cedar-wood stills are magical to behold. One local man, Tatsuya Tsudome in Kagoshima, who is nearing retirement, has the skill to repair these wooden pot stills in the traditional way, using bamboo ties to hold the barrels together. "The still has to be repaired regularly, because if the ties loosen you could have a dangerous accident. It's not the most convenient way, but it gives a softness to the spirit," says Yusaku Takenouchi of the Shirakane distillery. The fermented moromi mash is only in the cedar still for a few hours, but a hint of cedar flavor comes through in the final product.

The traditional pot still is a very simple contraption: a pipe pushes hot steam from a steel tank directly into the fermented moromi. As the fermentation heats up, the alcohol begins to vaporize, as it has a lower boiling point than water. The alcohol vapor rises into a narrow neck leading to a worm tub or *jakan* ("snake pipe") where a coiled tin pipe immersed in water condenses the alcohol vapor back into liquid. Some of the older wooden stills include a "thumper," which catches moromi that splashes up through the neck of the still if the steam does its job too well. Modern stills, which are much more carefully temperature controlled, skip this safeguard,

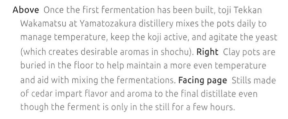

Above Once the first fermentation has been built, toji Tekkan Wakamatsu at Yamatozakura distillery mixes the pots daily to manage temperature, keep the koji active, and agitate the yeast (which creates desirable aromas in shochu). **Right** Clay pots are buried in the floor to help maintain a more even temperature and aid with mixing the fermentations. **Facing page** Stills made of cedar impart flavor and aroma to the final distillate even though the ferment is only in the still for a few hours.

and also sometimes heat the fermentation indirectly by steaming the hull of the still rather than injecting steam into the fermentation directly. The type of neck will vary depending on the flavors and aromas the maker hopes to achieve; even in relatively small distilleries, different stills may be used to produce different brands.

Unlike Western spirits, and in the true Japanese tradition of *mottainai* (no waste), in shochu-making the "heads" (what comes out of the still first) are not cut, or are cut very little. For Western spirits, in contrast, the heads—alcohols like methanol and volatile organic compounds like acetone, which are not safe for human consumption—are discarded rather than being captured in the storage tank. Shochu makers tend to let enough distillate run out to clear the last batch from the pipes, but retain most of the heads. The first pint or so, which is the most volatile, is discarded, but everything else is kept.

Typically, by the end of distillation the resulting *genshu* (undiluted alcohol) shochu will be between 37 and 45 percent alcohol by volume. By Japanese law, if it is over 45 percent it cannot be classified as honkaku shochu (with the resulting tax breaks). Most sweet-potato shochu is around 37

to 38 percent, while rice and barley styles are usually closer to 43 to 44 percent. This is largely determined by the "tails"—the last alcohol to come off the still—which stay flavorful longer in sweet-potato fermentations than in rice or barley fermentations. As they are much lower in alcohol than the heads or the "hearts" (the middle of the distillation run), the overall alcohol percentage is decreased the longer the tails run.

Of course, shochu distillers have their own language for all of this. "After about one hour of heating [the still], what we call the *hanatare* [first drops] starts to emerge, drip by drip (this is sometimes bottled separately). It looks like morning dew. This is why so many shochu brands have the word *tsuyu* [dew] in their names. Then it comes out like a fountain. This is called the *hondare* [main drops] and finally we get the *suedare* [last drops], which carries the character of the rice and sweet potato most strongly," says Takenouchi.

A further distinction from Western distilleries is the use of the vacuum still for alcohol production. Vacuum stills have been used for centuries to make perfume. By boiling the ferment at a lower temperature (like a home pressure cooker) perfumeries can capture the delicate, almost ephemeral aromas of flowers and other botanicals used in perfume production. In 1972, the Kitaya distillery (also a sake brewery) in Fukuoka prefecture first turned the perfumer's vacuum pot still to a use that was much more relevant to alcohol lovers. They began making *genatsu* (vacuum distillation) shochu, which retains the lighter, more elegant flavors and aromas that are lost when *joatsu* (atmospheric distillation) is employed in shochu production. This vacuum

Maturation

Shochu did not, until recently, have a culture of aging spirits to rival that of Okinawa's awamori or Western traditions like whisky or brandy. The spirit was routinely left to sit for between three months and a year before reaching consumers, but longer aging was not widespread. Only enough time was given to allow the volatile compounds to degrade into more mundane compounds and off-gas from the liquid. For most brands today this is still true; the raw distillate rests in large glass-lined stainless-steel tanks that retain the spirit's flavors without adding any additional flavors or aromas from the aging process.

A more traditional maturation process is aging in *kame* (clay pots) much like those buried in the floor and used for the first and second fermentations. These pots, however, live above ground, often resting on sand floors or framed in wood casing to avoid breakage during earthquakes. The pots are unglazed, which allows the clay to breathe so those volatiles can blow off, while also imparting a minerality to the spirit that would otherwise be missing. And just like Speyside Scotches that have a briny quality, shochu that is pot-aged near the ocean has a salinity that is absent from shochu made inland.

The popularity of whisky during and after the American occupation of Japan after World War II caused shochu makers to realize the potential of barrel aging. Many makers are aging their product in wood casks—either repurposed whisky, brandy or wine barrels, or casks of virgin oak. Some are also experimenting with cedar, *mizunara* (Japanese oak) and other woods native to Japan. Again, Japanese law plays a role in how long the spirits are aged: shochu cannot be darker than a certain shade; otherwise it's classified (and taxed) as whisky. This creates a

distillation approach was rapidly adopted throughout northern Kyushu, leading directly to the first "shochu boom" starting in 1976 when Nikaido, a vacuum-distilled barley shochu, broke out of Kyushu and became all the rage in Tokyo. Genatsu shochu has become a very popular style for rice and barley fermentation, but not so much for sweet potato, where *imo kusai* (literally "sweet-potato stink") is a sought-after characteristic in the traditionally made sweet-potato shochu coming out of natural gas-heated cedar stills held together precariously with bamboo fronds.

ARBITRARY AMERICAN LIQUOR LAWS

The vagaries of US liquor laws have spurred the creation of products that are only sold on the US market. In California, the most populous state in the US, Japanese shochu can be sold in a restaurant with a beer and wine (soft liquor) license if it's 24 percent ABV or less and it has the word *soju* on the label. In New York State, these same rules apply, but only if the liquor is made in Korea. Since shochu makers are not going to produce one style for export to California and another style for export to the rest of the US, much of the shochu available in the US is 24 percent ABV. Furthermore, American consumers are completely confused about what shochu is, since soju is Korean and usually multiply distilled like vodka, with sweeteners and citric acid added to improve flavor. The rational thing, of course, would be for US states to make consistent rules about requirements for alcohols that can be sold with a soft license. Proof is certainly a much better marker than production process; in many states no distilled spirit can be sold with a soft license, no matter how low the ABV. Currently, some high-proof beers now range to over 60 percent ABV—far beyond the legal limit for shochu.

problem for shochu makers, because production licenses for shochu and whisky are different, and very few companies hold both. Barrel aging imparts a golden hue, so makers are usually limited to about three years before their distillate gets too dark to sell legally (it cannot register higher than 0.08 on a light spectrometer). Some also blend barrel-aged shochu with clear tank-aged shochu of the same vintage to lighten the color.

Three years is a magic number in aging, since at that point shochu can be labeled as *koshu* (古酒, old alcohol—the same name used for aged sake). Koshu tends to sell for a higher price and is sought after by aficionados. Some producers

have now released 10-, 20- or even 30-year-old koshu. As you can imagine, they sell for several times the price of more recent vintages from the same producer.

Dilution

Shochu is nearly always diluted prior to sale; this is virtually always done after aging, between a day and a month before bottling. This serves the dual purpose of allowing producers to store products more efficiently and also to sell a product that better suits that Japanese preference for an alcoholic beverage that can be consumed with food. Undiluted shochu, at 37 to 45 percent alcohol would, burn out the taste buds more easily than diluted shochu. Most shochu is diluted to 25 percent ABV, which has become the standard due to Japanese tax laws—once it's over that level, the tax rate goes up. Local tastes also factor into the decision regarding dilution. The east coast of Kyushu—namely Oita and Miyazaki prefectures—has a long tradition of drinking shochu that is 20 percent ABV, and many producers sell 20 percent ABV versions of their 25 percent ABV shochu exclusively in those prefectures. While Kyushu produces the vast majority of all shochu, Japan's northernmost island, Hokkaido, also produces local shochu at 20 percent ABV.

One notable exception is *kokuto* (black sugar) shochu from the Amami Islands off the coast of Kagoshima. Producers there were exempt from the graduated tax rules governing other shochu producers. As a result, they developed a tradition of bottling at 30 percent ABV. When their tax break was canceled in 2008, many of them thumbed their noses at the government and continued to sell 30 percent ABV shochu just as before (though far more 25 percent ABV kokuto shochu is available now than it used to be).

Undiluted genshu shochu is a style sought after by many shochu lovers, but it's usually reserved for after-dinner drinking as a digestif. This higher-proof shochu tends to have a higher price tag, but is produced in relatively low quantities, so the tax burden on the producers is mitigated.

A few producers also ignore the tax ramifications and produce shochu in curious alcohol percentages. This is usually done to meet some specific taste or aroma target. One such example is Mizu Shochu (美鶴乃舞; the full name is Mizunomai), which is a 35 percent ABV shochu developed for the international market. The thinking was that 20 to 25 percent ABV shochu would be unpopular as a cocktail base, but at 35 percent, Mizu Shochu is pushing into vodka or rum territory. Tasting a variety of test samples with Jesse Falowitz,

"GIFT-SHOP" SHOCHU

During the shochu boom, many local tourism offices throughout Japan realized they had a potentially popular gift shop purchase if only they could convince the powers that be that their famous local crop was worthy of the *honkaku* shochu designation. Dozens of prefectures applied for, and received, permission to make new styles of shochu, which were usually contracted from Kyushu makers who had ready production capacity. These include a dizzying array of styles from seaweed, green tea, flowers, mushrooms, cactus, aloe, and even milk—yes, milk shochu. All of these ingredients, lacking starches to convert to alcohol, start with a rice and/or barley fermentation with the main flavoring ingredient added at some point during the second fermentation.

The two most popular styles of these *omiyage* (souvenir) shochu are Beniotome (紅乙女), a roasted sesame shochu from the Beniotome distillery in Fukuoka, and Tantakatan (鍛高譚), a shiso-leaf shochu from Hokkaido. Tantakatan is not considered a honkaku shochu, but is still extremely popular. Beniotome is honkaku with the rice and barley fermentation finished with up to 20 percent roasted sesame seeds in the second fermentation. Beniotome smells and tastes like the popular Japanese dessert, black sesame ice cream. If don't have a sweet tooth but you like the flavor of that ice cream, Beniotome may be the perfect dessert substitute. For US consumers, who still have no concept of what shochu actually is, Mizu has made inroads in this category with beautiful 35 percent ABV lemongrass and green tea expressions, both made with organic ingredients harvested near the distillery in Saga prefecture.

Left Traditionally, aging is done in clay pots called *kame* (bottom photo), much like those buried in the floor and used for the first and second fermentations (top photo). These pots, however, live above ground, often resting on sand floors or framed in wood casing to avoid breakages during earthquakes.

spirits run, because after that you have a distillate that can be trusted to comply with your flavoring techniques, whether that be barrel-aging a whisky or adding juniper and other botanicals to make gin. Japanese shochu production takes a very different approach, as it uses the stripping run for the final product. Due to this process, shochu is packed with flavors and aromas, many of which come from organic compounds that have been carried over into the distillate on the backs of the alcohol molecules.

While these organic compounds provide the flavors and aromas shochu drinkers seek, they also introduce volatility to what would otherwise be an inert substance (the distillation process kills all living organisms in the fermentation). The oils that come through that first distillation are still organic, and therefore can turn rancid just like any other oil that's left to sit for too long. Imagine drinking stale nuts and you'll understand just how unappealing rancid shochu could taste. Thus, filtration is generally used to remove most of the oils from the genshu.

Filtration methods range from a porous cloth bag over the end of a hose, intended only to catch relatively large solids that have made their way into the spirit, to complex modern filtration systems utilizing charcoal and other microfilters that remove virtually everything that's not truly liquid. (Activated charcoal filtration is prohibited.) More intense filtration yields less flavor and aroma, but longer shelf life. Highly filtered shochu is essentially immortal: while the flavor may dull over time, it will not spoil.

This is not true of *muroka* (無濾過, unfiltered) shochu, which has a stable shelf life of a few years. In fact, many traditional producers of muroka shochu will not sell these

the American entrepreneur behind Mizu Shochu, showed that the 35 percent version really provided the greatest flavor and aroma balance while avoiding the burn of higher proofs.

On the other end of the spectrum, lower-proof shochu has also gained traction, as some producers, particularly in southern Kyushu, have begun experimenting with diluting down to a wine or beer proof. The most intriguing of these to date is Q from Kuroki Honten in Miyazaki, a blend of several genshu styles, both barrel and tank aged, that is diluted down to 12 percent and served chilled like a white wine.

Filtration

In virtually all major Western distilling traditions using pot stills, the spirit is made with multiple runs through the still. The first run, known as a stripping run, is intended to strip the alcohol from the ferment. The second run is called a

products outside their home prefecture, because they believe bartenders elsewhere in Japan do not know how to properly care for their unfiltered varieties. Indeed, if a muroka shochu is chilled in a refrigerator, clouds of oil will congeal and float around inside the bottle like legless jellyfish. You definitely will not see these styles outside of Japan, though a few lightly filtered brands are available, including Manzen's eponymous brand, Manzen (萬膳). It's not easy to find, though—the entire allocation to the United States is just a few hundred bottles per year.

If you do manage to get your hands on some muroka shochu, it's a good idea to turn the bottle on end at least once a month. This will help mix any surface oils back into the liquid to help preserve the flavor and aroma. This becomes more vital as the amount of shochu in the bottle is reduced. Consider making a reflexive habit of turning the bottle before pouring a glass of any shochu. It's never a bad idea, and others will be impressed with your knowledge and dedication to preserving the product.

Bottling

Traditionally, shochu was sold out of the maker's shop. Families would bring their empty ceramic storage vessels to the shop for refilling. This was obviously an economical process for the makers, but not so much for the buyers. Eventually makers started selling shochu in smaller ceramic jars, and finally moved to glass bottles. Some brands are still sold in ceramic, such as the popular Kame Shizuku (甕雫), a very light 20 percent ABV sweet-potato shochu made at the

Kyoya distillery in Miyazaki. This brand is a popular gift because the handsome ceramic pot can be reused for making pickles or storing kitchen staples such as rice or salt. Rumor has it that it's going to start being exported soon.

Today shochu is almost always sold in glass bottles of 720, 900 or 1800 milliliters (24, 30 or 60 fluid ounces). Traditionally only clear glass was available, so bottles were wrapped in paper to prevent sunlight from spoiling the oils in the lightly filtered shochu. These days clear or green glass is often used for shochu that is highly filtered, but brown or black glass is often used and paper wrapping is still favored for muroka shochu. In larger factories, labels are applied by machine, but many small distilleries still label their bottles by hand. The speed and perfection attained by those assigned this task are remarkable to behold. The famous Hyakunen no Kodoku (百年の孤独, whose name is the Japanese translation of the title of the Gabriel Garcia Marquez novel *One Hundred Years of Solitude*), a barrel-aged barley shochu bottled at 40 percent ABV, is enfolded in paper by women who can hand-wrap a bottle perfectly in less than 20 seconds.

MAIN STYLES OF HONKAKU SHOCHU

Unlike, say, rum or brandy, honkaku shochu is defined by its method of production rather than its ingredients. In fact, honkaku shochu can legally be made from more than 50 ingredients. Almost any imaginable starch source is fair game, running the gamut from rice and barley to the root of the kudzu plant. With two exceptions, fermentable sugars are prohibited—after all, what would the koji do if there were no starches to break down? The exceptions are the previously mentioned *kokuto* (black sugar) shochu from Amami and palm dates (nobody seems exactly sure why these are legal). With more than 6,000 brands on the market at any one time, the variety is nearly infinite. However, there are a few established traditions.

Rice Shochu

Most 16th- and 17th-century writings describe shochu as a rice-based alcohol. This makes perfect sense, since Japanese sake had been produced for more than a millennia prior to the introduction of distillation to Kyushu. Further, since it's difficult to make reliably delicious sake in warm climates, it

STRONG ZERO

Perhaps nothing annoys shochu aficionados more than the fact that *korui* shochu is technically named "superior" shochu while *otsurui* (another name for honkaku shochu) is designated as "usual" shochu. However, there is little disagreement that *chu-hai* (shochu mixed with fruit-flavored syrup and sparkling water) are a great use for korui shochu; unless made with fresh fruit, honkaku shochu is wasted in such a concoction. The selection of canned chu-hai in convenience stores is greater than the beer offerings owing to the seemingly endless number of fruit flavors that Japanese will buy to mask their cheap alcohol. The high sugar content can result in a wicked hangover if you're not careful. However, Suntory has found a way to avoid that with Strong Zero. The "zero" means no sugar is added, and the "strong" refers to the 9 percent ABV. These surprisingly refreshing canned chu-hai pack a punch and have become extremely popular in Japan.

seems likely that distilled sake produced in Kyushu was the first foray into making shochu. The distillation would serve to mute or eliminate the off flavors and aromas that might creep into a warm-weather fermentation.

Today the best-known rice shochu is Kuma Shochu from Kumamoto prefecture in central Kyushu. As with champagne or cognac, the World Trade Organization (WTO) has recognized Kuma Shochu has having a special geographic indication (appellation of origin status). This means nobody outside the city of Hitoyoshi and the district of Kuma-gun in Kumamoto can make Kuma Shochu. As a result, there are 28 distilleries in a region of just 30,000 people. These distilleries must use local water from one of the most beautiful and pristine rivers in Japan, the Kumagawa. Rice koji and pure rice are also required as the main ingredients to earn this prestigious designation.

Exploring Hitoyoshi's distilleries demonstrates just how varied Kuma Shochu can be. Even though it's made with only four ingredients—water, rice, koji and yeast—the flavors and aromas are almost endless. Nearly half of all Kuma Shochu is produced by the Takahashi distillery, whose Hakutake

Shiro (白岳しろ) brand is easily the bestselling rice shochu worldwide. Light and easy drinking due to the use of white koji and a vacuum still, Hakutake Shiro is a favorite with younger city dwellers throughout Japan.

On the other end of the spectrum is the smallest distillery in Hitoyoshi, Jufuku Shuzo, which still makes rice shochu completely by hand. Stepping into this *sakagura* (distillery), you would think you just stepped into someone's old, worn home. In a sense, it is—the family residence is attached to the distillery, and you have to pass through a clay-pot aging room to reach the front door of their house. The president, Kinuko Jufuku, is a legend among shochu makers as one of

Right Rice shochu production relies very heavily on traditional sake-making methods, often using identical equipment right up until distillation.

Left The clay pot aging room at the Jufuku distillery in Hitoyoshi, Kumamoto prefecture, where all of their rice shochu is made by hand. They age in smaller pots so that less product is lost in the event of an earthquake. The curtained doorway in the back leads to the family's home.

(武者返し), is an ode to the styles of yore. Black koji and atmospheric distillation make for a big, full-bodied revelation; the limited filtration allows those rich flavors to linger for a long time. Look for the rare "black label" Mushagaeshi, a 10-year clay-pot-aged variety that's simply decadent.

If Jufuku is the salt of the earth—the unassuming descendant of humble farmers who happened to make delicious shochu—Torikai is an otherworldly being. The family can trace its heritage back more than 1,000 years to Kyoto, where they were bird keepers among the priestly class. The family was sent to Kumamoto to establish a new temple in the 9th century and has been there ever since. Over the years they set up many successful businesses, and the family wealth grew. When Kazunobu Torikai took over the business in 1974, he consolidated, selling off all other production interests in order to focus exclusively on shochu. This became his obsession. His goal was to make the most refined, elegant rice shochu possible. Working with a professor from Sojo

the first (and toughest) female *toji* brewers. She's now turned over the daily operations to her son, who would not look out of place at a Mr. Universe contest (you can see him on page 6). He's a hulking man who throws around 110-pound (50-kilogram) bags of rice the way most of us would move around 5-pound bags of sugar. The distillery sits in a modest neighborhood of the town. Unless you know what you're looking for, you could easily mistake it for a retail shop or one of the many crafts establishments still common in small towns throughout Japan. Their signature brand, Mushagaeshi

THE LAST SAMURAI: A TRUE SHOCHU LOVER

Contrary to popular belief, Tom Cruise was not the "last samurai." That epithet goes to Saigo Takamori (1828–77), born in the Satsuma domain in southern Kyushu, a low-level samurai who rose to prominence after defending the emperor during an uprising, and was named head of the Imperial Guard. In 1871 he led the forces that took Edo Castle and ended the shogunate, ushering in the Meiji Restoration, which modernized Japan practically overnight. After helping modernize Japan's army, Saigo-don (as locals called him) resigned in 1873, disillusioned with the new regime, and returned to Satsuma to open a military academy, which drew thousands of unemployed samurai into his militia. In 1877 he led an army of disaffected samurai to revolt against the new government in what is known as the Satsuma Rebellion, which ended with the modern military he helped create routing him and his troops at the Battle of Shiroyama. Details of his death are hazy, but of one thing there is no doubt: Saigo-don loved his shochu. No fewer than a half-dozen shochu brands claim to have been his favorite, and it's entirely possible he loved them all. He remains a legendary figure in Kagoshima, and locals are more than happy to raise a glass to his favorites.

University, he developed Ginka Torikai (吟香鳥飼), which was released in 1994. This is essentially a premium *ginjo* sake that is distilled prior to bottling, full of yeasty anise notes and an unexpected depth of umami. Ginka Torikai remains their only brand. Torikai hasn't been idle, though. In the intervening years he's become a conservationist, using his substantial fortune to buy up a few thousand hectares of mountains that feed the Sozu River (a tributary of the Kumagawa) when the local government was considering a proposal from a waste management company to turn one of the valleys into a landfill. He needed to protect his water source.

Kasutori Shochu

Through much of the modern era, shochu was regarded as a poor man's drink in Japan. No shochu had a rougher reputation than kasutori shochu, which is made from *kasu*, the solid lees left over after sake-making.

Kasutori shochu had a long history as a laborer's drink in premodern Japan. It was produced all over the country, not just in the traditional heartland in the south—mainly, it seems, because of its usefulness to agriculture. In 1696, the agricultural text *Nogaku zensho* (The complete book of farming) recommended the use of sake kasu as a fertilizer for rice. The alcohol had to be removed first, as it degrades soil quality and harms plant roots, and the best way to accomplish this was to distill the sake lees. This resulted in a wonderful circle of life in which the waste from distilling grew the rice that made the sake that left the lees that were distilled. Early on the spirit seems to have been widely used as an antiseptic, but by the late Edo period working-class drinkers had taken it up.

In Fukuoka prefecture there is a long history of the famously uncompromising style of kasutori shochu known as *sanabori* shochu. For this style—made for the sanabori rice harvest-festival—rice husks and sake lees are mixed and steamed in a very rustic still known as a *seiro mushi* (imagine a wooden pork-bun steamer with a condenser on top). This mixture allowed for direct distillation, because the rice husks provided aeration for the otherwise solid sake lees. If you can find sanabori shochu today (there are none currently on the market, though a few distilleries are still holding old stock in hopes of a revival), you'll find it might best be described as "a kick in the teeth." The most enthusiastic drinkers worked as farm hands or foresters, or in the coal mines. The advent of very cheap *korui* shochu in the Meiji era challenged the popularity of kasutori among laborers, but many continued to mix sanabori with the characterless korui shochu.

Immediately after Japan's defeat in World War II, however, the reputation of kasutori in particular, and shochu in general, took a nosedive, even among the working class, as it became associated with the violent and desperate subculture that sprang up around black markets. With little money, no hope, and horrific memories from the war, these people drank, as one black marketeer put it, "trying to forget a life that hung suspended like a floating weed." This dangerous subculture came to be known as "kasutori culture," even though the black-market liquors were often unrelated to real kasutori. An infamous drink at the time was the *bakudan* (bomb), a mixture of methyl alcohol and disguising chemicals; it, and other cocktails like it, killed at least 384 people in 1946. Negative associations stuck to kasutori and to shochu in general, and people turned to more glamorous foreign liquors like whisky for their pleasures when they got more money in their pockets.

Younger drinkers with no memory of the postwar years have now rediscovered shochu, and the kasutori tradition is producing much to intrigue them. For instance, the aged Kaito Otokoyama (開当男山) 1984 kasutori is unlike just about any other rice-based spirit, being reminiscent of a very earthy dark sherry. At the other extreme, a growing number of distilleries are making delicate and sophisticated kasutori from premium *ginjo* and *daiginjo* sake lees, which are re-fermented with additional koji, yeast and water for a few days before distillation. When they are distilled in a vacuum still, like Kitaya's Nihon no Kokoro (日本の心), they smell very

Above Sake lees, the solids left over after sake production, are used to make shochu. The waste left over after distillation can then be used for fertilizer for the next rice planting.

much like a ginjo sake while still retaining the dry flavor of shochu.

Unfortunately, kasutori shochu remains difficult to find in much of Japan. Sake lees have become popular as a cooking ingredient for marinating meats and other uses, and the Japanese skincare brand SKII makes extensive use of sake kasu (hence the "SK" in the name). In an example of history repeating itself, lees from all varieties are now used in a variety of ways to minimize waste—creating biofuels, feeding livestock and, yes, fertilizing crops.

Barley Shochu

Not long after shochu production began in Kyushu, barley became an alternative material for fermentation, which saved the more valuable rice harvest for use as food. The Japanese word *mugi* can mean wheat, barley, oats or rye, but most mugi shochu is made from unmalted barley (*omugi*) of the two- or six-row variety. Other grains, like millet, have been distilled in places such as Akune in Kagoshima since the late 17th century. The most famous production center of barley shochu is on the island of Iki, off the north coast of Kyushu.

One of the origin stories of shochu production suggests that the first stills were set up on Tsushima, an island with a long history of trade between Korean and Japanese fisher-men. Nearby Iki would naturally have been an early adopter of the new technology. As with so many innovations in the history of the world, necessity was the mother of invention. Strict surveillance of the rice crops by Iki officials in the

1700s forced the island's enthusiastic farmer-distillers to concentrate on barley. By the late 19th century, there were 55 barley shochu distilleries crammed into the island's 142 square kilometers—that's more than one per square mile. Today only seven remain, but the fame of barley shochu from Iki has spread worldwide. Like Kumamoto's Kuma Shochu, Iki Shochu (壱岐焼酎) has received WTO appellation of origin status and uses a strictly defined method to produce its famous natural sweetness. Rice is used for koji in the first fermentation. Roughly twice as much barley is then added to start the second fermentation. Distillation is usually atmospheric, making for a richer flavor and stronger aromas.

The other major area of mugi shochu production is Oita prefecture in northeastern Kyushu. A relative newcomer to barley shochu, Oita historically concentrated on sake and rice spirits, but in the mid 1970s, a company called Nikaido Shuzo released two kinds of barley shochu: Kicchomu (吉四六) and Nikaido (二階堂). Sanwa Shurui, a merger of four Oita sake-brewing families, followed suit with the now-iconic iichiko (いいちこ) brand. Iichiko's slogan, "Shitamachi no Napoleon" ("downtown Napoleon" with "downtown" in this context meaning "among the common people"), conveys a similar meaning to the Japanese that a boast of being "the Cockney's cognac" would to the English. It was a refreshing departure from shochu's old inferiority complex, referring to the drink's unpretentious image, but proudly challenging comparisons with any of the much vaunted foreign alcohols.

Shochu from Oita tasted different, too. Unlike Iki's, it used barley for koji production and both fermentation steps. Vacuum distillation kept the smell fresh and the taste very smooth. In the 1970s this new style fueled the first major spike in honkaku shochu consumption since the war. The brand iichiko, released in 1979, quickly surpassed Nikaido in sales as its light, elegant flavor was taken to another level through further innovation. Borrowing from Scotch traditions, Sanwa Shurui began blending different *genshu* (undiluted alcohol) shochu to make elegant, sophisticated styles of iichiko, creating a line of products that are all relatively similar in profile, yet quite different when tried side by side—remarkable for a brand sold in every convenience store in Japan.

Of note, this all-barley shochu production process was pioneered by the Yanagita distillery in Miyazaki, whose *toji* brewers taught the process to visitors from Oita. Those visitors returned to Nikaido and turned that distillery into a massive enterprise, while Yanagita remains a small family-

run company making delicious 100 percent barley shochu, the most famous of which, called Aokage (青鹿毛), smells and tastes unmistakably of chocolate. This innovation did save the family business, as the nearby Kirishima distillery subsequently took over the shochu world with their now-ubiquitous Kuro Kirishima sweet-potato shochu.

Sweet Potato Shochu

In perhaps the greatest twist on the concept of terroir in modern alcohol traditions, the WTO has bestowed appellation of origin status on Satsuma Shochu—that is, sweet-potato shochu made in Kagoshima prefecture from locally grown sweet potatoes (*imo*). The twist, of course, is that sweet potatoes are not indigenous to Kagoshima, Kyushu or Japan. In fact, South American sweet potatoes did not arrive in Kyushu until 1705, well after the distilling technology that created shochu was imported. In that year, a Yamagawa fisherman named Riemon Maeda brought sweet potatoes back from Okinawa, which had in turn obtained them from Chinese sellers who had received them from Portuguese merchants who had brought them from South America.

The volcanic soil in southern Kyushu is some of the worst in Japan, unsuitable for rice and many other grains, but farmers quickly discovered that sweet potatoes love the minerals in the ash. Fortunately for residents of the Satsuma domain, local farmers enthusiastically embraced sweet-pota-to farming, limiting the worst effects of a massive grain crop failure in 1732. Riemon Maeda remains a folk hero for saving thousands of peasant's lives (tens of thousands died in other parts of Kyushu). Imo shochu is just an added bonus.

When you visit Kyushu, you might be struck by just how ingrained shochu is to the local culture. However, it's only when you get to Kagoshima prefecture that you discover the depth of the passion for the drink. If you take the *shinkansen* bullet train from Tokyo or Osaka, Kagoshima is the last stop south on the Sakura Super Express. Before you even leave the ticket gate inside the station you stumble across Satsuma Bar, a casual café with bento boxes and more than 100 kinds of sweet-potato shochu for as little as ¥210 ($1.89, £1.44, €1.62) for the daily special. And it's a healthy pour. In fact, many locals do not know there are styles other than sweet potato. They may be aware of barley shochu, because a few Kagoshima producers do some barrel-aged barley styles, but when you mention rice shochu they reply, "You mean sake?"

Imo shochu really was the most southern of blue-collar drinks for most of its history, but that changed between 1996 and the early 2000s. In 1996 the WTO decided that Japan's alcohol taxes unfairly discriminated against foreign spirits, a momentous decision that would raise the price of a 2 quart (1.8 liter) bottle of honkaku shochu from 183 yen to 464 yen and cut the whisky tax in half. A crisis meeting was called among the Kagoshima shochu producers. Yuichiro Hamada, the head of a medium-sized imo-sho-chu distillery, stood up in front of his fellow producers and shocked everybody. What Hamada said was met with stunned silence, according to the Japanese writer Takashi Nagai. "This is not the end of the world," he breezily told the gathered crowd. "What this means is that the Scotch whisky industry has told the world that it regards Japanese shochu as its equal! This could be one of the greatest opportunities for us to tell the nation what imo shochu is!" Many in the room were furious. A number of older men stood up to condemn him. Imo shochu was a common man's drink, they said. It should never try to rival whisky.

Left Currently, sweet-potato shochu represents fully half of all honkaku shochu sales.
Below Kokuto shochu can only be made in the Amami Islands from dried black sugar and is usually bottled at 30 percent alcohol.

Koichi Sato, head of another distillery in neighboring Miyazaki prefecture, says, "Until then, everyone believed honkaku shochu was for the ordinary people and mostly consumed in Kyushu. There were some distillery owners who even believed their own product to be a cheaper substitute for korui shochu." The stricter tax regime forced the industry to try to reach more lucrative markets in big cities, and there they found young consumers with few preconceptions about the drink. It helped that, from 2003, there was a series of reports in the media about the supposed health benefits of honkaku shochu. Sales grew exponentially, and more importantly, Hamada's prediction that shochu could become a premium product was conclusively proved correct. In 1998, 85,885 gallons (325,109 kiloliters) of honkaku shochu were sold, climbing to 141, 822 gallons (536,856 kiloliters) by

2005; currently sweet-potato shochu represents fully half of all honkaku shochu sales. Today Hamada's distillery is one of the largest producers in Kagoshima.

The boom has tapered off recently, but imo shochu, in particular, is now widely regarded as a connoisseur's drink.

The once-derided "stink" of a traditionally made imo shochu is now sniffed intently in hundreds of specialty bars around the world. An entire industry has grown up around shochu specialists, the equivalent of wine sommeliers. Yet if you visit southern Kyushu, there is still an abiding sense that imo shochu should never be a posh person's tipple. Nevertheless, a premium bottle can now sell for hundreds of dollars in Tokyo. In fact, a single glass of what is now the most famous sweet-potato shochu, Mori Izo (森伊蔵), was recently listed on a New York City menu for $57 (£44, €52) for a single glass, which would have bought you about 16 gallons (60 liters) of the stuff before the WTO whisky tax decision. When you tell this to locals in rural Kagoshima, they smile broadly and shake their heads at the absurdity of city dwellers.

Kokuto Shochu

Another liquor born of the struggles of ordinary people is the black-sugar (*kokuto* in Japanese) shochu of the Amami Islands, which trail off the coast of Kagoshima prefecture toward Okinawa. The spotless white beaches in today's tourist brochures make it look like a tropical paradise, but life has been hard for much of the history of this viper-infested, typhoon-swept archipelago. Its most famous product, since samurai times, has been sugarcane. The powerful Satsuma domain, led by the Shimazu clan, received permission from the shogunate to take the islands from the Ryukyu Kingdom (modern day Okinawa) in 1609. They subsequently turned the islands into a massive sugarcane plantation, which made Satsuma one of the wealthiest domains in Japan despite being one of the furthest from Edo (Tokyo).

The islanders seem to have sought respite from their labors with millet- and rice-based spirits in the past. They knew early on that the sugarcane also made great alcohol, but their samurai overlords came down very hard on anyone who tried to distill it. Oral tradition has it that the samurai foremen used to round up all the distilling equipment on the island between January and June, the sugar-producing season, for fear that the valued commodity would evaporate up the necks of the islanders' stills.

Black-sugar shochu left its illegal past behind during World War II, when an American naval blockade made sugar exports impossible. Production accelerated after peace. In 1947, rice distilling was banned in Okinawa because of food shortages, but there were surplus stocks of sugarcane in Amami; that year, the total production on Amami's main island reached 47,551 gallons (180,000 liters).

The islands were under direct American military control after World War II but were returned to Japan in 1953. Instead of taxing Amami's sugarcane liquor at the exorbitant rates then applied to "foreign" spirits, the Japanese government gave it a special designation as *kokuto* (black sugar) shochu, which benefited from a special tax rate. To this day, sugarcane shochu can only be made in the Amami Islands; otherwise, it must be labeled and taxed as rum. Kokuto shochu differs from rum in that it must be made with rice koji, and while the product from the 18 Amami distilleries is vaguely reminiscent of rum, it is usually less sweet, with a distinct umami note added by the koji.

It should also be noted that, unlike rum, which can be derived from many different types of sugar (cane, molasses, brown sugar), kokuto shochu is made exclusively from "black sugar," blocks of sun-dried molasses that are added to the rice-koji ferment for the second fermentation. (Incidentally, there's a running debate between one of our authors and

Left Yamatozakura is the smallest all-handmade shochu distillery in Kagoshima prefecture where the young toji, Tekkan Wakamatsu, oversees all aspects of production "Never take shortcuts on the little things," he cautions. "Because if you do, you may start taking shortcuts on the big things."

noted shochu expert Christopher Pellegrini, who wrote *The Shochu Handbook*, the very first English-language guide to shochu, about whether to translate *kokuto* as "black sugar" or "brown sugar." We use "black sugar" here, since the kanji for black (黒) is used in the kanji for kokuto shochu (黒糖焼酎); also, the sugar used in production of kokuto shochu is quite a bit less refined than what Westerners think of as brown sugar. Look for Christopher Pellegrini's next book to see if he concedes.

Other Styles of Shochu

Well over 90 percent of shochu production consists of the abovementioned styles, but other varieties are worthy of note. Prior to the introduction of 100 percent barley shochu to Oita prefecture, the few distillers in Oita not using rice were fixated on making *kuri* (chestnut) shochu. Chestnuts are not easy to work with, so many shochu makers moved on to barley production, but those who persisted make a shochu that yields a rich, nutty flavor.

A relative newcomer is buckwheat shochu, developed in 1973 at the Unkai distillery in Miyazaki prefecture, now the biggest seller of nontraditional honkaku shochu. Buckwheat shochu is being produced by makers in Miyazaki, as well as in Honshu's Nagano prefecture. Historically, the main challenge with making soba shochu was suppressing the powerful aromas and flavors of the buckwheat, but modern vacuum distillation and maturation techniques produce a remarkably mild drink. Ever innovating, Takara Shuzo has released a 100 percent buckwheat shochu, Towari (十割). The

Above Mushagaeshi, the main brand from the Jufuku distillery, is delicious many different ways, but here it's served straight, at room temperature. **Below** The variety of shochu styles is nearly endless. In specialty bars such as Otsu (乙) in Fukuoka, the knowledgeable staff can point you in the right direction.

scientists at this large alcohol producer were able to cultivate koji spores on buckwheat, even though it is not a grain but the seed of a plant in the marigold family. The resulting all-buckwheat shochu is rich and luscious.

In Hokkaido, famous for its white potatoes (the kind we think of for french fries in the West), *jagaimo* white-potato shochu has become a popular style. The sweet, mellow spirit has hints of steamed potatoes and is nearly always bottled at 20 percent alcohol. Several other grains, tubers and root vegetables with adequate starch content are used in shochu production as well, albeit in very limited quantities.

HOW TO DRINK SHOCHU

Unlike sake, which can at times seem to have all of the pomp and circumstance of the Japanese tea ceremony, blue-collar shochu has few pretensions. However, there are some recommendations. Each method may compliment different types of shochu in different ways, and experimenting to find your own preferences is part of the fun. We'll go from the simplest to most involved preparation.

Sutoreto (straight)

Most premium shochu distillers recommend you try their spirits straight in order to fully capture the flavors and aromas they offer. As shochu is diluted before bottling, it is much more palatable to drink straight than some other distilled alcohols. People often use tiny *choko* cups for shochu; as long

as you control the refills, these have the great benefit of encouraging moderate drinking. A variation is *atsukan*, in which the shochu is heated in a small carafe before drinking. Much as when sake is heated, this enhances aromas and can be quite warming on a chilly night. Atsukan is a popular way to serve Kuma Shochu in Hitoyoshi, Kumamoto.

Oyuwari (mixed with hot water)

It's likely that shochu was originally sold at full proof and customers diluted it to their taste. There is a long history of drinking hot beverages in Asia, and Japan is no exception. Hot tea, hot sake and yes, hot shochu, all have long traditions. A way of achieving dilution and heat at the same time is to mix shochu with hot water. This is popular in Kagoshima prefecture, where you'll find old men drinking *oyuwari* shochu in the middle of the hot summer. The "proper" way to make oyuwari is to heat your water to approximately 130°F (55°C), determine your preferred shochu-to-water ratio (anywhere from 1:9 to 9:1 is fine, but 3:7 to 6:4 are most popular), and slowly pour the shochu into the hot water. The

convection this provides releases the aromas of the shochu. If you prefer not to have strong aromas, you can reverse the process and pour the hot water into the shochu, which will suppress the aromas. Just make sure your water isn't too hot. Many Western restaurants unfamiliar with oyuwari preparation will use water heated as for hot tea, but this will scald the shochu, create off flavors and burn off some of the alcohol (alcohol boils at about 173°F [78°C]).

Maewari (mixed beforehand)

To add yet another layer to shochu drinking, there is *maewari*, which is essentially dilution in advance. Maewari is usually prepared 24 hours to two weeks before serving. The shochu-to-water ratio can be anywhere from 9:1 to 5:5. It may be served hot, chilled, at room temperature, or over ice. The added dilution again changes the character of the shochu, but is significantly affected by the mineral content of the water being used—use bad water, get bad maewari. Shochu is made with very soft water, so you'll generally want to use a very soft water to make your own maewari.

Left *Maewari* aging pots rest on the counter of the bar Tokuri in Shinjuku, Tokyo (see page 138). Old-school shochu makers complain that most Tokyo bars don't know how to properly serve their brands, but Tokuri is not one of those places.

Rokku (on the rocks)

Ice came to Japan long after hot water and distillation, so drinking shochu on the rocks is a relatively recent invention. (Of course, by "recent," we mean over a century ago.) With modern shochu, which is already diluted, this results in very easy drink, not nearly as stiff as a whisky or vodka on the rocks. *Rokku* is by far the most popular way to drink shochu in Japan today. Another variation on the Kumamoto atsukan shochu is to pour the hot shochu over a large ice ball. This completely changes the character of the spirit in unexpected ways. However, this is an extremely uncommon practice. Neither of the authors have ever seen it outside Hitoyoshi.

Mizuwari (mixed with cold water)

If 25 percent ABV shochu on the rocks is too stiff a drink for you, *mizuwari* is a nice option. Mixing with water to the proportions used for oyuwari shochu can make the shochu very easy drinking. With both water and ice, you can quickly get down to a beer-strength drink as the ice melts. Thanks to the single distillation, mizuwari shochu can still have a surprising amount of flavor; it's an excellent way to enjoy shochu alongside lighter-flavored foods such as sushi.

Sodawari (mixed with soda)

Another common way to enjoy shochu, which has recently begun to trend, is mixing it with sparkling water. With ice, a sodawari can be very refreshing in the summer heat; the carbonation serves to make some flavors pop. Red or purple sweet-potato shochu mixed with soda can be fun to try, sometimes tasting of grape soda or other unexpected flavors.

Tsumetai (chilled)

Like keeping vodka in the freezer, there is a style of shochu that's almost always served from a frozen bottle and poured over a single large ice cube. That's *hanatare* shochu. A few distilleries bottle those "first drops" off the still and sell it as a separate product. It is usually found in a tall, slender 12 fluid ounce (360-milliliter) bottle at around 44 percent ABV. It is quite hard to find, and is often sold at a higher price than a 2 quart (1.8 liter) bottle from the same distillery. Low proof shochu is also sometimes chilled in a refrigerator (don't put it in the freezer or it'll turn solid) before service.

We recommend you try shochu in all these different ways to find your own style and figure out which brands taste best to you one way or another. Mixed with one shochu, soda will make it sing; with another it crushes the flavors. Some make amazing oyuwari, while others are too funky. Ice can make some richly flavored shochu bitter, while mixing with cold water makes the same shochu elegant. In short: explore.

Chu-Hai

All of the above ways of drinking shochu are variations on the theme of dilution and temperature. Another very popular way to drink shochu is in a *chu-hai*—an abbreviation of "shoCHU HIGHball"—which is shochu mixed with just about anything you like. This is most commonly korui shochu mixed with fruit-flavored syrup and some sparkling water. In fact, canned chu-hai are a common convenience-store drink that is both affordable and delicious, though if you drink too much of the stuff with sugar added, hangovers are inevitable.

However, many Tokyo bars and Japanese restaurants overseas have begun making premium chu-hai in which honkaku shochu is mixed with fresh fruit juices, sometimes squeezed tableside. The shochu is usually a vacuum-distilled barley or rice shochu that does not compete with the fruit flavors. This has perhaps been perfected by Mizu, the 35 percent ABV international market brand that now has its proprietary chu-hai on menus all over the United States and Canada. That said, black-koji sweet-potato shochu with fresh peach or pear juice and soda makes for an amazing chu-hai.

Top Sodawari is a summer refresher and goes with all sorts of shochu styles if you get the proportions right.

Bottom The bar Juban (see page 139) in New York is a great place to learn about the shochu and they'll make you an excellent fruit chu-hai if you ask politely.

泡盛

Awamori

Okinawan Moonshine

Below Okinawans are voracious drinkers and their reputation on the mainland is legendary.

Facing page, top Aged awamori is sought after by collectors and aficionados alike. You never know what you'll find on the shelves of an old Okinawan bar.

Facing page, bottom Newer vintages of awamori are often sold in clear 20 oz (600 ml) bottles.

AWAMORI HISTORY AND CULTURE

For most of its history, Okinawa was an independent country known as the Ryukyu Kingdom. The Ryukyu people were very active traders throughout the Pacific; they had strong economic relationships with Japan, China, Korea and even far-off Siam (modern-day Thailand). Their geographic positioning made them well suited to be a hub for trade across Asia. In keeping with its name, the Ryukyu Kingdom was ruled by a king, with a royal family and a strict aristocracy. Life for the peasants was hard, with typhoons, poisonous tropical creatures, and harsh class divisions. Nevertheless, they made the most of their lot in robust communities.

In 1606, Tadatsune Shimazu, lord of the Satsuma domain in Japan, received permission from the shogun to invade Ryukyu and turn it into a vassal state. The Japanese were prohibited from building seafaring vessels during this period, but Shimazu was allowed to do so for this purpose. The invasion, which took place in 1609, succeeded in less than a month, as approximately 100 ships carrying 3,000 samurai were able to systematically dismantle the Ryukyu defenses using superior firepower and military tactics. As was common with other vassal states paying tribute to stronger powers at the time, the king was allowed to keep his position, but was expected to share his wealth with the Satsuma domain. This was a better deal than Shimazu gave to the people of the Amami Islands, which were turned into a sugarcane plantation (see page 61), but the decision was practical. The Ryukyu Kingdom, made up of hundreds of islands covering thousands of nautical miles, was almost impossible to directly supervise. Better to have the Okinawan king continue keeping his people in check while paying tribute.

Today Okinawa is part of Japan, but is the only Japanese prefecture with no territory within the four main islands. The other 46 prefectures on Japan's four main islands may include one or more of the 6,848 outlying islands that are Japanese territory, but Okinawa is the only one that is made up entirely of outlying islands. The Ryukyu islands stretch from just south of Kyushu to Taiwan. Okinawa prefecture comprises 160 of these islands, of which 49 are inhabited. So remote is Okinawa that the southernmost island, Yonaguni, is closer to Taiwan than it is to the nearest Ryukyu island.

Japanese people from the mainland still think of Okinawans as Okinawan, not as Japanese. This may be just as well, as the Okinawans are proud to be Okinawan and find mainlanders a little stuffy. Okinawa is very much a tropical

paradise: you're much more likely to see adults in shorts and colorful shirts there than in the rest of Japan.

As to their local booze, the Chinese imperial envoy Tung-yen Li, who visited Okinawa in 1800 for the crowning of the boy king Sho On, recounted that two big pots of the local spirit, awamori, appeared on their doorstep every morning. The stuff was good enough—another envoy lavished praise on it—but the locals seemed to expect them to drink it at an inhuman rate. The delegation did its best, but each morning two new pots would be waiting for them. Eventually, Tung-yen Li admitted, they had been forced to write to the Okinawan royal family: the alcohol was a very nice, but the envoys would be obliged if the king could send a little less.

The British captain Frederick William Beechey was also defeated by Okinawan hospitality at a reception held by a local official in 1827. "During the whole time we were closely plied with sackee in small opaque wine glasses, which held about a thimble full, and were compelled to follow the example of our host and [empty our glasses]: but as this spirit was of a very ardent nature, I begged to be allowed to substitute Port and Madeira, which was readily granted, and we became more on a footing with our hosts, who seemed to think that hospitality consisted in making every person take more than they liked."

If these accounts give the impression of a culture lost in mindless drunkenness, they are a little unfair. In the 1800s alcohol was considered safer to drink than water due to sanitation concerns, and many great Americans and Europeans of the time were known to have drunk beer, wine or even whisky from morning to evening while still managing to be productive enough to be remembered by history. The first American president, George Washington, spent a nearly 10 percent of his presidential salary on alcohol, and in 1799 his estate bottled more than 10,830 gallons (41,000 liters) of whisky. The German philosopher Karl Marx was known to ride donkeys through neighboring towns after benders while at university, and later drank his way through London with other German intellectuals of the day. Writers Charles Dickens and Mark Twain were also known for their drinking. When his son started at Cambridge, Dickens sent a care package that included 102 bottles of various wines and spirits, lest his son become thirsty. Mark Twain, a noted bourbon drinker, later discovered a taste for cocktails, and claimed to have one before breakfast, lunch and dinner. He's also known for his exhortation to "never refuse to take a drink—under any circumstances." So it is not so surprising that Okinawan royalty would ply their visiting dignitaries with vast quantities of their local brew.

In truth, Okinawan awamori was always one of the islanders' finer pleasures, bound up with elaborate social rituals and spirituality. Traditionally, it was aged for years in large earthenware pots kept by the highest-ranking families. It was said that the head of an aristocratic household might let a trusted servant keep the keys to the safe, but never to his awamori storehouse. A mature awamori—some had reached 150 to 200 years when the oldest stocks were wiped out in World War II—was a precious thing. No one who actually tasted ancient prewar awamori is alive any longer, but the

American traveler Bayard Taylor got a rare chance to try some from the royal family's cellars in 1853. He wrote: "It was old and mellow with a sharp, sweet unctuous flavor, somewhat like French Liqueur."

The Origins of Awamori

The exact beginnings of awamori-making are hard to pinpoint, but we do know that the people of Ryukyu were enthusiastic drinkers long before they learned the art of distillation. A Chinese reference to the islands in 636 AD said the locals drank a type of wine, and the *Omoro soshi*, a collection of Okinawan poems written between the 12th and 16th centuries, contains several references to *miki*, a variation on *kuchikamizake* (see page 20) in which grain is chewed and then spit into a container to promote fermentation. In 1477, we get a priceless snapshot of medieval Okinawan alcohol culture from a group of Korean sailors shipwrecked on the far western island of Yonaguni. They were kept for half a year on Yonaguni and only encountered a weak, cloudy chewed alcohol like the miki mentioned in the *Omoro Soshi*. Once transferred to the larger but still remote Miyako, the castaways drank more sophisticated unfiltered brews. When they reached the center of Ryukyu civilization on the main island of Okinawa, they found clear filtered alcohols and a very strong yellowish brew that was highly prized by the Okinawans.

We don't know whether that yellowish alcohol was an early example of distilled alcohol in Okinawa or just a strong matured wine. The first clear evidence of distilled spirits comes from the Chinese envoy Chin K'an in 1534: "The alcohol the king gave was clear and powerful. It came from Siam and is made the same way as Chinese distilled

Left A warm welcome at Urizun bar in Tokyo (see page 141). Wherever you go to experience a little bit of Okinawa you're sure to find a smile and plenty of awamori.

alcohol." While K'an attributes a Siamese origin, Okinawans were trading all over the South Seas at the time and were notorious for their interest in alcohol of all descriptions in every port. About 15 years before K'an visited Okinawa, the Portuguese adventurer Tomé Pires noticed Okinawan merchants in Malacca scouring the markets for the strongest booze: "Among [them] Malaccan wine is greatly esteemed. They load up large quantities of one kind which is like brandy, with which the Malays make themselves [so drunk as to] run amok."

There are certainly similarities between Thai *lao khao*, traditionally a distilled rice-based spirit, and awamori, so it's possible that there is a link between these distilling traditions. However, the Thai liquor uses glutinous sticky rice while awamori uses steamed Indica (long-grain) rice for its koji fermentation. Lao khao also uses a Chinese-style yeast ball rather than the isolated black koji used in Okinawan awamori. Despite these dissimilarities, the idea persists that Okinawan awamori is descended from Thai distilling traditions. Both were flexible regarding ingredients added to the ferment; among Okinawans, millet was commonly used as an inexpensive base ingredient for awamori until Japanese regulations discouraged it. Of course, all this is speculation, since no written records exist regarding production methods for either tradition. Today most Thai lao khao is made from sugarcane, and is more akin to rum.

What is clear from the early reports is that distilled alcohol in Okinawa was, from the start, an aristocratic drink. The famous Ryukyu courtier and reformer Sai On (1682–1761) felt that distilled alcohol (which by then was being produced domestically) was perfectly acceptable for consumption by the Okinawan elite or for export to Japan, but said that commoners should not drink it. During the 18th and early 19th centuries, it was decreed that distillation could only occur within sight of the castle walls, so awamori production was limited to the Sanka area immediately southeast of the walls of Shuri Castle. Only 40 individuals were given permits, and all distilling was done under royal patronage: the stills and the ingredients were owned and loaned out by the king, and all of the liquor had to be returned to him, save for 1½ gallons (5.4 liters) left as payment with each maker. Unlicensed distilling was a capital offense, and the culprit's family would be exiled to a prison island.

We have no way of knowing exactly how much home-brewed awamori passed under the noses of the Okinawan authorities. The geography of the archipelago, with hundreds

A DRUNKEN POETRY SLAM?

People from the island of Miyakojima, to the south of Okinawa's main island, have a reputation for eloquence. There is a good reason for this. It is called the *otori*: islanders gather in a circle and the first among them, called the *oya*, gives a speech. When they have finished, the oya drinks a shot of awamori and sends the glass around the circle to be filled and emptied by all present. The next person in the circle then becomes the oya, followed by the obligatory speaking and drinking, and so they continue into sozzled and word-heavy evenings. It is a testament to the importance of alcohol in traditional Okinawan society that, when one Miyako village decided to abolish the otori because it forced excessive drinking, the villagers elected to hold an otori to celebrate their progressiveness! Not all drinking customs of Miyakojima encourage overindulgence, however: some people still pour the first glass of a newly opened bottle on the earth. They call it *kami no mono*, "the gods' property."

of islands separated by hundreds of miles of ocean, makes it seem unlikely that distilling was, in practice, limited only to the Sanka district. Many of the outlying islands have their own distilling histories, and some of those activities seem to have been officially tolerated. However, until the late 19th century, it is fair to say that the drink of most normal Okinawans was not distilled but brewed, and had not advanced much since the days of the chewed miki beer encountered by the Korean castaways on Yonaguni. Fumi Miyagi (1891–1990), noted Okinawan historian and author, writing of her childhood on the Yaeyama Islands in the early 1900s, recalled a beverage she called *mishi* (likely a local dialect variation of "miki"). During the rice harvest, there would be a big pot of mishi in the middle of the field for everyone to drink from, she said. It was the women's job to do the chewing. "They would say, 'Today, it is my mishi turn,' and they would brush their teeth carefully before they went out."

The worlds of aristocratic and peasant alcohol collided on occasion. Chewed alcohol was an important part of some island festivals, and in 1756, the Chinese imperial envoys were served it at court (they stopped drinking as soon as they were told how it was made). In fact, a miki festival persisted in Okinawa into the 1930s, and by all accounts it is still a form of home brew on some remote islands. Takuya Sunagawa, president of the Taragawa distillery on the island of Miyako, remembers miki being served at his local shrine when he was a child, which would have been in the 1970s. Much of the elite's distilled awamori, on the other hand, was doled out by the king in rations to officials and noblemen who would then share it, in the form of gifts and hospitality, with others lower in the social pecking order. In this way, the spirit seeped down through society. But in general terms, the rural brewing and urban distilling continued as two separate traditions until the 1870s, when the formal annexation of Okinawa by Japan and the fall of the Okinawan royal family brought an end to the old restrictions on distilling outside Sanka. An explosion of distilling followed: by 1893 there were 447 distillers across the islands and less than a quarter of them were in Sanka. By the early 20th century, awamori could genuinely claim to be the "people's drink" for the first time in its history.

The Rebirth of Awamori

World War II completed the revolution by nearly extinguishing the old aristocratic tradition. On October 10, 1944, a massive air raid damaged Shuri Castle heavily. The following year the Battle of Okinawa, which killed more than 100,000 local civilians, smashed what little was left. Between May 24 and 26, the huge naval guns of the battleship USS Mississippi reduced the old castle to dust; Sanka, the traditional center of awamori-making nestled under the castle walls, was destroyed. Ancient stores of aged awamori, some of it well over 100 years old, were gone forever, and the stocks of black koji spores necessary for making awamori were lost. After a desperate search, a straw mat with traces of koji on it was

found under the rubble of one distillery and, after several failed attempts, the mold was successfully resuscitated.

Such technical issues were the least of the distillers' problems. At the end of the war, when the US occupied the islands, they banned awamori production due to rice shortages. The Okinawans were not easily dissuaded: the US military reported brown sugar, palm, corn, wheat, fruit and even chocolate moonshine being made, and on outlying islands, where distilling had not been stopped, production was in full flow. In March 1946, locals sent a delegation to the authorities pleading for the ban to be lifted, and the Americans eventually relented. Initially, they set up five closely regulated factories making only molasses-based spirits, but two years later they allowed private companies to apply to make awamori. They received 229 applications, and 79 working distilleries were established. Only 11 of these could trace their roots back to the prewar industry. The new awamori map would have been unrecognizable to an 18th-century Okinawan: there were distilleries on almost every sizeable island, many with roots in village cooperatives.

The postwar story of the Tsukayama distillery is a sadly common one. Distilling since 1927 in the same building, the original owner died in the war and his eldest son, a soldier stationed in the Solomon Islands, succumbed to disease before being issued his transfer papers to return home at the war's end. The distillery was shuttered and became a shelter for homeless families after the conflict, as every other building in the area had been flattened. The facility was subsequently commandeered by the occupying Americans, first as a bakery, then as a local headquarters. In 1949, the determination of the old master's wife, Tsuru Tsukayama, brought it back to its original use: she summoned her second daughter Sada and Sada's husband, who had been a classmate of her late son, home from Kyushu to start making awamori again. The operation has not changed much since then: three men still carry out all the production (about half of Okinawa's distilleries employ fewer than ten workers).

Facing page At the Tsukayama distillery, a staff of just three men carry out all of the production.
Left Nico Nico Taro is a revival brand from the Ikema distillery in Miyakojima, which received its distiller's license in 1949 thanks to the US military.

Just as the Tsukayama distillery needed to reestablish itself, awamori had lost its image as a highly regarded spirit. "In those days, the drink got a bad reputation," says Akiyoshi Miyagi, owner of Awamori Kan, an iconic awamori bar in Okinawa. "It was partly to do with competition from whisky, but it was also to do with the image that surrounded awamori itself. People here, not just the Americans but the Okinawans too, didn't want to drink the old spirit, and to be honest, it wasn't always that good."

The advent of bottling and the emergence of bottled brands from the early 1950s brought different problems. Awamori is rich in rice-derived fatty acids; these are important for lending character and mildness to a matured spirit, but can also produce unwanted smells and flavors. Traditional earthenware pots disperse these aromas naturally, but glass bottles, if not handled properly, shut them in. Many islanders turned to whisky and neutral spirits like the popular Shirasagi brand in the 1960s. Awamori production declined nearly 40 percent between 1958 and 1963, and the number of distilleries fell from 118 to 85.

Since America returned Okinawa to Japan in 1972, the number of active awamori distilleries has fallen further to a current total of only 46, but there has also been a gradual rebuilding of the old pride. Miyagi started buying and maturing the Okinawan liquor in 1987; even then, he says, the

spirit was being dismissed by many. A series of initiatives, including a project to document the history of awamori and a committee to encourage long maturing of awamori, have helped remind people of the drink's heritage. Although it saw a spike in popularity across Japan in the early 2000s, with sales outside Okinawa growing 50 percent every year at one point, this has not been sustained. Nonetheless, awamori has regained its place as a key part of Okinawan culture and is sold as such not only on the islands, but across Japan. Perhaps most significant in the long run is the emerging consensus among producers that the future of awamori lies in producing top-quality spirits. Rules on the labeling of matured awamori have been sharpened up and an increasing number of premium drinks are reaching the market.

AGING AWAMORI

If you get the awamori bug, you could try maturing it yourself. You need clay pots, preferably unglazed ones with a rough texture (see below). Okinawans never wash their pots with soap—only with water. Pour the strongest awamori you can find into the pots and cover them. The lids need to be airtight. The Japanese-language guide *Chishiki zero kara no awamori* (The First Book of Tasting Awamori), by the *Nihon Shurui Kenkyukai* (Japan Alcohol Research Institute), recommends the following for home aging: place two layers of cling film under the pot lid, fasten them in place with tape, then cover the lid with two more layers of cling film and tie them down with rope. Keep the jars in a cool, dark place and move them gently every two or three months. Once a year, open the pots and follow the *shitsugi* method (see page 75). Or better yet, break out the oldest pot for a house party, pour it from your *gari-gari* bottle into your *chibugwa* cups (see page 77) and impress your happily inebriated guests when you demonstrate your shitsugi method in front of them.

MAKING AWAMORI

Landing at the airport in Miyakojima, an island of about 50,000 inhabitants, it's clear that you are now very far away from Tokyo. It would be akin to a flight from New York City to St. Kitts and Nevis, though perhaps a bit shorter. Nevertheless, when you emerge from the airport you find yourself surrounded by palm trees. Unlike other parts of Okinawa, which still have a large American military presence, Miyakojima is pristinely Okinawan. It caters to tourists who flock from around the world for the famous scuba diving, but even this is minimal. There's a single business hotel in the

town center across the road from a beach, but not much more. The local dialect can be inscrutable even to native Japanese, and non-Asian faces draw stares from children and adults alike.

The largest producer on the island is the Taragawa distillery, which makes the popular Ryukyu Ohcho (琉球王朝) brand. "Large" is relative, of course. Taragawa has a team of just five men making its awamori and produces a little more than 264,000 gallons (1,000 kiloliters) per year. The distillery is surrounded by sugarcane fields, and the signs—and scars—of sugarcane cultivation are everywhere (the president of Taragawa is missing several fingertips due to a childhood accident). Next to the distillery is a small hillside that shelters the company's aging cave. The natural limestone cave has been improved to store hundreds of clay pots and bottles of awamori. The distillery was established in 1948 at this location after the founder had a dream in which he was instructed to dig a well. When he did, he found water that was ideal for awamori production, and Taragawa was born. They use a production process common to virtually all awamori today.

Making the Koji

Just as with sake and shochu, awamori production begins with koji propagation. Awamori used to be made from all sorts of things, including millet, local rice, sweet potatoes and sugarcane, but today it is almost always made with long-grain Indica rice imported from Thailand, harking back to Okinawa's long trading history with Siam. Broken rice that cannot be sold as food is used, allowing producers to procure high-quality rice for a fraction of the cost of unbroken grains. The broken grains create more surface area, allowing for more efficient koji propagation. Indica rice is less sticky than Japanese rice, but easier to turn into sugar and therefore alcohol.

The rice is one of the three main characteristics that distinguish awamori from mainland Japanese shochu. The other two distinguishing features are that all awamori is made with black koji (*kurokoji*), and that the koji mold is propagated on all of the rice from the start, rather than in two stages as is done for shochu.

The rice is first washed and then steamed for 45 to 50 minutes in a large stainless-steel drum. The rice is then cooled and mixed together with black koji mold spores (*kurokoji-kin*). As explained in previous chapters, the purpose of the koji mold is similar to the malting of barley in beer and whisky-making: to convert the starches in the rice to sugars which can later be turned into alcohol when yeast is added to the fermentation. For awamori, the koji-inoculated rice is usually spread out and left for about 24 hours for the mold to propagate. However, some traditionalist awamori makers, including Taragawa, still use the *hinekoji* method, which allows a special type of black mold to propagate for three days. This creates a drink with a strong flavor and aroma that its makers say is well suited to long maturation.

Fermentation

The *moromi* (fermentation) in awamori production happens in a single ferment, unlike the two-stage process used in shochu production. The koji-inoculated rice, water, and yeast are added to a large tank and left to ferment for 10 to 20 days. The longer the fermentation, the more careful the producer needs to be, as the yeast needs to remain alive and active longer to keep off flavors from emerging. Higher fermentation temperatures result in a faster ferment and richer aromas and flavors, while lower temperatures take longer, but create milder, easier-drinking spirits. The mash ends up at about 18 percent alcohol, or around the alcohol percentage of an undiluted sake.

Distillation

Awamori distilling is pretty basic: steam is simply injected from a boiler directly into a stainless-steel still containing the fermented moromi. But there are all shapes and sizes of stills on Okinawa. At the modern Helios distillery they run three

This page Black koji (above) is an ancient mold that grows at will. As such it gets all over everything at awamori distilleries including the aging pots and the distillery's exterior walls, giving the buildings a nice patina.

large copper stills not unlike those in a Scottish whisky distillery. At the old Zuisen distillery in Shuri—one of only four currently operating in the old Sanka awamori district—they have a complicated stainless-steel device in which the moromi fermentation mash is indirectly steam-heated in a side-arm before flowing into the main still. Other distilleries use modern vacuum stills which produce a lighter spirit; on the other side of the technological coin, some distilleries, including the Takamine distillery on the island of Ishigaki-jima, are operating old direct-fired stills. Look for their Omoto Homura brand (於茂登炎), with the last character for "flame" dominating the label.

The proponents of all these types of equipment claim they improve their end product, but of course the basic process is same as any other pot still: the alcohol in the mash turns to vapor, rises through the neck of the still, and is turned back into liquid in a condenser. Most awamori distillers collect distillate at about 44 per cent alcohol, but will often dilute it down to 30 percent or lower before bottling. Notable exceptions are the three distilleries on Yonaguni (the island where the Korean sailors found only chewed *miki* in the 15th century), which are now famous for their ferocious 60 percent *hanazake* spirit—so strong that it cannot legally be labelled awamori. Look for the Donan (どなん), Maifuna, (舞富名), or Yonaguni (与那国) brands.

Maturation

The best things in life come to those who wait, and awamori is no different. Okinawans call their matured spirit *kusu* (*koshu* in standard Japanese), which means "old alcohol." Many people will tell you that kusu tastes mellower and richer than unaged awamori, but in truth, the taste varies markedly with the nature of the original spirit and the methods of maturation. One old categorization described three different types of kusu: the first was characterized by the "aroma of a white plum," the second had an "aroma of cheek"; the third, the "smell of a male goat." We can't pretend to know what those classifications meant—there can definitely be a little funk in some kusu, though generally it is milder and smoother than

LOVE POTIONS?

Japan has a long history of herbal medicines from China being introduced to the country. Umeshu itself is an indirect result of the introduction of cured plums to Japanese medicine. A surprising number of these concoctions are designed specifically to address male virility; some of them appear to be quite potent. Perhaps no more aggressively virile concoction exists in modern Japan than *habushu*, awamori in which a pit viper has been drowned. The snake's venom is diluted by the alcohol, bringing down to a nonlethal dose at which it acts as a stimulant. If you think this is it hard to believe, we urge you to try it yourself—though we recommend only drinking a small amount, because you'll be as wired as if you'd had a pot of coffee. Use with caution! If drinking pit-viper booze is a step too far, in parts of Kyushu you can find wasps drowned in shochu, which gives a similar, though somewhat less aggressive, buzz.

standard awamori. These odd classifications simply give an idea of the variety of flavors that maturation can impart to an awamori.

The islanders seem to have been aging spirits for almost as long as they have known how to make them. In fact, they may have been aging wine long before distilling arrived. The *Omoro Soshi* contains references to storehouses that some scholars think may have been used for holding wine, and a Korean eyewitness in 1461 said he visited an alcohol warehouse in Naha which had three separate sections for one-year-old, two-year-old, and three-year-old goods. Awamori aging was certainly well established by 1719, when the Japanese scholar and politician Hakuseki Arai came across a seven-year matured awamori. In fact, they must have been laying down stocks for much longer aging around that time; a 1926 report mentions awamori in Shuri that had been aged for 200 years.

The traditional way of maturing awamori is the *shitsugi* method, which is similar to the *solera* method used for sherry: a series of earthenware pots holding awamori of

Facing page, top Open fermentations with Thai rice and black koji are left to make alcohol for about three weeks. They bubble away like mad most of the time.

This page Most awamori is aged in subterranean limestone caves in clay pots of varying sizes.

different ages are kept beside each other in a storehouse. When spirit from the oldest jar is drunk, awamori from the next-oldest pot is added to replace it. What is taken from that pot is, in turn, replaced from the next-oldest jar and so on down to the youngest container, which is filled with newly distilled spirits. This has the benefit of allowing the kusu to be exposed to air and to interact with other spirits, promoting changes in the alcohol. The rough earthenware pots also accumulate residues and themselves give flavor to the alcohol over time. The pots are porous (though less so than oak barrels), and acquire some terroir depending on where they are stored. Awamori aged near the ocean can pick up a brininess like an island Scotch, while those stored in dank limestone caves can take on an earthy minerality.

Left Clay aging pots for home maturation of awamori are an everyday retail purchase in Okinawa.
Below 1.8 liter (2 quart) bottles of awamori rest in an aging cave awaiting the 20th birthdays of the kindergarteners whose photos are on the labels.

are also aging awamori in oak casks. The result at Helios is so whisky-like in smell and appearance that the Japanese government currently insists that they lighten the color to avoid confusion. In fact, there are now almost as many variations in aging methods are there are distillers. At Zuisen in the Shuri district, they hold classical music concerts on site, theorizing that the music will affect maturation. The Onna distillery places pots 400 meters under the sea for a day, claiming it makes their Shinkai (しんかい, deep sea) brand more rounded and fragrant. There's no limit to how producers will try to gain an edge on the competition.

A unique feature of awamori culture is that families living near a distillery can buy and fill their own clay storage pot and leave it in the distillery's aging cave; whenever they need it, they call up the distillery and have it delivered to their home. When it's empty, the distillery picks up the pot, refills it, and puts it back in storage until the next festivity. Parents will buy a pot for their newborn children and give them the 20-year-old spirit—which has been aging in the cave all the while—as a birthday present when they're old enough to drink. At the Taragawa distillery on Miyakojima, when elementary-school field trips visit the distillery (there is no moral compulsion against alcohol consumption in Japan, so this seems completely natural to virtually everyone), each child gets their picture taken; a bottle of awamori with that photo imprinted on the label is set aside to wait for them in the aging cave until they retrieve it upon adulthood.

Okinawa (and neighboring Kyushu) is a popular spring-training location for professional Japanese baseball teams. The Orix Blue Wave team trains in Miyakojima, and one table in the Taragawa aging cave is reserved for their clay pots. At the start of spring training, the pots are delivered to the players' hotel rooms. They are collected when the team heads home to Osaka. It is not known if former Blue Wave star Ichiro Suzuki still has his own pot awaiting his return.

Unfortunately, the shitsugi system is also ideally suited to cheating, as any shitsugi-aged kusu is actually a blend of awamori of different ages. The oldest spirit in a "100-year-old" awamori will indeed be a century old, but it will also contain younger spirits. Depending on the speed of the shitsugi process, it might actually contain a surprisingly small amount of 100-year-old alcohol. Some makers made the most of this when rules were lax. A code of conduct introduced in 2004 has cleared up the ambiguity. It states that 50 percent of the alcohol in any awamori labeled as kusu must be over three years old, and all of the alcohol in bottles labeled with age statements (e.g., "10-year-old awamori") must be at least the stated age.

Many makers have abandoned the shitsugi method. Some retain the jars but do not use the method. Others are using stainless steel or enamel-lined tanks because they want to avoid the earthy notes introduced by the traditional pottery. A number of makers, including the Helios distillery in Nago,

HOW TO DRINK AWAMORI

As you may have surmised, Okinawans are voracious drinkers and their reputation on the mainland is legendary. Many Japanese will not even try awamori, citing its strength. When they're told it's almost always bottled weaker than whisky, they're skeptical until shown the label. Even then, the look of worry doesn't leave their face until they've enjoyed a glass and realized they're not (yet) falling-down drunk.

The classic way to drink awamori is straight. Most early sources talk of small thimble-like cups called *chibugwa*, which are indeed the best vessels for tasting awamori. Many bars now use gorgeous Ryukyu glass tumblers or fancy brandy-tasting glasses, but there's something about the feel of a tiny pottery chibugwa that helps concentrate the taste buds on the alcohol. These diminutive cups are usually served alongside a *gari-gari*—a small narrow-necked carafe with a ceramic ball inside—filled with awamori. The ball is silent until the vessel is empty; then it makes a "gari-gari" sound, signifying it's time for a refill. This was a necessity in the past when awamori was a highly sought-after delicacy carefully meted out by the royal family. Furthermore, as in Japan, pouring for your neighbor has long been an Okinawan sign of hospitality and friendship. However, due to the rarity of fine kusu awamori, stingy hosts were known to occasionally pretend to pour for their drunken guests even when the carafe was empty. This "honesty pebble" in the bottom of the vessel keeps everyone honorable even when they're drunk or feeling stingy.

If awamori is too much for you straight, don't worry. Most people now drink it on the rocks or mixed with cold water as a *mizuwari*. In fact, on Miyakojima, mizuwari is the standard way of drinking awamori. A room-temperature mizuwari is best for bringing out the flavor, but some find it easier to drink if ice is added. Vary the proportion of water according to your taste and the strength of the liquor (try 4 parts awamori to 6 parts water if you have a standard 30 percent spirit).

Another method, recommended by distiller Hajime Sakimoto for her 60 percent Yonaguni *hanazake*, is to drink it straight after chilling in the freezer. She says this makes for a sweet, thick liquor that goes well with salty foods. You can also drink awamori mixed with hot water as an *oyuwari*. This custom may have been introduced by Japanese samurai from the Satsuma domain, as it became quite common in the Edo period. Ideally, the water should be between 158°F (70°C) and 176°F (80°C) when it is poured into the glass. Shake the bottle and pour the awamori into the water. Okinawans often prefer a stronger mixture than they serve on the mainland: a 1:1 ratio of water to liquor is common for 30 percent awamori. Finally, unaged awamori (*ippanshu*) is often drunk mixed with fruit juice, particularly citrus juice.

Top The traditional way to serve awamori is straight, in a small ceramic carafe with thimble sized ceramic cups. Here it's served with *rafute*, an Okinawan dish of braised pork belly.

Bottom The popular Kumesen brand comes in a variety of styles and alcohol percentages. The black bottle is a 43% alcohol 7-year-aged kusu awamori.

梅酒
Umeshu

*Plum Liqueur and Other
Fruit Ferments*

THE HISTORY OF FRUIT FERMENTS

Excavations of the prehistoric village at Sannai-Maruyama (3,900–2,300 BC) in Aomori prefecture have challenged the idea that Japan's first alcohol arrived with rice farming sometime around 1,000 BC. In the waste pits at Sannai, archaeologists found unexpectedly large quantities of fruit seeds, including those of wild *yamabudo* mountain grapes, elderberries, raspberries and mulberries. The crucial detail that has led some experts to suspect something more interesting than large-scale berry eating was going on is the huge number of dead fruit flies found in the same dumps. Unless the villagers were in the habit of chucking away tons of uneaten fruit, the presence of the flies indicates that the grapes and berries were allowed to ferment before consumption. And why would anyone allow fruit to ferment? It seems the early Japanese, who kept up a fairly large settlement at Sannai-Maruyama for 15 centuries, were getting together for little fruit wine between boar and deer hunts.

Modern fruit ferments in Japan have nothing in common with those prehistoric drinks. In fact, the most popular modern Japanese fruit ferment, umeshu (meaning "plum alcohol," often called plum wine in English), is not mentioned in Japanese writing until 1695, when it comes up in the *Honcho-shokkan*, a culinary encyclopedia of sorts. While

not particularly appealing raw; in fact, their pits contain cyanide. They're also very high in natural citric acid. If not pickled, they can be cooked down to make them palatable.

These fruits were first preserved and used as medicine in ancient China more than 2,000 years ago, and arrived in Japan sometime about or before 700 AD in the form of *ubai*, a dried and/or smoked plum used to remedy fatigue and aid digestion. Ume trees may have been native to Japan, but it does not appear that the fruits had a use before that time. Cultivation began quickly upon the introduction of ubai—the earliest book of Japanese poetry, the *Man'yoshu* (759 AD), has no fewer than 118 poems that mention the ume tree or its flowers. In fact, one passage reads, "When the spring comes, let's take an ume branch for your hair, and have a merry drink." (Whether that merry drink was umeshu is anyone's guess.) The Japanese eventually developed their own pickling techniques and made umeboshi pickled plums, which proved to be a great boon to nutrition and health. In fact, local lords planted ume groves throughout their domains during the violent Muromachi period because the samurai believed the salt-pickled fruit increased stamina and sped recovery. Umeboshi are small and easy to carry, and their high citric acid content aids the breakdown of lactic acid in fatigued muscles (not that anyone knew about that then). Even today umeboshi are considered rejuvenating.

The most popular ume variety today is the *nanko-ume*, which was developed from a single sapling identified in Minabe village in Wakayama prefecture in 1902. This tree was carefully nurtured by the Takada family in the village and was chosen as the best ume in a prefecture-wide competition in 1950. The nanko-ume is sought after due to its thick, soft pulp and high natural acid content. Wakayama prefecture currently accounts for approximately 60 percent of the more than 100 million tons of ume harvested each year; a majority of the harvest consists of nanko-ume from orchards planted from that first sapling. Most of the ume harvest is used to for umeboshi; the remainder is used to make umeshu.

1695 predates many things that Westerners consider old, that's actually the latest first mention of any of the traditional Japanese alcohols described in this book.

It's not likely that it took the Japanese until the 17th century to realize that they could soak plums in sake or shochu to make a boozy sweet-and-sour drink. It's more likely that this was a largely rural home-brewing technique that fell under the radar of official scribes of the era.

UMESHU

The base of umeshu is the *ume* plum. These are most often used to make *umeboshi*, the pickled plums that are ubiquitous in Japanese bento box lunches and many other dishes. Ume are not like sweet Western plums, with their delicate skin and soft, juicy flesh; rather, they are tart, hard-skinned and dense. They're more closely related to apricots, and are

Umeshu Home Brew

Umeshu is simple to make, so many Japanese families concoct their own. Seemingly every family has its own recipe for making umeshu at home, but it almost always comes down to three ingredients: ume, rock sugar and white liquor (*korui* shochu, page 44). These ingredients are so ubiquitous that rock sugar and white liquor are usually sold side by side in grocery store displays. Homemade umeshu may be much better or much worse than what's on store shelves. As you can imagine, a Tokyo housewife living in a high-rise block will not have the same access to nice fresh plums as the farmer's wife in the countryside. Her umeshu will invariably suffer even if she follows the same recipe step by step.

In order to give you a leg up in making your own umeshu, we've enlisted the help of Japanese farm-kitchen chef Nancy Singleton Hachisu, who went to Japan after college to study Japanese for a year and never came back. She's now lived in rural Japan for more than 30 years and has written several cookbooks, including *Preserving the Japanese Way*, which includes a recipe for umeboshi. Here, in her own words, are her instructions for making umeshu.

UMESHU SOUR "PLUM" CORDIAL

Umeshu, also known by the misnomer "plum wine," is the traditional cordial made in every farm household from native sour plums, which are really members of the apricot family. My husband's parents made any number of unsweetened (or minimally sweetened) medicinal cordials by steeping various wild sour berries or even ginger or

Above Japanese farm-kitchen chef Nancy Singleton Hachisu has lived in rural Japan for more than 30 years and makes her own umeboshi. **Facing page** Nakata Foods makes a standout selection of umeshu.

ginseng in a clear, cheap spirit (shochu). These cordials are used to perk you up when feeling droopy or as a homeopathic remedy for colds. Umeshu, on the other hand is served "on the rocks" in a little roly-poly tumbler—and was even given to children in my husband's childhood. While umeshu is the best-known cordial made from fruit in Japan, I also like to make apricot, blueberry, and raspberry, all readily obtainable in other countries (ume will be harder to find). The basic technique is the same no matter what the fruit or berry. The ume should be starting to yellow with some pink spots on the skin.

Makes about 2 quarts (2 liters)

INGREDIENTS
2 pounds (1 kg) ripe ume (sour or fresh plums)
1 pound (500 g) organic granulated sugar or white rock sugar (*korizato*)
2 quarts (1.8 to 2 liters) white liquor (see note) or plain vodka

Note: "White liquor" is a relatively recent marketing term, coined when shochu was considered cheap plonk for lowlife types. However, by Japanese law it is illegal to make umeshu at home with an alcohol of less than [yes, *less* than] 20 percent ABV (40 proof), so most white liquor is sold at that strength.

Method:

1. Destem, then wipe but do not wash the ume, and place them in a large clean jar or sealable crock. Add the sugar and the liquor, and screw on the cap or seal the crock well. Shake or stir vigorously to distribute and help dissolve the sugar.

2. Let the fruit and liquor macerate for at least 3 months in a cool, dark place. Shake or stir occasionally. Taste after three months, and if the liquor is sufficiently infused with ume, it is ready to serve. The flavor of this cordial deepens and mellows with age, and will keep practically indefinitely.

3. Serve cold over ice, as an aperitif, or mix with soda water for a refreshing summer cocktail.

Large, multi-quart clear plastic jugs with colored tops and handles to make pouring easier have long been the standard umeshu-making vessel across Japan. Today, it has become increasingly popular for young people to make their umeshu in attractive glass jars and in smaller batches, often experimenting with adding other fruits as well. This may be at least part of the reason for the recent decline in sales of commercial umeshu. More young people have taken up the tradition of making their own rather than buying it off store shelves.

Commercial Umeshu

Commercial umeshu is made with essentially the same process, but on a massive scale. For example, Nakano BC, a Wakayama umeshu producer, steeps about 500 tons of ume at a time across their 56 fermentation tanks. They have a chemistry lab and team of scientists dedicated to monitoring the acidity and sugar content in each tank in a highly choreographed process that tells them exactly when to end the steeping so their product remains consistent. Their umeshu is usually ready after about 18 months of maturation. Nakano BC was the bestselling sake brewer in Wakayama before branching out into umeshu in 1979. Their Kishu Umeshu Konanko (紀州梅酒 紅南高) brand recently took home the top prize at Japan's biggest umeshu competition, enhancing their market position. Today their umeshu and other fruit-based liqueurs account for about half their sales.

The largest producer of umeshu is Choya, which began selling umeshu in 1959, at a time when home umeshu-making was illegal under Japanese alcohol laws (it became legal in 1962). As of 2011 Choya was the sixth-largest liqueur brand in the world, just behind Southern Comfort. By 2015 they'd declined to 11th, with sales dropping by more than a third; still, they sell nearly 2½ million gallons (10 million liters) of Choya umeshu each year. The shift in sales likely reflects a shift in the domestic umeshu market rather than a loss of sales overseas. Choya currently exports to more than 70 countries worldwide. The cylindrical bottle with the ume at the bottom is iconic at Japanese restaurants around the world. Umeshu is extremely popular in other Asian countries, especially Korea, China, and Thailand. Its sweet-and-sour flavor and healthy image makes umeshu particularly attractive to young women from those countries.

A third company, Nakata, from the Kishu region of Wakayama, started as a trading company in 1897 before turning to umeboshi production in 1916 and umeshu later in the 20th century. They have fully embraced the Kishu region's legacy of sustainable agriculture, which started more than four centuries ago when the lord of the Tanabe domain allowed peasants to plant ume orchards in the mountains. They were encouraged to keep the surrounding forest in place to protect the orchards; this environment has allowed for a sustainable agricultural model for more than 400 years. The forests provide protection for the trees and a home for the honeybees that pollinate the ume blossoms each spring. The quality of the local ground water is also maintained through this symbiotic relationship; Tonda no Mizu, the local mineral water, is renowned throughout Japan. Nakata uses this water for all its umeshu products, which have now won several international awards.

In the domestic umeshu market in Japan, sales have seen a big shift over the past couple decades. In 1998, sparkling umeshu (a modern interpretation) held a 43 percent market share. By 2017 this had declined to just 9 percent; however, overall umeshu sales increased by 59 percent between 2003 and 2011, largely driven by traditional umeshu. As with seemingly all drinking trends in Japan (except beer, which is forever and always the most common beverage of choice), the umeshu wave receded, with the industry giving back about half its gains by 2017. This may have been partly due to the newfound love for home umeshu-making among younger Japanese, but a larger factor was likely at play.

During the boom, the Japanese government realized that umeshu sales had grown massively while ume harvests and umeboshi consumption had remained flat. Deeper investigation revealed that many producers were no longer using any ume at all in their umeshu. Rather, they had begun using artificial flavorings and coloring to produce an umeshu-like beverage at a fraction of the cost. When the government cracked down on this, much of the carbonated umeshu shifted to the *chu-hai* market (see page 65), which is not regulated to nearly the same extent as traditional alcohols.

In 2015, umeshu producers and their umbrella regulatory agency agreed to use the designation *honkaku* umeshu (authentic plum alcohol) only for umeshu made with ume, sugar and alcohol. Anything that has additional additives or replaces the ume with chemicals can still be called umeshu, but cannot carry the "authentic" designation. Sales figures for umeshu compared to honkaku umeshu are not available, though this will assuredly improve the reputation of the premium brands, as happened when the honkaku designation was given to shochu produced in a traditional fashion.

Some producers age their umeshu for up to 10 years in ceramic pots or wood barrels. These long-aged umeshu really mellow out and become smooth and luxurious, and can cost quite a bit because of the long aging. The barrel-aged umeshu Nakata comes in a one-year or five-year version; the latter is in a handsome wooden box. Other producers are experimenting in other ways. Some add pureed steeped ume to the bottle, which imparts an almost smoothie-like texture and a viscous mouthfeel (Choya's iconic brand aside, many standard umeshu brands are sold without a plum inside the bottle). Most are shelf stable, and under proper storage conditions should last as long as most other alcohols made from distilled spirits. However, sake-based umeshu is more perishable, and should be finished within a few months of opening.

Today many producers of premium Japanese alcohols ranging from sake to whisky make their own lines of umeshu using their high-quality products as the base rather than white liquor as many large umeshu producers do. Eigashima Shuzo (see page 97), a sake, shochu and whisky producer, makes a whisky-based umeshu, Akashi Ume (明石梅) which has been described as "an

Top, and facing page Commercial umeshu is produced on an industrial scale with computerized temperature and acidity control as well as very high standards of hygiene during bottling.

This page *Kajitsu-shu,* or fruit liqueurs, come in a seemingly endless variety of styles. If you name a fruit, Japan probably makes alcohol out of it.

Old-Fashioned in a bottle"; several Japanese wineries make brandy-based umeshu, too. Awamori producers have also followed this trend, serving up higher-proof umeshu with the deep earthy richness of their rice-based spirit. Nanbu Bijin, a premium sake maker from Iwate prefecture, has created a no-sugar-added umeshu, Nanbu Bijin No Sugar, which makes sense since sake has residual sugars already.

OTHER FRUIT LIQUEURS

As archeologists at Sannai-Maruyama discovered and Nancy Hachisu hinted in her recipe, Japan has a rich history and drinking culture around fruit-based alcohol, or *kajitsu-shu* (果実酒). These are typically produced in the same way umeshu is, but with quite a wide variety of styles. Apart from *chu-hai*, which usually contain only artificial fruit flavorings, most kajitsu-shu at this point is made with real fruit, and often contains some sediment or puree, much like the rich umeshu does. Citrus-based kajitsu-shu are often sparkling and are primarily made with regional citrus such as yuzu, *dekopon* (Kumamoto navel), *mikan* (Satsuma orange) or grapefruit. *Ringo-shu* (apple liqueur), *momo-shu* (peach liqueur), *budo-shu* (grape liqueur), and *anzu-shu* (apricot liqueur) are also popular.

Another emerging style is a mash-up between umeshu and kajitsu-shu in which additional fruits are added to an umeshu base. Kumamoto shochu maker Takahashi Shuzo's Umepon (うめぽん) combines local ume and dekopon citrus in a liqueur that took top honors as the best new product at the 2016 New York Restaurant and Food Service Show. These new styles have proved especially popular among young female drinkers due to their sweetness, flavor and relatively low alcohol content.

MEDICINAL ALCOHOL

If fruit liqueurs aren't for you, or if you enjoy the odd European-style herbal digestif, why not try *yakushu*, or medicinal alcohol? The use of alcohol as medicine has a long history in Japan (as it does in the West, where distilled spirits originally spread across Europe in this guise). Shochu and awamori have long medicinal traditions; when Western-style wine arrived in Japan in the late 19th century, it quickly found itself repackaged as a medicine.

The most famous yakushu contains snakes (*habushu*, see page 74), lizards, turtles and other animals. While habushu may be a bridge too far for many, various Chinese and Japanese herbs can be steeped in alcohol to make medicinal drinks that supposedly brighten the skin, prevent hangovers, improve vitality or cure insomnia. Ingredients for these infusions run the spectrum from anise to insects; ginger and lemongrass are popular. While these may not be for everyone, they're certainly interesting, and they too can be made at home by steeping an ingredient in white liquor or the honkaku shochu or awamori of your choosing.

Perhaps what sets all of these Japanese fruit liqueurs apart from Western liqueurs, apertifs and digestifs is that they're made to appeal directly to a Japanese taste and sensibility. There is definitely a focus on freshness when it comes to kajitsu-shu, as evidenced by the attention paid to the quality of the ume and the production methods for umeshu, which still dwarfs other styles of kajitsu-shu in terms of sales and popularity. And yakushu also tends to incorporate Asian spices and herbs rather than Western ones. Once you start down this path, you'll find an entire world to explore.

PART TWO
WESTERN ALCOHOL TRADITIONS IN JAPAN

洋酒
Yoshu

In this section we'll look at Japanese interpretations of Western alcohol: whisky, beer, wine and cocktails. Unlike the Japanese alcohol traditions, which are opaque and confusing to many outside Japan (and even to many Japanese), we're going to work under the assumption that most readers are familiar with how wine, beer and whisky are made, though we'll touch on the processes a little bit. Other than that, we'll focus primarily on history, brands, trends and what the Japanese have done to make these products appealing to drinkers.

Japanese Whisky

Improving on Perfection

Below A Japanese woodblock print shows three men, believed to be Commander Anan, Commodore Perry and Captain Henry Adams, who opened up Japan to the West. The text being read may be President Filmore's letter to the Emperor of Japan. **Above** An Ichiro's Malt whisky is served at Uchu's bar in New York (see page 145).

Facing page A selection of Eigashima whiskies at Bar Leichardt in Fukuoka (see page145), but what is that on the left? That's actually Asakura, a spirit made in the spirit of the Takamine process (see boxed text, page 87). It cannot legally be called whisky in Japan, but you would never be able to tell the difference.

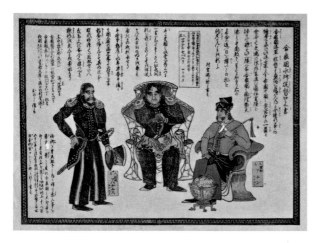

THE HISTORY OF JAPANESE WHISKY

American commodore Matthew Perry arrived with his fleet of black ships to negotiate the opening of Japan on July 8, 1853. He left a letter of terms and returned six months later for the emperor's decision. Upon returning, he brought a barrel and an additional 109 gallons (416 liters) of American whiskey as a gift for the emperor and his subjects. By all accounts, a good time was had by all (the emperor's share was never delivered). The *New York Times* reported that the "toddy flowed" at a meeting of US officers and senior samurai, one of whom "became quite merry, hugging the Commodore most affectionately in his happy moments." But once the Americans had gone home, the smitten Japanese were left with no idea how to make the golden spirit. That didn't stop them from trying.

Despite this American introduction of whisky to Japan, even the earliest attempts to "make" whisky were labeled with the Scottish "whisky" rather than the American "whiskey." Rather than becoming a passive consumer of American trade goods like the whiskey presented by Commodore Perry, the government of this fully fledged civil society sent out a delegation of scholars and government officials to learn from the West. The Iwakura Mission (1871–73) traveled throughout the US and Europe, returning with knowledge and goods—including, perhaps apocryphally, a case of Old Parr Blended Scotch from Britain. (The Greenlee brothers, who produced Old Parr, started their blending company in London in 1871 and trademarked their Old Parr brand in 1909. It's possible, of course, that the brand existed prior to trademark, and the new brand was somehow presented to the Iwakura Mission as a gift, but that seems hopelessly unlikely; anyway, the truth is lost to history.)

A FALSE START

In a twist of fate, the first Japanese whisky wasn't made in Japan at all. In 1879 a young Japanese scientist named Jokichi Takamine was part of the first graduating class of Kobu University in Tokyo. After studying abroad and returning to work in the Japanese Ministry of Agriculture and Commerce, Dr. Takamine was sent to the 1884 World's Fair in New Orleans as part of the Japanese delegation, where he fell in love with American Caroline Hitch. He went home to make his fortune in the phosphate business before returning to America to marry Miss Hitch. They had children in Japan before settling in the Chicago area where he started a company focused on improving agricultural technologies. At the Peoria distillery, owned by the local whisky "trust" (which controlled the local market), he experimented with a maltless whisky fermentation process, which threatened the livelihood of the local maltsters. The innovation made the local papers in September 1891 and two weeks later the distillery burned to the ground. Not dissuaded, Takamine perfected his maltless whisky process and in May 1894 sold it to the whisky trust who implemented it in December 1894. Two months later the trust went into receivership and was later dissolved in a political climate that was vigorously trust busting. The maltless whisky making process? Japanese koji spores grown on wheat bran—a similar process to that used for sake, shochu, and awamori. Unfortunately for almost everyone who loves alcohol, the barreled whisky was likely blended into other products and consumers never knew what they were drinking. Koji whisky was stillborn.

The Early Years of Japanese "Whisky"

There was a very limited supply of foreign imports in early Meiji Japan, so the slack was taken up by domestically produced imitation "whiskies." These were "whisky" only in the sense of being a bottle with the word "whisky" on the label. They were part of a wider "Western alcohol" (*yoshu*) industry that capitalized on enthusiasm for the newfangled alcohols by employing trickery in the chemistry lab rather than actually learning how to make them.

Everything about these early Japanese whiskies was fake; the bottles that survive show what might charitably be described as a "playful" relationship with authenticity. "Holy" whisky proclaimed itself a "Special Quality Old Scotch Whisky," but immediately below that, proudly boasted that it was distilled and bottled by the Eigashima Company in

Japan. "Lady Brand," displaying what looks like a European operatic diva against a backdrop of the hills of lowland Scotland, was also an "Old Scotch Whisky."

Fortunately for our livers, none of this early fake Japanese rotgut survived, but an account of a bizarre encounter in 1918 in Hakodate, Hokkaido, offers a sense of its potency. Japan was not much involved in World War I, which was then playing out its last macabre act in Europe, but one day in September two troopships containing nearly 4,000 American soldiers sailed into Hakodate port. The soldiers were destined to spend the next two years in Siberia fighting Bolsheviks (one of the more obscure chapters in US military history), but that night they had only two things on their minds: women and alcohol.

One enterprising bar enlisted a foreigner with a sense of humor to try to pull in the troops, erecting a sign in English that welcomed the visitors as follows:

> Notice!! Having lately been refitted and preparations have been made to supply those who give us a look-up, with Worst of Liquors and Food at a reasonable price, and served by the Ugliest Female Savants that can be Procured. This establishment cannot boast of a proprietor, but is carried on by a Japanese lady whose ugliness would stand out even in a crowd. The Cook, when his face is washed, is considered the best looking of the company.

Major Samuel L. Johnson, who had been sent ashore with the enlisted men, was soon back on the ships, reporting chaotic scenes to his fellow officers. "All the cheap bars have Scotch whisky made in Japan," he said. "If you come across

Left It's possible that Eigashima's White Oak distillery made the first real whisky in Japan, but this is impossible to verify. As a result, Masataka Taketsuru (left) is credited with first creating Japanese whisky, and rightly so, as he trained in Scotland before returning to Japan to help found Suntory's Yamazaki distillery. He then set off on his own to create Suntory's biggest rival, Nikka.

any, don't touch it. It's called Queen George, and it's more bitched up than its name. It must be eighty-six per cent corrosive sublimate proof, because 3,500 enlisted men were stinko fifteen minutes after they got ashore. I never saw so many get so drunk so fast."

Captain Kenneth Roberts, who was part of a team sent to round up the paralytic soldiery, described the scene: "Intoxicated soldiers seemed to have the flowing qualities of water, able to seep through doorways, down chimneys, up through floors." It was not just enlisted men; some of the officers also fell victim to Queen George and were later disciplined. Roberts and his men spent hours trying to get the men back on the boats: "When we slowly edged a score of Khaki-clad tosspots from a dive and started them toward the ships, then turned to see if we had overlooked anyone, the room would unbelievably be filled with unsteady doughboys, sprung from God knows where, drunkenly negotiating for the change of American money or the purchase of 'juss one more boll of Queen George.'"

The ships hurriedly left Hakodate without the coal they had come for. At the next port, Otaru, only a few troops were allowed off. Queen George seems to have had her say there too: an American soldier smashed a bottle over the head of a Japanese policeman.

While whisky giants Suntory and Nikka would have you believe that Japanese whisky-making began with the collaboration between Masataka Taketsuru and Shinjiro Torii in 1923, an arguably authentic whisky was being made by Eigashima Shuzo in Hyogo prefecture before those two men even met. This facility was established in 1888 when the family received a license to produce sake and shochu. As whisky was gaining popularity in Japan, the family began experimenting with making it in the early 20th century. Not

knowing how to malt barley, they may have manipulated the koji-growing process to work with barley rather than rice. This ferment was first sent through a pot still in 1919 and immediately put into barrels, and White Oak whisky was born. We have no way of knowing how this early distillate tasted or smelled, since none of it survives, but apart from the lack of malted barley, it met all other definitions of whiskey if not Scotch whisky.

A Mission to Scotland

The "official" history of Japanese whisky begins about two months before the debacle in Hakodate and about a year before White Oak was first barreled. In July 1918 Masataka Taketsuru, the son of Hiroshima sake brewers and a promising chemist who had developed a reputation for making non-explosive spirits for Settsu Liquor Company, boarded the SS *Tenyo Maru* with his family and colleagues waving dockside. His boss at Settsu, Kihei Abe, had decided the time had come to try to make whisky the proper way, and had hand-picked Taketsuru to take on an audacious mission: travel to Scotland and bring back the secrets of Scotland's distillers. In fact, he would bring back more than secrets.

Taketsuru studied first English and then chemistry at the University of Glasgow to improve his understanding of distilling. He became acquainted with medical student, Ella Cowan, whose brother was interested in Japanese martial arts. Taketsuru was invited to the Cowan family home for Christmas 1918, and there he met and fell for their older sister, Rita Cowan, who had recently lost her fiancé in the trenches of World War I. He would propose to her the following Christmas, and she would accept.

But we're getting ahead of ourselves. Once Taketsuru felt he was ready, he began his whisky education in earnest. On April 17, 1919 he boarded a train to Elgin, near the heart of the famous Speyside whisky region. He recalled singing Japanese folk songs to calm himself on the journey. The journey was not easy. He was turned away by several hotels, because, as he explained in his typical understated way, "some people were afraid of foreigners." When he approached the famous whisky authority J. A. Nettleton for guidance on learning the whisky trade, Nettleton demanded a prohibitive fee.

Despite these frustrations, Taketsuru was not so easily dissuaded. He obtained a map of Speyside's distilleries and began knocking on doors. Eventually, three miles south of Elgin at the Longmorn Distillery, the general manager, James Grant, agreed to give him a week's worth of work experience. Longmorn by this time had become a key component in blended whisky; the Grant family ran production until 1970, when Longmorn became part of The Glenlivet Distillers Ltd. Next, Taketsuru spent three weeks at the Bo'ness distillery in West Lothian, where he learned to make grain whisky in Coffey (continuous distillation) stills.

He spent the second half of 1919 in Bordeaux studying winemaking before returning to Scotland to propose to Rita at Christmas. They married in January 1920 and moved to Campbeltown, a port town with easy water access to Glasgow, which was the largest whisky-producing region in Scotland as late as the 1880s. Taketsuru undertook a five-month stay at Hazelburn, the largest distillery in Campbeltown. Throughout all these experiences he wrote down everything, from the precise temperatures at which maltose and dextrose are created during the mash to the wages of the cooper. His voluminous notes would go on to become the bible of Japanese whisky making.

By the time Taketsuru's first bottle of whisky was sold, two of the three distilleries where he had studied would be lost to history. Bo'ness was purchased in 1921 by the Distillers Company Limited, a whisky trust that controlled more than half of all Scotch production and manipulated supply and demand to keep prices high. They closed Bo'ness in 1925 to limit demand, and it never reopened; its last buildings were destroyed by fire in the 1990s. Hazelburn, despite being the largest distillery in Campbeltown, was purchased by rival Mackie & Co. in 1920 and shuttered a year later. Mackie simply wanted the large warehouse and dockside location. The distillery was acquired by the same whisky trust that bought Bo'ness, and was reopened as the White Horse distillery in 1924, but it closed again for good in 1927.

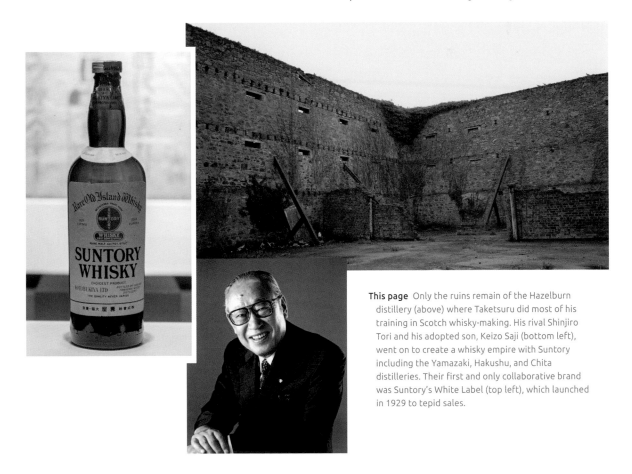

This page Only the ruins remain of the Hazelburn distillery (above) where Taketsuru did most of his training in Scotch whisky-making. His rival Shinjiro Tori and his adopted son, Keizo Saji (bottom left), went on to create a whisky empire with Suntory including the Yamazaki, Hakushu, and Chita distilleries. Their first and only collaborative brand was Suntory's White Label (top left), which launched in 1929 to tepid sales.

This page The Yamazaki whisky distillery (right), bordering Kyoto and Osaka, was opened in 1923 and has remained in continuous operation ever since. The original stills were heated by fire (bottom right) and labels were applied by hand by a cadre of female employees (bottom left) at a time when women were just beginning to seek employment outside the home.

Today, apart from the malt house, which has been converted to an office building, only ruins remain.

Taketsuru and Rita left the British Isles in October 1920, traveling by ship to New York, by train to San Francisco and by ship again to Yokohama. Returning to Japan, Taketsuru found a nation in recession. His employers were more interested in making a quick profit than the enormous investment required to build an authentic whisky distillery, so he quit his job. His Scottish wife was left to support them by doing the one job that seemingly every foreigner living in Japan does: teaching English. Fortunately, unemployment did not last long. Word of Taketsuru's journey to Scotland reached the visionary businessman Shinjiro Torii, who had decided to open a whisky distillery in Yamazaki, a town situated on the Kyoto-Osaka border. The area seemed to have everything a good whisky distillery needed: pure water, a temperate climate and easy access to several large cities with

thirsty customers who were curious about Western drinks and—perhaps most importantly—who had the money to afford them. Torii signed Taketsuru to a 10-year contract at the same salary he'd been offering to Scottish whisky makers to move to Japan.

With Taketsuru's help, Suntory's Yamazaki distillery opened in 1923. Early attempts were fraught with failure, and enormous sums were put into perfecting the fermentation, distillation, aging and blending of a uniquely Japanese whisky. Finally, in 1929, Suntory released Shirofuda ("White Label"), which is rightly known as the first authentic whisky ever made in Japan. The release was met with disappointing sales, and Taketsuru was demoted to managing one of Suntory's beer breweries in Yokohama. He quit in the last year of his contract.

With hindsight, the relationship seems to have been doomed from the beginning. Torii's goal all along was to create a whisky unique to the Japanese palate—one that reflected the national character. Taketsuru, on the other hand, had fallen in love with traditional Scotch and had decided that the only way to make great whisky in Japan was in the Scottish tradition. As we will see, as is often the case with conflicts between legends, both men were correct.

Rita, never idle, had continued to learn Japanese and teach English. Fortunately for Taketsuru, one of her students was the wife of a wealthy securities investor who decided, with some other partners, to back Taketsuru in opening his own distillery. The backers were skeptical of his choice of the sleepy hamlet of Yoichi on the remote and underdeveloped island of Hokkaido for the distillery's location. Nevertheless, his passion and certainty persuaded them, and his company, Dai Nihon Kaju (later shortened to "Nikka"), was formed. His Yoichi distillery opened in October 1934 and produced its first product, Nikka, in 1940.

Meanwhile, Suntory stayed busy. Torii continued to import and produce whisky, and in 1937 released Kakubin, which can only be described as the most popular Japanese whisky in the history of Japanese whiskies. Even today, more than 80 years later, the brand is still on shelves in seemingly every bar, restaurant, liquor shop, supermarket and convenience store in Japan. In no small part, Kakubin is responsible for the success of Suntory, which purchased American whisky conglomerate Jim Beam for US$16 billion (¥1.8 trillion, £12.2 billion, €13.6 billion) in 2014, becoming the third-largest spirits producer in the world as of this writing.

Taketsuru's Nikka went in a different direction. Using the pristine water, cool climate, ample coal and peat bogs of Hokkaido, Nikka established itself as the maker of

premium Scotch-style whiskies. Fortunately for the survival of this small distillery in an enclave on a remote island two to three days' travel from the major urban centers of Japan, the Japanese Imperial Navy had developed a taste for whisky. When Scotch imports dried up with start of World War II, Nikka was contracted with making whisky for the thirsty sailors. So vital was whisky to the naval war effort that the Nikka distillery was designated a war industry, which allowed access to precious resources such as coal and barley. A garrison of troops was stationed nearby to make sure the whisky flowed without interruption.

Hiroyoshi Miyamoto, general manager of Suntory's Yamazaki distillery, says: "When we were at war, every industry had to provide all of their goods to the military.

This page Taketsuru and his wife Rita (top) were inseparable in life and in death. After her passing he poured himself into opening a second distillery, Miyagikyo (bottom), in rural Miyagi prefecture.

It was only because the navy wanted whisky to be made that the industry could survive." For the rest of the population, whisky was a complete mystery, according to Tatsuro Yamazaki, the legendary owner of Bar Yamazaki in Sapporo (see page 128): "A tiny minority of the elite—top business-men and bureaucrats in Marunouchi—seem to have known about whisky before the war. Alcohol meant sake and few people knew that whisky was drunk in the navy. We were only told about it after the war."

Taketsuru is rightly known as the father of Japanese whisky, and Rita its mother. She stayed by his side for the rest of her life, even through the war years when she was suspected of being a spy for the Allies. When she died in 1961, Taketsuru was heartbroken. He refused to even attend her funeral, instead asking that her ashes be brought to their bedroom where he could mourn in privacy. He outlived her by 18 years, but today they are buried together on a hill overlooking the Yoichi distillery. His knowledge helped found the two great rival empires of Japanese whisky: Suntory and Nikka. This adversarial start to the industry has had lasting repercussions even as other Japanese whisky makers have joined these pioneers.

MODERN JAPANESE WHISKY

The alcohol- and amphetamine-raddled existentialist philosopher Jean-Paul Sartre was an early convert to Japanese whisky. On a visit to Japan in 1966, as Japan's student revolution began to tear society apart, Sartre pronounced the food inedible but developed a great liking for the country's take on whisky, according to his biographer David Drake. The French philosopher and his partner, the feminist Simone de Beauvoir, swigged through gallons of the stuff during their visit. De Beauvoir was also impressed, noting in her memoir *All Said and Done* that on one occasion they had ordered a bottle to their hotel room, and pronounced it "very good." Other fans included Ian Fleming, who advocated the Japanese version in the 1964 James Bond novel *You Only Live Twice*, and the heiress and art collector Peggy Guggenheim, who was fond of decanting cheap Japanese brands into Scotch bottles for her parties. Some of these early endorsements have a touch of condescension about them ("By Jove, it's actually quite decent!"), but nowadays it is possible to say, quite categorically, that no serious whisky critic would challenge the right of the Japanese drink to be considered on an equal footing with its American, Canadian, Irish and Scottish counterparts.

By the 1970s, whisky was everywhere in Japan. If you were to choose a drink to symbolize the rapid economic growth in the four decades after the war, it would have to be whisky. It started off as an unattainable object of desire, enjoyed only by the US Occupation forces and rich businessmen. "Just after the war, the Scotch whisky that was most generally known was Johnnie Walker, Red and Black. Black was the symbol of luxury," says barman Yamazaki, who at that time was serving American servicemen in Tokyo clubs. "White Horse was also quite well known, and other labels started to come in." But the general poverty and punitive import taxes kept this whisky well out of the reach of most Japanese. The real shift came in 1955, with the opening of a chain of reasonably priced whisky pubs: the Torys Bars. "People started to drink whisky mainly because Suntory's Torys whisky was so cheap. It was almost the same price as a cup of coffee at a Torys bar," says Yamazaki. These bars were created by Shinjiro Torii's adopted son, Keizo Saji, and were styled after English pubs, but with the centerpiece being drams of whisky rather than pints of beer. There were more than 1,500 Torys Bars at their peak popularity, of which a handful still remain, though none can claim original provenance.

Throughout this development, Japanese whisky stayed remarkably loyal to the Scottish roots put down by Taketsuru. There have been experiments with Japanese bourbons, but by and large, Japanese whisky has always tried to be Scotch, using Scotch methods and ingredients. The product has not always been as pure as it is now. In the 1960s, Japanese blended whiskies often contained neutral spirit rather than grain whisky, and there are accounts of significant amounts of wine being found in some bottles. However, throughout this period, hundreds of distillery workers were sent to learn their craft in Scotland, building a reserve of knowledge that is now serving the industry well.

In 1964, only about 13 million gallons (50,000 kiloliters) of whisky were being consumed annually. By 1983, this number had risen to 100,300,000 gallons (380,000 kiloliters), more than six pints (three liters of spirit for every person—adult and child) in the population. With protectionist policies limiting foreign imports to the very well-heeled, it was the domestic industry, led by Nikka and Suntory, that met much of the demand. The distilleries that are now winning gold medals for their single malts were originally set up to slake a raging domestic thirst for a more ordinary dram, sold for a few yen a shot. In 1956, the Karuizawa distillery began production, and between 1969 and 1973, the opening of the Miyagikyo distillery by Nikka, Fuji Gotemba by Kirin and the enormous Hakushu distillery by Suntory increased Japan's production massively. Japan was the fourth-biggest producer of whisky in the world, behind Scotland, the US and Canada. It was producing three times more whisky than Ireland.

This page During Japan's rapid economic growth after the war, the Tory's Whisky brand (above) from Suntory brought affordable whisky to the common man. It was served in Tory's bars, the last of which, Juso Tory's in Osaka (left), closed due to fire in 2014. It has reopened in a new location, though the original patina is lost.

The end of the whisky boom started in the late 1980s and continued into the 21st century, with sales in 2007 representing just 20 percent of the 1983 peak. A variety of factors were at play. Between 1986 and 1996 the European Commission and the World Trade Organization pressured the Japanese government several times to change its tax schemes. This resulted in an end to the usurious tax rates on foreign spirits and balanced the tax rates between whisky and shochu relative to alcohol percentage. While this made domestic Japanese whisky more competitive with shochu, it also resulted in a precipitous drop in the prices for foreign whiskies, flooding the already competitive whisky market with extremely high-quality Scotch just as consumer tastes began to change. The first and second shochu booms drew millions of younger drinkers into the arms of the traditional Japanese spirit. While whisky was now priced more competitively, it was still more expensive per drink. This hypercompetitive environment motivated the Japanese producers to develop the excellent products that are now receiving international attention. The fourth-largest whisky industry in the world is competing fiercely for a shrinking but increasingly sophisticated domestic market and a rapidly growing export market that demands the highest quality.

A series of victories in international competitions over the past two decades has washed away any condescension toward Japanese distillers. The dam broke in 2001, when a 10-year-old Yoichi whisky won the "Best of the Best" award in an international blind tasting organized by the British publication *Whisky Magazine*. Since then, the country's two top producers, Nikka (which owns the Yoichi and Miyagikyo distilleries) and Suntory (Yamazaki and Hakushu), have joined the ranks of the most medal-bedecked whisky makers in the world. In 2003, a Yamazaki 12 won a gold award at the

International Spirits Challenge. The next year, a Hibiki 30 blended whisky from Suntory won the overall trophy at the same competition and, in 2005, a Yamazaki 18 won a double gold medal at the San Francisco World Spirits Competition (SWSC). The killer blow to old-world whisky snobs was struck in 2008. At the World Whisky Awards (WWA) in Glasgow, the Japanese not only won the prize for best single-malt whisky in the world (Yoichi 1987), but also the award for the world's best blended whisky (Hibiki 30). The top single-malt prize at the WWA has since gone to a Yamazaki 1984 Limited Edition (2011) and a Yamazaki 25 (2012), while at least one Japanese blended whisky has won its category every year between 2007 and 2017. Rather than simply competing in these categories, Japanese whisky seems to be expanding its reach, with a Fuji Gotemba Single Grain 25 winning the 2016 WWA "Best Grain" category and Chichibu's Whisky Matsuri 2017 winning the 2017 WWA for "Best Single Cask." Yes, that's right. The best single cask of whisky bottled in 2017 was from a Japanese distillery that opened in 2008.

This explosion of popularity has come at a steep price. At the time of writing this book, virtually all Japanese whisky distilleries have ceased releasing age-statement whiskies except for competition or in very limited releases at auction. This is because 10 to 15 years ago, when Japanese whisky was extremely unpopular, the producers had reduced their production to just a day or two a week, because they could not afford to keep producing and barreling product they were not sure they could sell. Those unproduced whiskies would be going into age-statement bottles today. Instead, the small amounts that were produced are going into blends to

keep up with very high demand. There are indications that some age-statement whiskies will be released in time for the 2020 Summer Olympics in Tokyo, but for now most of us will have to enjoy some of the very nice non-age statement whiskies that are available, such as Hibiki Harmony (SWSC 2016 double gold medalist) and Nikka Taketsuru Pure Malt.

MAKING WHISKY

Making malt whisky is a relatively simple process compared to shochu and awamori. However, this really only refers to the production of the distillate itself. The real magic of whisky is what's done with it after it comes off the still.

Malting

In the Scottish tradition, most Japanese whisky starts with malting barley, the process of warming the barley seeds to trick them into believing spring is coming so that they begin to sprout and convert their stored starches (complex carbohydrates) into simple sugars. In a cruel trick, the barley is then immediately roasted to kill the seedlings before they can grow. However, now all of that malted barley is full of sugars that can be accessed by hungry yeast to make alcohol.

Peating

Malted barley may or may not be peated. Peating barley is the process of exposing the malted barley to smoke from burning peat, which gives the grain the rich smokiness

associated with some full-bodied highland Scotches. Japanese whiskies come in both peated and unpeated examples, though much of it is only lightly peated.

The Wash

The malted barley is soaked in warm water for several hours to release the sugars. The wash is gently agitated, like a washing machine on a delicate cycle, to release as much sugar as possible.

The Mash

The liquid from the wash is moved to a fermentation tank, where yeast is added. The yeast is very happy in the warm sugary water and begins converting the sugars to alcohol over a two- to four-day period in which the alcohol content of this mash rises to approximately 5 percent.

The Stripping Run

The mash is moved to a pot still to begin the distillation process. The first run, or stripping run, removes the alcohol from the mash by boiling. After this, the distillate, known as low wines, is approximately 30 percent ABV.

The Spirits Run

The stripping run is then moved to another pot still (or returned to the same still after cleaning, in a single-still operation) to perform the spirits run. This step gives the distillate a more neutral flavor and aroma and ups the alcohol percentage to between 65 and 70 percent. The method of heating the still, the shape of the still, the angle of the neck and many other factors play a role in the flavors and aromas that are captured in this raw distillate.

Aging

Once the distillate is finished, it is moved to barrels (usually oak) for aging. Barrels in a wide variety of sizes, shapes and origins are used for making whisky, the most common of which include repurposed American bourbon barrels, virgin barrels of white oak imported for the purpose, sherry butts, and wine casks. *Mizunara* (Japanese oak) is sometimes used, though it's highly porous, so there's a lot of evaporation, and it takes a long time to age to a nice flavor.

The Japanese Whisky Style

While Taketsuru endeavored to make Scotch whisky, he did so after learning predominantly in Speyside and Campbeltown, which have their own unique profiles. As such, Japanese whiskies tend not to be too overly peated like Islay Scotches, nor do they have the briny overtones associated with some of the Island Scotches. Rather, they are generally fruity and lush, which incidentally goes well with Japanese tastes (this was Torii's original goal). While the two men went their separate ways, and Nikka is certainly much more traditionally Scotch-like, Suntory is incredibly well made; the strengths of each of their distilleries are quite distinct.

However, their rivalry resulted in a unique twist that differentiates Japan's whisky-making from Scotland's. Since there were really only two major players, and they did not like each other very much from the beginning, there was not much of an avenue for making blended whisky. Scotland has a long history of Scotch whisky distilleries trading barrels with each other for blends or selling barrels to bottling companies that blended their own brands. Remember the whisky trust that bought up Bo'ness and eventually Hazelburn? That company was also involved in making blended

brands. In Japan they had no such option, and were thus forced to install multiple still designs and make multiple styles of whisky within the same distillery in order to create their own blends. Only once Nikka and Suntory had grown into powerful whisky makers could they start acquiring barrels from other distillers for blending. How did they do that? They bought Scotch whisky barrels from Scotland and blended them into their Japanese whiskies, eventually buying entire Scotch distilleries that now exclusively make whisky for blending into Nikka and Suntory products.

Blended whisky and lighter-profile single malts lend themselves to dilution to a large degree, and since Japanese drinking culture is naturally intertwined with food, it makes sense try to make whisky more food-friendly. In the 1950s and 1960s it was served *mizuwari* style (with ice and water); some people still drink whisky *oyuwari* (with hot water) in the winter. The most common way of drinking whisky today is as a highball, the highly diluted Japanese version of a whisky and soda. Variants include the "half up" (whisky and soda in equal measure over ice) and the "twice up" (whisky and water in equal measure, no ice).

Legend has it that when Japanese whisky was in the doldrums in the mid-2000s, Suntory realized that two bars were selling more of their whisky than any other in Japan: Samboa in Osaka and Rockfish in Tokyo. A visit made the reason clear—they were serving whisky highballs. In fact, at Rockfish, 90 percent of sales consisted of Kakubin highballs in the Samboa style (Rockfish's bartender had learned his craft at Samboa). Suntory quickly put its marketing team to work and launched a campaign featuring popular young actresses enjoying Suntory highballs. Within a couple of years the whisky highball was all the rage. Domestic sales surged, and have continued to climb to the point where Suntory has now released canned Kakubin highballs that you can drink at home without the trouble of keeping soda on hand as a mixer. And if you're particular about the dilution percentage, they are offered in both 7 percent and 9 percent ABV versions.

JAPANESE WHISKY DISTILLERIES

There are currently 17 active whisky distilleries in Japan, most of them making single malts. The information in brackets at the head of each entry below shows the date of establishment and the name of the parent company

White Oak (1919, Eigashima Shuzo)

White Oak is a very small distillery in Hyogo prefecture. Eigashima Shuzo, the sake and shochu company in charge, has a plausible claim to being the oldest Japanese whisky distillery. They began selling whisky in 1919, after Suntory's "Torys" whisky was first marketed but before the Yamazaki distillery was built (Shinjiro Torii seems to have used imported whisky or whisky imitations before building Yamazaki). Eigashima does not claim to have been making authentic whisky from that date, but the operation certainly has a long history. It also has a fantastic location, right next to the sea. If it was a Scottish distillery, the seaside rooftops would be painted with their brand name and the charismatic location would be used furiously in its advertising. Eigashima has always been a sake-first company, however, with whisky being a seasonal side business. Their seaside properties are falling into ruin while they limit their whisky operation to some newer buildings away from the shore. That is not to say their whisky is bad. For a long time they produced only cheap blends, but in 2007 they released their first single malt, called Akashi. It had a nice rounded flavor with notes of licorice and bread. With the recent rise in the popularity of Japanese whisky, White Oak has finally begun to take whisky-making seriously, doubling its whisky production between 2013 and 2016 and stopping shochu production altogether. Its first age-statement whisky, a five-year-old sherry-cask single malt, has been released, with more age-statement single malts poised for release soon.

Yamazaki (1924, Suntory)

Yamazaki is the oldest Japanese malt whisky distillery. It is situated just outside Kyoto at the confluence of the Katsura, Kizu and Uji rivers, and nestled up against forested hills rising out of the Kansai plain. The area has long been famous for its superb water—the 16th-century tea ceremony master Sen no Rikyu had his tea house just down the road because he esteemed it so highly. Yamazaki has 16 pot stills in a variety of designs; like many of the big Japanese distilleries, it is able to make whisky in a wide range of styles. This is necessary because Japanese distillers, unlike their Scottish counterparts, do not commonly trade whisky between companies to balance their blends. Everything has to be made in-house. In general, however, Yamazaki single malts show a tendency towards a soft and delicate fruitiness, often with sweet spice and incense aromas. Casks of Japanese oak (*mizunara*) are used at the attached Ohmi aging cellar, which lends distinctive flavors of incense, vanilla and coconut to some of the whisky. Yamazaki's products, as well as those from Hakushu, are used in Suntory's famous Hibiki blended whisky, which seems to pick up an international award nearly every year (and is probably best known in the West for its starring role in Sophia Coppola's popular film *Lost in Translation*).

Below The Yamazaki distillery may be the most iconic in Japan. It's also one of the easiest to get to—a short walk from JR Yamazaki train station between Kyoto and Osaka—but book your tour in advance. Tickets sell out.

Left Harder to get to, but worth the trip, is the Nikka Yoichi distillery in Hokkaido.

Yoichi (1934, Nikka)

Set up ten years after Yamazaki, Yoichi is Japan's other iconic prewar distillery. It is perched on the northern shore of Japan's northernmost island, Hokkaido. The sight of the silent warehouses, long icicles hanging from their eaves and almost subsumed into the landscape by the snowdrifts, is an abiding view of this most northerly of Japan's distilleries. The cold climate means that Yoichi's whiskies mature more slowly than those from the distilleries on the main island. Yoichi still uses six old coal-fired pot stills, a method that founder Masataka Taketsuru learned in Scotland but which has now died out in that country. None of the main distilleries produce very peaty whiskies, compared to the peat monsters that come out of some parts of Scotland, but Yoichi is perhaps closest to that style. Its whiskies are the most uncompromising and "masculine" of Nikka and Suntory products, but there are also rich stewed fruit, nut and coffee notes to balance the assertiveness. Taketsuru and his wife Rita are buried together on a hillside overlooking the distillery.

Asaka (1945, Sasanokawa Shuzo)

Established in 1765 in Fukushima prefecture, Sasanokawa actually obtained its whisky license in 1945, but until the 1980s was producing only second- or third-grade whiskies (i.e., whisky-like products mixed and colored with anything that could be found). In the 1980s, they began buying whisky barrels from Scotland (cheaper than having new casks made) with the whisky still inside. They blended this with a small amount of their own in-house distillate and bottled it as their own product. This is completely legal in Japan (see sidebar, page 98). In 2004, they agreed to store the barrels of the nearby Hanyu distillery (the progenitor of Ichiro's Malt) when Hanyu was sold and dismantled. This led to their own

Above Masataka Taketsuru was obsessed with finding the perfect location for his second distillery. Rural Miyagi prefecture fit the bill with its perfect climate and pristine waters.

interest in making authentic malt whisky; new copper stills were installed in 2015. Their current line of products, branded as Yamazakura (mountain cherry blossom) are still Scotch whisky blended with a little bit of old stock from Hanyu. This will have to satisfy consumers until the new malt whisky being produced authentically for the first time has had time to age.

Saburomaru (1952, Wakatsuru Shuzo)

In Toyama prefecture, a sake brewery has been making whisky sporadically since 1959, much of it in a French *allospas* continuous distillation still. A fire in 1953 delayed everything quite a bit. They've never released more than 3,000 bottles in a single year, and only in 2013 did they release their first age-statement expression, a 20-year-old single malt. In 2016, they released Sabuonomaru 55, a 55-year-old allospas-still-derived whisky aged in wine casks, the oldest single malt

MADE IN JAPAN?

It is not too much of a stretch to say that, if a bottle has the words "single malt" and "Made in Japan" on its label, it is almost certainly a quality product from a distillery with a sophisticated understanding of Scottish-style whisky-making. There are notable exceptions, however. Due to the lax rules around Japanese whisky labeling, a Matsui "distillery" has begun marketing Kurayoshi whisky in bottles with age statements presenting them as 8- to 33-year-old pure malts; prices range from the equivalent of around $50 (£38, €45) to upward of $1,400 (£1,082, €1,255) per bottle in Japanese duty-free shops across the country. While the age statements may be true, the product inside is low- to mid-quality malt whisky imported from Scotland and bottled in a blending facility in Tottori prefecture. No actual Matsui distillery exists. Sadly, desperate tourists searching for age-statement Japanese whiskies, which are becoming increasingly hard to find, are being taken advantage of on a daily basis. In fact, in one liquor-shop chain, the 12-year-old Kurayoshi single malt is selling alongside a 12-year-old blended Nikka whisky for a 25 percent premium. Only one is actually made in Japan.

ever released in Japan. The company now has plans to add a copper still to its stainless-steel pot still, which should improve its whiskies over time.

Miyagikyo (1969, Nikka)

Miyagikyo opened in 1969, just before Suntory's Hakushu, and its eight pot stills and one enormous column still (a design commonly used to make multiply distilled spirits like vodka) provide much of the malt and grain whisky that goes into Nikka's mass-market blended brands. It also makes some elegant single-malt whisky. This was the first place Taketsuru visited on a tour of the Miyagi countryside. He realized immediately that the location, sandwiched between the Hirosegawa and Nikkagawa rivers and surrounded by mountains, was perfect for whisky distilling; he canceled the rest of the tour. How much the name of one of the confluences (Nikkagawa, or "Nikka River") played a role is anybody's guess. In 1999 Nikka moved their grain-whisky Coffey still to Miyagikyo, where they subsequently released Nikka Coffey Malt Whisky, an expression that could not be created in Scotland due to regulations. Miyagikyo whisky is often, though not always, markedly softer and milder than the product from Yoichi.

Hakushu (1973, Suntory)

Perched in the Japanese Alps, Hakushu is among the loftiest malt whisky distilleries in the world. At more than 2,200 feet (670 meters) above sea level, it is over twice the altitude of Scotland's highest, Dalwhinnie. Hakushu takes its water from beneath Kai-Komagatake ("Pony Mountain"), the impressive granite peak on whose forested coattails it sits. During the heady days of the early 1980s, according to the whisky writer Ulf Buxrud, a total of 36 pot stills on two separate sites in the forest at Hakushu were in full production. Changes in taste

Top left Using the pristine water, cool climate, ample coal and peat bogs of Hokkaido, Nikka has established itself as the maker of premium Scotch-style whiskies.

Top right The distinctive twin roofs of the Hakushu distillery stand out in the forest beneath the peaks of the Japanese Alps.

Bottom A distillery worker keeps a sharp eye on his still as it makes new pot whisky.

and technology resulted in the original Hakushu distilleries (#1 and #2) being decommissioned in the 1980s. Today, 16 stills at the new Hakushu East site (#3, 1981) are running nonstop. Like other Japanese distilleries, Hakushu produces whisky in a variety of styles, but many of its single malts have a clean, playful taste, with sweet, fruity flavors often balanced by well-controlled pepper or aniseed notes.

Fuji Gotemba (1973, Kirin)

Started as a collaboration between Japanese beer giant Kirin, grain-whisky giant Seagram's, and malt-whisky specialist Chivas Brothers, Fuji Gotemba has a unique history in Japanese whisky. As iconic locations go, it's hard to beat a distillery hidden in the forest at the foot of Mount Fuji. At over 2,000 feet (600 meters) above sea level, Fuji Gotemba's elevation makes it cooler than the great Kanto plain stretching below toward the east. Summers are hot and humid down in the flatlands, but the distillery's temperatures range only a few degrees higher than those in Scotland. Fuji Gotemba's water comes from the rain and snow runoff from Mount Fuji itself. Analysis of water from the distillery's very deep wells has suggested it is snowmelt from up to 50 years earlier. Its single malts, sometimes labeled "Fuji Gotemba" (富士御殿場) and sometimes "Fuji Sanroku" (富士山麓), tend to be relatively light, and are elegantly balanced.

Below The Chichibu distillery's Ichiro's Malt series is ever changing and never boring. The company produces some of Japan's most interesting new whiskies.

Chita (1973, Suntory)

The Chita distillery was set up by Suntory in collaboration with the National Federation of Agricultural Cooperative Associations. It has four column stills making various configurations of grain whisky (corn and six-row barley). No aging is done on site; rather, the raw distillate is shipped to other Suntory facilities for aging. Chita is not open to the public, likely because dedicated grain distilleries resemble steampunk industrial nightmares rather than riverside oases of craftsmanship.

Mars Shinshu (1985, Hombo Shuzo)

Hombo, maker of Mars Whisky, has a love-hate relationship with whisky production, seemingly missing each wave and buying in on each downturn. In 1960 they acquired Fuji Wine Company in Yamanashi prefecture (today Mars Winery) and began making whisky on site in the same year, but pulled the plug in 1969 after slow sales. The stills were moved to their headquarters in Kagoshima, where a small amount of Mars whisky was produced between 1978 and 1984. The whisky boom of the 1980s led them to open the Shinshu distillery in Nagano prefecture in 1985. Situated in the Japanese Alps, 2,618 feet (800 meters) above sea level, Shinshu is the most altitudinous whisky distillery in Japan. Unfortunately—and true to Hombo's luck with whisky—within four years whisky sales plummeted due to new tax regulations that doubled the price of their whisky while reducing the price of foreign competitors. Shinshu was shuttered in 1992 when they ran out of barrel-aging space. To sum up, they had produced whisky at three different sites for a combined 25 years between 1960 and 2010. In 2011 Hombo reopened the Shinshu distillery and replaced the very decrepit stills with exact replicas (with a few minor concessions to modern convenience and reliability). With its high elevation and seasonal production (only during cold months), Shinshu occupies a unique place in Japanese whisky, with strongly peated whiskies aged more slowly due to elevation. Some distillate is aged at Hombo's Kagoshima headquarters and at their shochu distillery on Yakushima Island (a World Heritage Site whose landscape inspired the famous anime film *Princess Mononoke*).

This page The Nukada distillery from the Kiuchi brewery is new to the whisky game, but they've been making excellent sake for nearly two centuries and fine craft beer for more than two decades so we have every hope they'll figure whisky out as well.

Chichibu (2008, Venture Whisky)
At the other end of the scale from the old Yoichi and Yamazaki distilleries is Chichibu, which was only set up in 2008. Compared to Suntory and Nikka's operations, the Saitama distillery has a tiny production capacity (a thirtieth of Yamazaki's). It has not even put out any properly matured whisky yet. However, the Chichibu experiment is one of the most important things to happen to Japanese whisky in the last decade. The owner, Ichiro Akuto, who makes great whisky, comes from an old sake-brewing family that began distilling whisky at the Hanyu distillery around 1980. Unfortunately, the domestic whisky market started to implode during the 1980s and the firm was forced into bankruptcy in 2000. Akuto has led it through a phoenix-like rebirth, selling whiskies from the old Hanyu stock under the "Ichiro's Malt" brand, with clever playing-card names for each whisky ("Queen of Hearts," "Two of Clubs"). Early Chichibu releases have been non–age statement whiskies, but don't let that dissuade you—they are excellent early expressions of single malts. The annual Chichibu Matsuri distillery festival has become a must-attend event for whisky lovers from around the world.

Okayama (2011, Miyashita Shuzo)
This outfit has been making sake since 1915 and shochu since 1983. In 1994 they became one of the pioneers of Japanese craft beer, and began experimenting with distilling beer and then barrel-aging it. Their Doppo Beer Spirits, aged 10 years in oak, was a hit upon release. They began barrel aging some of their barley shochu, and in 2011 acquired a whisky makers' license. The early experiments didn't turn out well as they were using a stainless-steel shochu still rather than a copper whisky still. In 2015 they acquired a hybrid copper still and continued experimenting. The results of the shochu-still experiments have not yet been released, while early copper expressions (new-pot, six-month, and one-year) have been released in limited quantities. They are unique in that they are dedicated to

using local barley—some 50 percent of their malt comes from local farmers. Most other producers procure their malt from overseas sources.

Nukada (2016, Kiuchi Shuzo)
Best known overseas for its Hitachino Nest beer, Kiuchi actually started as a sake brewery in Ibaraki prefecture in 1823. They began making beer in 1996 and set up a distillation facility in 2003 to reduce waste. Their first distillate was a *kasutori* shochu (page 57) made from their sake lees. They installed a hybrid whisky still 2015 and released the first product in 2016, which was actually a distilled beer liqueur (Kiuchi no Shizuku). The first whisky runs, in a handful of casks, are still aging; as of 2018, no whisky has been released to the public. This isn't an attempt to capitalize on the Japanese whisky boom, though—Kiuchi had been planning to produce whisky for more than a decade. The idea was inspired by the company president's involvement in the revival of an heirloom strain of Japanese barley, Kaneko Golden, which is now used in their Ancient Nipponia craft beer and may eventually appear in their whisky expressions.

Akkeshi (2016, Kenten Co., Ltd.)

The second whisky distillery in Hokkaido after the famed Nikka distillery was the brainchild of a Tokyo-based import-export company CEO. Frustrated with the difficulty of acquiring high-quality Japanese whisky, he decided it was time to make his own. He set up shop on the east coast of Hokkaido, in the town of Akkeshi, with plans to make Islay-style malt whiskies that would play on the heavier side of Japanese whiskies. All equipment was imported from Scotland; the aging facility will be in the dunnage style, with barrels stacked four high on a concrete floor (Scottish dunnage distilleries often have dirt floors). Since a large firm is backing this distillery, there has been no rush toward early releases. They seem content to wait and release their product when it is deemed ready.

Shizuoka (2016, Gaia Flow)

When the CEO of a Japanese renewable energy company goes on a whisky tour in Scotland, strange things happen. Taiko Nakamura, already a whisky fan, was so inspired by his 2012 visit to Scotland's Kilchoman whisky distillery that by 2016 he had rebranded Gaia Flow as a spirits company and built a whisky distillery in his hometown of Shizuoka. While this may not be great news for renewable energy, it should prove highly entertaining for whisky fans. The distillery

acquired equipment from the defunct Karuizawa distillery, including one of the stills, the malt mill, the destoner, and a hoops press machine; these will be partnered with original equipment ordered from Scotland. The entertainment factor is that the distillery was built with tours in mind—visitors can walk through the production process without being in the way and then enjoy a dram in the second-floor tasting room, which overlooks the distillery floor. While no product has been released at the time of writing this book, we do know that Nakamura intends to depart from other recent Japanese whisky ventures by making Shizuoka's whisky on the lighter side.

Mars Tsunuki (2017, Hombo Shuzo)

Hombo, owner of the Mars Shinshu Distillery, surprised the whisky world by announcing that, in addition to barrel-aging whisky at the traditional family headquarters in Kagoshima prefecture, they would also open another distillery, Mars Tsunuki, on the same site. This distillery is situated next to their mothballed seven-story column still where the family made its fortune producing multiple-distilled shochu back in the 1920s. This clean, light distillate was so well received by the brewers' association of the day that it was offered as a gift to the emperor; as a result of this, it rocketed to the top of national liquor sales. Hombo used the newfound wealth to expand their business in a myriad of ways, with ventures into wine, whisky, beer and even into soft drinks. The Tsunuki distillery went online in 2017 with two pot stills; its first products are slated for release in time for the 2020 Tokyo Olympics.

Kanosuke (2018, Komasa Shuzo)

Within a year of Mars Tsunuki opening in Kagoshima prefecture, a location best known for sweet-potato shochu, rival shochu maker Komasa opened its own whisky distillery. The newest whisky distillery in Japan, it sits beside the ocean. The tasting room has ocean views; guests can enjoy a walk down to the water before or after a tour. Komasa is not a newcomer to spirits making—it has been making the very popular Mellowed Kozuru barrel-aged rice shochu for decades, and several members of the team have earned whisky-making degrees. The distillery's first new pot was bottled and released in April 2018, on the first day it was open to visitors.

Karuizawa

The active distilleries listed above account for the vast majority of Japanese whisky on the market, but one prominent name is missing: Karuizawa. This distillery was owned by the Kirin corporation, which acquired it as part of a takeover of Mercian wines in 2006. Unlike Kirin's Fuji Gotemba, however, it was mothballed and all of its stock was sold to venture capitalists, who have made a fortune releasing single casks at a time, often only available at auction, with resale sticker prices comparable to the cost of a business-class flight from London to New York.

For much more information on specific brands and bottlings from these distilleries and to learn more about all things Japanese whisky, we recommend *Whisky Rising* by Stefan VanEycken, the first definitive guide to Japanese whisky ever written. It's so definitive that the original English version has been translated back into Japanese, because no such guide existed in that language. For something a little less encyclopedic, but approachable and chock-full of useful information we also recommend the book *Japanese Whisky* by Brian Ashcraft.

It doesn't appear that the Japanese whisky craze will be abating any time soon, though all waves of enthusiasm eventually crash on the shore. Hopefully these distillers will be well positioned to weather the inevitable downturn in demand so they can continue to produce world-class whiskies and build on the reputation they've established over the past couple decades. There's no doubt we should all look forward to the day when Japanese whiskies of known provenance can be purchased for prices commensurate with their quality alongside the finest Scotch whiskies in the world.

Above and left Kanosuke is the new kid on the block and the purpose-built distillery is a testament to modern efficiency while also having a beautiful seaside location. The Komasa Mellowed Kozuru shochu distillery can be seen just beyond the Kanosuke distillery building.

JAPANESE GIN?

There may be no spirit more English than gin, despite its origins in genever and other European traditions. The juniper-forward spirit uses a wide variety of botanicals in exact proportions to produce a vegetal, herbaceous and usually very refreshing drink. As with craft gin in the US and UK, which has recently seen a rapid increase in popularity, Japanese gin has become a thing just within the past few years. The first mover, at least for export, was Kinobi, a wholly Japanese gin made in Kyoto (in the city itself, which is very uncommon for alcohol producers). The Kyoto distillery was the brainchild of the investors behind Japanese whisky distributor, Number One Drinks, Ltd., who famously bought up the old stock of Karuizawa whisky and bottled and sold it at auction. They used the proceeds from to build their own distillery and create Kinobi. As a gin, it is flavored with juniper—not a traditional Japanese ingredient, but a requirement for gin—as well as shiso, green tea, ginger, bamboo leaves, cypress wood, yuzu and *sansho* pepper. Sansho is the most distinctive of these ingredients, being a relative of the peppercorn that gives Szechuan cuisine its numbing quality. Sansho does the same thing without the fiery heat; when you drink Kinobi (and other Japanese gins made with sansho) you get a tingle on your tongue.

For those unfamiliar with gin, it's often made with the botanical ingredients macerated in grain alcohol in a single steeping tank, after which the maceration is distilled. Another method puts the botanicals in a mesh basket in the still neck, so the alcohol vapor captures their flavors and aromas as it passes through the basket. The Kyoto distillery goes a third way with Kinobi. They create eight separate macerations and distill each of the eight botanicals separately before blending these eight distinct base spirits. This allows them to balance the flavor and aroma profile based on yearly variation in ingredient quality (for example, some years sansho can be very strongly scented, and other years very mild). They can also create additional styles (Navy Strength, Green Tea Gin, etc.) by changing the ratios of these base spirits. Other Japanese gins have recently hit the market in Japan and overseas, but to date Kinobi appears to be the most balanced, likely due to the fact that the entire process is overseen by Alex Davies, a native of Sussex, England, who cut his teeth at the Cotswolds Distillery in the UK.

Juniper berries are the foundation of any proper gin, though here with some Japanese cypress wood chips thrown in for some local character.

Fresh ginger (pictured), green tea, sansho pepper, and other ingredients make for a distinctly Japanese gin.

Bamboo leaves are another ingredient that add a distinctly Japanese character to Kinobi Gin.

Left Both a pot still (left) and fractional column still (right) are in use at the Kyoto distillery, where each ingredient's maceration is distilled separately before blending, which gives the master distiller more control of his end product.

Below The separate distillates and subsequent blending allows the Kyoto distillery to produce a variety of styles without varying fermentation or distillation methods.

Properly macerating these raw ingredients in neutral alcohol can be backbreaking work.

Japanese Beer

*From Industrial Lager
to Microbrews*

Below When people think of Japanese alcohol they think of sake, but beer has been the best-selling drink for decades. Even geisha are known to enjoy a cold one now and again.

AUSPICIOUS BEGINNINGS

Beer has been in Japan for about 400 years. During the Edo period (1603–1868), Dutch merchants first imported it, then started to brew it for themselves at the port of Dejima in Nagasaki. They even presented some to the shogun in 1724. As far as the average Japanese drinker was concerned, however, beer really got its start with the Meiji Restoration, which modernized Japan extremely rapidly in the late 19th century. Some of the Japanese representatives who dealt with the American "Black Ships" in the 1850s were treated to beer during the negotiations; shortly afterward, the father of Japanese chemistry, Komin Kawamoto, became the first Japanese person to make his own beer, using an improvised setup in his back garden. His method was published in a textbook in 1860.

Over the next decade, as foreigners began flocking to Japan's newly opened ports, imported beer flooded the rowdy pubs and clubs in the foreign quarters. Bass Pale Ale, still a common sight in Japanese bars, seems to have been the dominant brand, but other British styles and a few Bavarian lagers were being distributed quite widely by the 1870s.

It was expensive. In 1871, the Nankaitei restaurant in Tokyo was charging three gold coins and 300 silver coins for one bottle. For the less affluent, there was a substitute: used beer bottles refilled with locally produced ersatz beer.

Nobody knows how the stuff was made, but we can be pretty sure its manufacture bore no resemblance to conventional beer-making. In 1871, the Tokyo city authorities issued an edict specifically banning fake Bass beer, but the pirate industry seems to have continued to stumble along. The Yokohama *Mainichi* newspaper complained that drinkers were prepared to drink any foul concoction so long as it carried an exotic enough label.

Commercial brewing in Japan got underway about the same time as the pirate bottling (and the two industries may have overlapped in some cases). One G. Rosenfelt (full name unknown) built the "Japan Brewery" in Yokohama in 1869, about the same time as a Japanese-run operation set up in Shinagawa, Tokyo. The next year, Dutchman J. B. N. Hecht's Hecht Brewery

This page More than 100 breweries existed throughout Japan by the late 1800s, before the industry was regulated. Sapporo and Yebisu (left) were two of the winners in the race to survive, while many others (below) were lost to history.

and Norwegian-American William Copeland's Spring Valley Brewery (which would become Kirin Beer) came on line in Yokohama. Breweries started popping up all over the country: Shibutani Beer in Osaka (1872), Mitsu Uroko beer in Kofu (1873) and a government-run brewery in Hokkaido in 1876. Notably, in 1890, with the help of a German brewmaster, the Japan Beer Brewing Company in the Ebisu neighborhood of Tokyo began brewing Yebisu, a brand that still exists today, believed to be the first Japanese beer to adhere to the Reinheitsgebot, or German beer purity law. At an industrial show in 1890, 83 beer brands from 23 prefectures were exhibited. By the end of the century, there were up to 150 breweries nationwide. This was the first Japanese microbrewing boom; sadly, its days were numbered.

THE RISE OF BIG BEER

There are many situations in which government intervention may have unintended consequences for consumer markets, and the Japanese beer market is but one example. Japan imposed it first beer tax in 1901 to help fund military campaigns in Asia. This immediately caused numerous smaller brewers operating on very narrow profit margins to close. The tax was ramped up over the next decade as the government pursued an aggressive policy of rationalizing the industry to increase tax revenues. It encouraged the merger of three of the largest firms into the Dai Nippon Beer Company in 1906; two years later, it imposed a minimum annual production volume of 47,500 gallons (180 kiloliters), which effectively outlawed the remaining small brewers who had managed to survive the increased taxation.

The policy of rationalization was extremely successful from the government's point of view. Beer tax revenues more than doubled in the five years following the introduction of the levy, significantly boosting an imperial treasury which relied on alcohol taxes for an astonishing one-third of its income in the early 1900s. In 1923, there was at least some diversity in the industry: in addition to the Dai Nippon Beer Company and Kirin Beer, there was also Sakura Beer, Kabuto Beer, Toyo Beer, the Anglo Japanese Brewing Company and Takasago Brewing. By the 1940s, however, even these medium-sized enterprises had been swallowed up, leaving only Kirin and Dai Nippon in the field.

If fans of small enterprise thought Japan's defeat in World War II would change the situation, they were bitterly disappointed. Dai Nippon was split into two companies in 1949, creating Asahi Beer and Nihon Beer (later to become Sapporo). In 1960s, the whisky giant Suntory reentered the fray, making a total of four large producers (the shochu maker Takara tried and failed at around the same time). However, alcohol taxes still accounted for a sixth of government tax revenues in 1955, and alcohol policy was (and still is) run

Left Modern Japanese beer is overwhelmingly factory produced and thirst quenching, but not necessarily interesting. The Asahi factory in Hakata can produce up to 20,000 cans of beer per minute and releases more than 800 million cans annually. However, craft beer is gaining a foothold with makers like Coedo, pictured here, producing some very nice styles.

the big brands using only malt for their premium beers.

Sapporo's premium product, Yebisu, an all-malt style that adheres to the German beer purity law, is considered a beer for special occasions by many Japanese. This is accentuated by the fact that the gold label is decorated with Yebisu-sama, the god of good luck. He holds a red carp (a lucky fish) under his arm; if you get one of the very rare surprise labels, he'll have a second red carp in his basket, making that particular bottle extra auspicious.

While all of these are lager-style beers, there is currently some differentiation among their bestselling products. Asahi Super Dry is a light, crisp lager that lives up to its "super dry" name. Its prime functions seem to be thirst quenching and palate cleansing, both of which it does very well. Kirin falls in this spectrum, but balances dry and sweet in nearly equal measures. Meanwhile, Sapporo tends toward the sweeter end of the spectrum. Suntory Premium Malts, an all-malt style, is clearly richer and more complex than the others. But these are, in the final analysis, only small variations on the pervasive light-lager theme.

from the tax office. The minimum production volumes were ramped up as the beer market expanded. The consistent effect of the government's policies was to foster a few huge conglomerates with fat profits capable of keeping the tax payments flowing.

The market was not uncompetitive; in fact, the big brewers fought like cats in a bag. At the top of the heap in the 1950s were Sapporo, with a network of themed bars in eastern Japan, and Asahi, with a lock on much of the west. Kirin, the smallest of the three brewers after the war, was forced to concentrate on the household market, but as drinking patterns changed and people started consuming more at home, Kirin overtook the two Dai Nippon fragments. It had 64 percent of beer sales by 1976. Asahi fought back from the late 1980s with the very light Asahi Super Dry. This brew led the beer market down the road of light, fizzy lager, and has now replaced Kirin's brands as the most popular beer in Japan. Recently, there has been a return to slightly richer styles, with many of

Right Modern Japanese beer factories look more like high tech pharmaceutical firms than alcohol producers. Their cutting edge technology allows them to produce massive quantities of very high quality products.

One aspect of Japanese mass-market beer is noteworthy and admirable, however: since the 1970s, virtually all beer sold in Japan—in bottles, cans or on tap—is unpasteurized. In 1967, Suntory released the first unpasteurized beer using microfiltration, and it became an immediate hit for its freshness. In 1968 Asahi followed suit, and within a few years every new brand released to the market was unpasteurized. This continues even today—so much so that when someone orders a draft beer in Japan, they don't say the Japanese equivalent of "draft beer" or "on tap," they say *nama*, which means raw or unpasteurized (as in *namazake*, page 38). Curiously, the word is only used to order draft beer, perhaps because there is not a direct translation for liquids served on tap. However, you can be sure that the kanji for nama (生) appears everywhere on Japanese beer bottles and cans.

The mass market beer is not bad, per se. Bryan Baird, an American who runs the craft brewery Baird Beer in Numazu, says, "I like industrial beer. It's refreshing and highly drinkable, but it all tastes the same. Less than 1 percent of what is possible in beer-making accounts for perhaps 99 percent of production in Japan; this has been the case for so long that it has become ingrained. When we started selling our real ales to the locals in Numazu, many of them were not prepared for the sort of beer experience we were providing. Beer, to them, was industrial lager and nothing else."

Frankenbeer

In 1994 the Japanese beer market suffered an enormous disruption when a Suntory laboratory scientist invented *happoshu* (literally "sparkling alcohol"), or "Frankenbeer," as it has been dubbed by Bryan Harrell, a leading foreign writer on Japanese beer. It is basically imitation beer that has a very low malt content. The reason for its runaway success is familiar: the telltale footprints of the Japanese government are all over the scene of the crime. Without getting too bogged down in the technicalities, Japanese tax law defines beer by its malt content; because beer is punitively taxed compared to other alcohols, there is a large tax benefit to be had by lowering the malt content and having your sweet yellow fizzy stuff defined as "sparkling alcohol" instead. Strangely, some famous Belgian beers, such as Chimay and Duvel, are also classified as happoshu under Japanese law, so it's not all fake beer.

This page Sapporo Beer's art deco Ginza Lion beer hall has remained essentially unchanged since the 1930s and is just as raucous as ever. Expats, locals, and tourists alike mix and mingle and enjoy German style pub food and a wide variety of beers from this large brewery.

Right Virtually all mass-market Japanese beer advertising focuses on the thirst-quenching aspects of the light lagers they produce.

The beer companies have not stopped there. In 1999, Shusaku Kashiwada, an engineer at Sapporo Beer, came up with the bright idea of making beer with no malt in it whatsoever, which would be taxed at an even lower rate than happoshu. The completely maltless Draft One (ドラフトワン) was released from its cage in 2003: a "beer" made from caramel and pea protein! Kirin and Asahi responded with soybean brews called Nodogoshi Nama (のどごし生) and Shin Nama (新生). Japanese beer writers, at a loss as to what to call this maltless style, vaguely refer to it as "third beer," implying that actual beer is "first beer" and happoshu is "second beer." Rob Bright, co-founder of the English-language Japanese beer website BeerTengoku.com, refers to this "third beer" as a "hodgepodge," perhaps because there doesn't seem to be any rhyme or reason to what it's made from or how it's classified.

Sales of these "Frankenbeers" now rival those of real beer in Japan. Longtime Tokyo resident Ben Johnson is fond of saying, "The Japanese may have the most sophisticated food palate on earth, yet the worst taste in alcohol," and in the case of beer, the Japanese consumer bears this out. A test-marketing campaign for Draft One in Kyushu in 2003 aimed to sell 170,000 cases of the beverage in a year; they sold 100,000 in a month. In the short term, the happoshu catastrophe has been thoroughly bad for Japanese beer quality. However, by flooding the bottom end of the market with cheap lager imitations, the beer companies have put themselves under pressure to create something distinctive at the top.

There has been a definite shift toward slightly richer all-malt styles from the major makers, and it is possible that this trend may eventually cause real diversity to emerge from the big companies. The brewers at the conglomerates are extremely capable, and whenever they are given the opportunity to make more exciting beer, they usually prove themselves. For instance, all have now released dark lagers made with roasted barley, and Asahi recently produced a

HOPPY: THE MOTHER OF INVENTION

In the wake of World War II, the Japanese alcohol industry was in tatters. Hundreds of people a year were dying as a result of drinking poisonous concoctions cooked up from unknown ingredients. Shochu had become nearly undrinkable, and beer was prohibitively expensive due to high taxes. To solve this drinking dilemma, the Tokyo confectioner Kokuka Beverage Company, then better known for its soda fountain, had a brilliant idea. Why not make a beer-like beverage that could be mixed with shochu to create a beer of sorts? In a nation with a history of ersatz beer, it could be marketed as such. Thus Hoppy was born. The first Hoppy was served in Akasaka in 1948 and quickly became an izakaya staple for the working class. It fell of out favor during the heady financial boom years, but has been making a steady comeback as people rediscover the refreshing drink. The iconic logo still appears outside many older izakaya around Tokyo. Hoppy is typically poured over a shot or two of *korui* (multiply distilled) shochu in a chilled beer mug to create a frothy beer-like drink that's surprisingly refreshing. If you want to actually taste the shochu, you should try it with honkaku shochu. Hoppy Black (made with roasted malt) goes best with black-sugar shochu (page 61) while the standard golden-hued Hoppy goes best with barley shochu (page 58).

Top left The bar Popeye in Tokyo (see page 146) has by far the largest range of beers in Japan. **Top right** Creamy stout from the Ginza Lion beer restaurant in Tokyo (page 147). **Above** If you're in Washington, DC, try Daikaya (see page 148) for a Japanese craft beer. **Left** Towa is a Tokyo soba shop (see page 146) with 12 kinds of beer on tap and plenty of bottled beer to choose from.

very good limited-edition strong stout. Over the past couple years, a fair number of macro craft beers have been offered by all of the large producers. In the end, they lack the complexity of real craft beer, but at least a wider range of options now exists in convenience-store coolers.

More significant, perhaps, is the effect the beer companies' gambit may have on Japanese government policy. Happoshu was a radical step: its entire purpose was to deprive the Japanese exchequer of billions of yen in beer tax. The basis of almost a century of Japanese alcohol policymaking was challenged by the very companies it was responsible for creating. The Finance Ministry and the big alcohol conglomerates had been at loggerheads on the issue since 1993. Finally, in 2017, the government changed the laws. As of 2018, the minimum malt content for beer was lowered from 65 percent to 50 percent, and a long list of new ingredients was authorized, including everything from fruits and spices to *katsuoboshi* (dried fish shavings). Between 2020 and 2026, taxes on beer, happoshu and maltless hodgepodge will be adjusted to the same rate regardless of production process.

THE CRAFT BEER BOOM

The events of 1994 were not all bad for the Japanese beer scene. In fact, that year could be looked back on as the best of times and the worst of times. In 1994 the government also lowered the minimum production requirements for a beer-making license. For the first time since the 19th century, small producers could seriously consider brewing. Echoing what seems to have been a universal trend over the past few decades, there has been an explosion of craft brewing

throughout Japan. Tatsuo Aoki, who set up the Popeye beer pub (page 146) in 1985, explains his perspective:

> Before the changes, you couldn't stock several types of cask beer. Each company would insist on it all being their stuff. I thought that was strange. From the mid 1990s, it started to open up. I could do what I had always wanted to do, which was to offer real variety to my customers.
>
> At first, it was a bit crazy. There were too many breweries set up. A lot of the sake makers and souvenir beer makers were getting involved. At its height, in the late 90s, there were more than 300 independent breweries operating, just a few years after a situation where there had been none. It was by no means all good stuff. You would find that the first batch was okay, because they would have a US or German expert over and the expert would have taken care of it but, after that, the quality tended to decline. But at least it was interesting. People were experimenting and there were a handful of makers who were making very good beer.

A lot of what was being produced during this early phase was *omiyage* (souvenir) beer that was intended to be brought home after visiting a particular region. These beers—some of which still exist—are usually made with ingredients associated with that region, like sweet-potato beer in Kagoshima or *sansho* pepper beer in Kyoto. They are generally not very good, but can be an entertaining flavor experience. Lacking the distribution network of other craft breweries, they form a relatively small part of today's market.

Since those early days, there has been a shakeup of the industry, with about a third of the original craft breweries

Top left The Nakameguro Taproom (see page 147), run by Baird Brewing, is widely acknowledged as one of the best craft breweries in Japan.

Above Hitachino Nest may be the most well-known Japanese craft beer overseas and they have now opened a series of brewpubs throughout the Tokyo area (see page 147).

closing or being replaced. At the lowest, approximately 200 remained; as of 2018, there are 278 licensed breweries with an additional 40 applications pending before brewery licensing laws change in 2019. The government recently began issuing happoshu licenses that require only 1,500 gallons (6,000 liters) per year be produced. In response, Popeye's Aoki and others have started very small breweries to supply individual beer bars or beer halls. Brewpubs have started popping up all over Japan; Rob Bright expects the number to double over the next five years as more and more small producers find it financially viable to brew and serve on the same premises.

At the other end of the spectrum, some craft breweries have begun expansion that's leading them into the multimillion-liter range of annual production. Yoho Brewing in Nagano, for example, is now nearly ubiquitous in convenience stores. Its Yona Yona Ale (よなよなエール), Suiyobi no Neko (水曜日のネコ, Wednesday Cat) Belgian style-ale and Indo no Ao Oni (インドの青鬼, Indian Blue Demon) IPA have led it into international markets and annual production in excess of 1,330,000 gallons (5 million liters).

Baird Beer has long been a leader in creativity, which has paid off in popularity. Starting in 2001 with an 8-gallon (30-liter) production tank in a taproom in Shizuoka, Bryan and Sayumi Baird were the first in Japan to release bottle-conditioned beers (a traditional style of carbonation), and have continued to innovate with fermentation types and serving temperatures, They also introduced seasonal beers to the Japanese craft-beer scene. They've also managed to open several taprooms, including the Nakameguro Taproom in Tokyo (page 147). All of this effort has resulted in international exports and the construction of a 500,000-gallon (2-million-liter) production facility that opened in 2014.

Above The craft brews from Tokyo's Y.Y.G Brewery (see page 147) run the spectrum from pilsners to easy-drinking IPAs to sour porters.

Another recent wrinkle in the Japanese craft-beer market is the entry of sake makers. Adept at highly sophisticated fermentation methods, some of them have been very successful at adding beer to their product portfolios. The most famous overseas is the Hitachino Nest brand, which is produced in Ibaraki by the Kiuchi Brewing Company. Sake brewers since 1823, they released their first beer in 1996 and won Japan's first international craft beer award in 2000, taking silver and bronze medals at the World Beer Cup in the US. They've since expanded their brewing capacity with a dedicated beer brewery opening in 2008. They were almost unknown in Japan, focusing almost entirely on the export market, until they opened two taprooms in Tokyo in 2016 and a third in 2018 (see Hitachino Brewing Lab, page 147).

"TORIAEZU NAMA"

On arriving in a Japanese bar, a patron will often tell the server, "*Toriaezu nama!*" which means, "A draft beer to start!" The word for beer is *biiru*, but draft beer is *nama* (page 109). "Toriaezu nama" is an institution in Japan: an easy, refreshing drink that can be ordered quickly on first arrival at a bar before everyone takes a look at the menu. You won't hear anyone asking questions like, "What types of beer do your have?" or "Do you have any bitter? Or an IPA, perhaps?" It's just beer—a cold, light substance that quenches the thirst, cleanses the palate and gets the toasts out of the way as soon as possible. Sales of beer in Japan far outstrip those of any other alcohol—about twice as much alcohol is consumed in the form of lager as is poured from sake bottles—but a sizeable proportion of that is served as a thirst quencher rather than a drink that is expected to have great individual character.

JAPAN'S BEER MUSEUMS

If you want to find out more about the history of beer in Japan, Japan's beer museums are worth visiting. Sapporo's Museum of Yebisu Beer in Tokyo (4-20-1 Ebisu, Shibuya-ku; tel. 03-5423-7255), pictured left, or Kirin's Yokohama Beer Village (1-17-1 Namamugi, Yokohama City; tel. 045-503-8250) will be most convenient for many visitors, but the Sapporo Beer Museum in Sapporo City Hokkaido (Kita 7-jo Higashi 9-chome, Higashi-ku, Sapporo; tel. 011-731-4368), pictured below, is also well worth a visit. All of these are large facilities run by Japan's big beer conglomerates offering professional presentations and slightly company-biased versions of beer history. The product tastings and inevitable attached bar and restaurant are part of the experience. For something completely different, however, go to Ishikawa Brewery in Fussa City, Tokyo prefecture (1 Kumagawa, Fussa City, Tokyo; tel. 042-553-0100; tamajiman.com). It is a tiny little place, with more of the very limited space in the museum devoted to their main business of sake making, but they have some interesting beer relics. On the grounds, they have an iron cauldron that was, until recently, being used to line a pond in a local garden. It turned out to be a relic from the company's brief dalliance with beer in the 1880s, one of dozens of forgotten enterprises all over the country. Try their Tama no Megumi Beer (多摩の恵) in the attached restaurant.

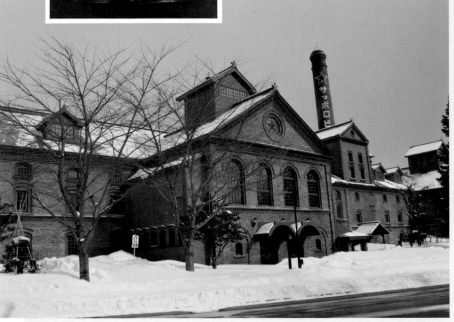

Collaboration brews between Japanese and foreign craft breweries are heightening the craft-beer trend. Perhaps the most compelling example to date is a collaboration between Hitachino Nest and Birrificio del Ducato of Parma, Italy, in which the Italian brewery sourced yellow and black koji from Hitachino Nest's sake brewery to create Koji il Riso. The black koji version is a punch-in-the-teeth sour, while the yellow koji version is dripping with honeyed sweetness. Drink it if you find it.

Hitachino Nest is far from the only collaborative Japanese craft brewer, however. Baird collaborated with Ishii Brewing and Stone Brewing Company to create a green-tea IPA in 2011, and in 2012 San Diego's Ballast Point brewers visited Coedo Brewery in Saitama to create the unique West to East IPA. This delightful one-off was made using Japanese rice, fresh yuzu citrus and yeast from Ballast Point's Brewery.

Early on, craft beer brewers in Japan seemed content with making imitations of other craft beers from around the world, particularly pilsners, wheat beers and stouts, thanks to the German and Czech brewers who were brought over early on to teach everyone how to make craft beer. This led to some tasty brews, but a lot of misses as well. No one really needs to try a garlic porter to know it's unpalatable, do they? IPAs rose to prominence in the early to mid-2000s, following in the footsteps of American craft-brew trends driven by increased communication between Japanese and American craft brewers. Nevertheless, according to Rob Bright, a distinct Japanese style has emerged. Japanese white ale has taken the Belgian white style and made it uniquely Japanese by using local citrus—usually yuzu. The use of rice is also common in Japanese craft beer. While American behemoth Budweiser uses rice to increase yields and lower prices, in Japan the purpose is to align with the Japanese palate and honor the local bounty. This is another aspect being emphasized in Japanese craft beer that mimics Japanese cuisine—the use of local seasonal ingredients. Such seasonal brews can be quite enjoyable, but they're made in very small quantities and can be hard to find.

And as you'd expect, the inevitable financial calculus has begun. Kirin was the first mover: in 2014 they became the first major brewer to buy a stake in a craft brewery when they acquired 30 percent of Yoho Brewing. In 2016 they went international, buying up 25 percent of Brooklyn Brewery, which has been exporting to Japan since 1990. Their Sorachi Ace beer, made with Hokkaido hops, has more complexity than 98 percent of the beer consumed in Japan (Japanese craft beer still makes up less than 2 percent of the domestic beer market). In 2017, Sapporo purchased iconic Anchor Brewing, which, with more than 100 years of history, has a rightful claim as the first American craft brewery. Asahi has gone in a different direction by buying up major European brands, including the well-known Pilsner Urquell, Grolsch and Peroni brands over the past few years.

In existence for less than 30 years, the Japanese craft beer scene remains nascent when considered in the context of the country's 3,000-year love affair with alcohol. The breweries are becoming more professional and the beers more sophisti-cated, and the craft-beer community is growing slowly but surely. There's still a long way to go before Japanese craft beer becomes a larger part of the Japanese drinking culture, but there's little doubt that, like seemingly all other Japanese alcohol traditions, craft beer will have its day. The growing interest and opportunity may be best exemplified by the growth in craft beer festivals. The 2017 Kyoto Beer

Fest was held in a shabby shopping street, far from the bustling tourist areas of the former Japanese capital. Yet even in this inconvenient location, thousands of people waited in long lines to try craft beers from all over Japan. (Particularly popular were the fruit beers, which must have looked especially refreshing on a sweltering summer afternoon.) Japan's craft beers certainly have far more to recommend them than the adjunct lagers that represent the lion's share of the market.

Below Craft brewing is now becoming extremely popular throughout Japan with many good craft breweries, such as Coedo (top), producing excellent beers in a variety of styles, and craft beer bars such as Before9 in Kyoto (bottom; see page 148) focusing on a variety of beers from around Japan.

Japanese Wine

*Gaining Respect
on the World Stage*

THE HISTORY OF JAPANESE WINE

Although wine has relatively shallow roots in modern Japan, the country's history of making wine may stretch back as far as 5,000 years—evidenced by the discovery of alcohol consumption at the prehistoric settlement of Sannai-Maruyama (see page 78)—further than any record of winemaking in France or sake-brewing in Japan. But after that, wine almost completely disappears from the Japanese historical record. In the late 1500s and early 1600s, it makes a brief reappearance with the arrival of Europeans in Japan; for a time, it seems to have been quite easily available to the country's elite. Although the evidence is far from conclusive, some sources claim that the warlord Nobunaga Oda even hosted a tasting party in 1569 to judge wines brought into the country by Jesuit priests. The subsequent closing of the country and banning of Christianity brought an end to wine's short heydey—its close association with Christian clerics and their sacraments probably did it no favors under the new regime. The early 18th-century botanist Ekken Kaibara wrote about *chinta* (from the Portuguese word for red, *tinto*) and other types of *budo-shu* (grape alcohol), but by that time, it was a foreign curiosity almost impossible to obtain in Japan.

Viticulture did expand rapidly in Japan during the Edo period (1603–1868) but grapes were desired as a delicacy for the table, not for wine. There are a number of myths about the provenance of Japan's unique *Koshu* (甲州) grape variety (not to be confused with *koshu* [古酒], which is aged alcohol).

Top Japanese wine growing regions are extremely diverse in climate and altitude.

Right The Koshu grape variety is the most well-known Japanese varietal internationally, with the white wines now winning international awards.

According to one story, while praying in Katsunuma in Yamanashi prefecture in the year 718, the famous Buddhist priest Gyoki had a vision of a buddha holding a vine, as a result of which, Gyoki planted grapes on the spot. Another story features a monk called Kageyu Amemiya, who noticed an unusual vine growing by the roadside in Yamanashi in 1186. Origins aside, we do know that Koshu

is a species of *Vitis vinifera* originally native to Europe, North Africa and Western Asia, and is probably descended from grape varieties exported along the Silk Road. It was likely brought into Japan along with Buddhism—hence its association with Buddhist priests long before the arrival of the Jesuits.

Cultivation remained on a very small scale until the early 1600s, when a famous medic named Tokuhon Nagata introduced the distinctive *tanajitate* or *tanashiki-saibai* overhead frames that are still a feature of Japanese vineyards. If you visit Japan's grape country in Yamanashi prefecture, you will find grapes hanging down above your head in almost every available space: there are even parking lots covered by the ubiquitous vine canopies. With this method, vines are spaced more widely than those in a European vineyard. Each vine produces huge yields, with its branches trained across overhead frames so that bunches of grapes hang down from the canopy. The method is labor intensive, but avoids damage in Japan's hot and humid climate and is ideally suited to producing the perfect table grapes that became an expensive luxury item in the Edo period—though it may be less suited, some argue, to producing good wine. Between 1601 and 1716, the number of vines in Yamanashi prefecture, only a day's journey from the shogunate's palaces in Edo, grew from 164 to around 3,000.

Right Kanae Nagasawa, the son of a Satsuma samurai, was the first Japanese citizen to make wine, first in New York, and then in California.

Top left Baron N Wine Bar in the Shiroyama Hotel, is in Kagoshima city, the hometown of Kanae Nagasawa.

Top right Muscat Bailey A grapes are the most common variety used for Japanese red wine.

The Wine King

Perhaps fittingly, the first great Japanese winemaker did not make wine in Japan. In 1865, 15 students and four emissaries from the Satsuma domain departed the port of Kushikino under the pretext of visiting outlying coastal islands on a botany tour. In reality, they were meeting a British frigate that would take them to London to study. This audacious journey was initiated by Tadayoshi Shimazu, the 12th and

final daimyo of the Satsuma domain, who had been beaten badly in a brief conflict with the British navy and then realized that Japan was destined for defeat unless it could modernize. At that time it was illegal for Japanese citizens to leave the country, but Satsuma had a long history of ignoring dictates from Tokyo.

The students, all sons of Satsuma samurai families, practiced English on their journey; when they arrived in London, all but one of them enrolled in university. They would go on to study economics, science, engineering, mathematics and political science, and on returning to Japan they would start the first Japanese stock exchange, Sapporo Beer, Tokyo University and the Department of Education, among other impressive accomplishments. For good measure, one even became an outlaw assassin. These young men would be instrumental in leading their country into the modern world. What about the one student who didn't enroll in university? At just 13 years old, he was deemed too young to start college in London. Instead, he was sent off alone to a boarding school in Scotland.

There, Hikosuke Isonaga (1852–1934), the genius son of a Satsuma samurai, adopted the alias "Kanae Nagasawa" by which he would be known for the rest of his life. He demonstrated his intellect by finishing at the top of his Scottish boarding-school class in subjects ranging from chemistry to English composition. Although Nagasawa excelled in school, he was lonely. When five of the older Satsuma students made the decision to follow spiritualist Thomas Lake Harris to his Brotherhood of New Life commune outside Buffalo, New York—a place that

happened to have a vineyard—Nagasawa happily followed.

Upon arriving in New York in 1867, Nagasawa became the first Japanese student to enroll at Cornell University, where he studied natural history. He then returned to Harris' commune where he helped with the winemaking. Shortly thereafter, the other five students quarreled with Harris and were asked to leave. The then 15-year-old Nagasawa decided to stay, as he was captivated by Harris and fascinated with winemaking. He would not return to his homeland for 30 years—and then only to visit.

Not content with the relatively inhospitable climate of western New York, Harris decided to establish a new commune in California, realizing it was ideally suitable for winemaking. The commune resettled north of San Francisco in the Santa Rosa Valley, where they established a winery on their Fountain Grove estate. Harris continued to lead his commune spiritually, while Nagasawa was put in charge of the earthly business of making money. The winery opened for business in 1882. Harris retired to New York City in 1892, leaving the Fountain Grove estate under Nagasawa's control.

By the turn of the 20th century, the Fountain Grove Winery was the largest winemaker in the United States, and soon began exporting to Europe and Japan. Nagasawa was renowned throughout California as the state's leading viticulturist, having created blends of Cabernet, Pinot and

Right Nagasawa's red octagon barn was a local landmark until destroyed by wild fires in 2017.

Zinfandel in a region that had previously only been producing Zinfandel. Nominally the head of the Brotherhood of New Life upon Harris' death in 1906, Nagasawa ceased the commune's spiritual activities and concentrated on winemaking. He also hosted elaborate parties for the group's members; the wine flowed freely in spite of Prohibition. Among the guests was none other than author Jack London, who had his own love affair with Japan and had visited Nagasawa's native Kagoshima (formerly Satsuma) as a young man; the poet Edwin Markham and botanist Luther Burbank also joined in.

Nagasawa never lost his sense of *bushido* (samurai spirit), as evidenced by an episode that occurred in 1909. In the wake of the San Francisco earthquake of 1905, the Japanese Imperial Navy sent a delegation to the city to aid with disaster relief. The group included Tadashige Shimazu, the son of the last lord of the Satsuma domain, Tadayoshi Shimazu. The younger Shimazu was no longer considered royalty, since the Meiji Restoration had ended the feudal structures of Edo-period Japan, but Nagasawa showed him extreme deference nonetheless, and invited him to stay at Fountain Grove. Upon arriving at the gates of the estate, the 57-year-old Nagasawa got out of his car, knelt on the ground, and bowed until his forehead touched the ground in repentance for abandoning his duty to the Shimazu family, who had sent him on his mission to England.

This sense of duty apparently pervaded his character, since California newspapers began referring him as "Baron Nagasawa" and "the Wine King" due to his samurai heritage. Later in life he became a leading judge for wine competitions throughout the state and was awarded the Order of the Rising Sun by the Japanese emperor in 1924

Prohibition in 1919 and the anti-Japan law of 1920 both hit Nagasawa hard. During Prohibition he switched to making grape juice to survive. Some of his nonalcoholic releases at the time apparently included nudge-and-wink warnings for consumers about how not to let the juice turn into wine. Unfortunately, by the time Prohibition ended, the estate was in financial distress, anti-Japanese sentiment was on the rise and his winery never returned to its former prominence. The 21st Amendment repealing Prohibition passed just a year before Nagasawa died in 1934 at the age of 82. Since he had never married or had children, he attempted to will his estate to his nephew (his sister Mori had moved to California to help out), but this was blocked by the local government, since the nephew was a child and his parents were not American citizens. The 1,000-acre estate was sold at auction for pennies on the dollar. To add insult to injury, his relatives would end up in an Arkansas internment camp during World War II. Just before the war, his ashes were returned to Japan and buried near his birthplace on a hillside overlooking the historic city of Kagoshima.

Kanae Nagasawa was all but forgotten in California and in Japan until President Ronald Reagan, a Californian, mentioned him in a speech to the Japanese Diet. Nagasawa has now been commemorated in the city of Santa Rosa with a bronze bust in the municipal offices and a nearby park named in his honor. His mark was still very much on the community until a 2017 California wildfire destroyed his original octagonal red barn (a local landmark) and the Paradise Ridge Winery, which had continued to produce Nagasawa Estate wines and housed a museum in his honor in its basement. With the fire, his museum and artifacts were lost to history. Fortunately, nearby Ridge Winery relocated some of his vines in the 1940s; it now produces a red wine called Monte Bello Historic Vines from those grapes.

In 2014, the Satsuma Students Museum opened in Kushikino, the municipality from which Nagasawa and his compatriots had left Japan 149 years earlier. His memorabilia are prominently featured. In 2018 the Baron N Wine Bar opened in the famous Shiroyama Hotel overlooking Kagoshima City. (Baron N, of course, is a reference to "Baron" Nagasawa, as the California papers liked to call him.) At the opening reception for this wine bar, descendants of Nagasawa's sister Mori attended from California. There they were able to meet distant cousins descended from his other siblings who had remained in Kagoshima and now run a *ryokan* (traditional Japanese inn) in the nearby Kirishima mountains.

Meanwhile, Back in Japan

The juicy purple grapes hanging in the Yamanashi vineyards were an object of unimaginable luxury for ordinary 19th-century Japanese, but wine seems to have scared the wits out of them.

"A boy brought a bottle and a cup at the command of the captain and put it onto the table," reported Renjo Shimoka, a local official sent out to the warship stationed at the mouth of Edo Bay in 1846 to tell the American captain James Biddle that Japan was closed to foreigners. "What was poured from that black bottle was a red, blood-like thing. I was taken aback and I started shivering, almost certain that the liquid contained some kind of poison. But I made the decision to give my life to my nation. I closed my eyes and drank it in one go."

When Commodore Matthew Perry arrived with his "Black Ships" seven years after Biddle's failed journey, a Japanese sailor sent onto the foreigners' ships had a similar tale: "I was given bread which had terribly smelly, hair-oil sort of stuff on it. It was disgusting. Then one person brought a glass containing a very dark red water. Everybody turned pale. What could it be other than human blood?"

But where the man in the street saw blood, Japan's modernizing leaders and capitalists saw opportunity. Almost immediately after the opening of the country there were attempts to make wine. At some time in the early 1870s,

Left The first nationally recognized brand of wine in Japan may have been Akadama from Shinjiro Torii, the same genius who brought us Suntory whisky. His 1922 ad campaign, showing a partially nude woman, created quite a stir.

Hironori Yamada and Norihisa Takuma set up a winery in Kofu, Yamanashi. Public interest was boosted in 1877 by a gift of wine and beer from Emperor Meiji to soldiers injured fighting the Satsuma rebellion, and Kofu-made wine was exhibited at the National Industrial Exhibition that year. However, Yamada and Takuma's business, which appears to have used sake-making techniques and tools to make its wine, foundered; the center of Yamanashi's fledgling viticulture shifted east to Katsunuma, where a group of farmers and merchants set up the Iwaimura Winery in 1877. The new company dispatched two young men—Masanari Takano, age 19, and Ryuken Tsuchiya, age 25—to France to find out about proper winemaking. Neither spoke any French. They learned their trade in a Bordeaux vineyard through sign language and a laborious process of translation by correspondence: sending questions in letters to Masana Maeda, an agricultural expert living in Paris, who would send the French translation by return post. The French wine makers' answers would then go through the same treatment. Tsuchiya said to his bosses in Japan: "We work morning to night, but since we can't even speak the language, we are little better than farm animals."

Despite the difficulties, they had learned enough that when they returned to Japan in May 1879, they immediately threw out the sake-making equipment. Proper winemaking machinery was installed at great cost, and the winery was churning out about 10,500 gallons (40,000 liters) of French-style wine annually by 1880.

Again, however, the enterprise ended in failure: Iwaimura Winery was shuttered only seven years after Tsuchiya and Takano's return from France. There are differing accounts as to why. Tsuchiya claimed the market was depressed and consumers were not ready for real wine. Kotaro Miyazaki, the company's marketing man, thought it was a problem with their product: vinegary, undrinkable and sometimes completely off. Competition was also growing faster than demand. A government-run winery opened in Hokkaido in 1879; Banshu Vineyard in Hyogo prefecture opened in 1884; and huge vineyards were established in Aichi prefecture during the 1880s. More importantly, a new type of sweetened and spiced wine was proving much more popular than the dry European-style product Iwaimura was trying to make. Denbei Kamiya, founder of the famous Kamiya bar in Tokyo, launched the sickly-sweet Hachijirushi ("Bee brand") wine in the mid 1880s. It was a simple formula: ship in gallons of dirt-cheap imported wine and fill it with flavorings and sugar to appeal to Japanese consumers. Much to the "real" winemakers' disgust, it sold very well.

Kamiya's initial tactic of using cheap imported wine might have crushed Japan's fledgling wine sector completely had it not been for a major cholera epidemic in 1886 that killed more than 100,000 people. In the resulting panic, opportunistic wine sellers began mixing wine with quinine and other medicinal additives and selling it as a miracle cure. A year after the epidemic struck, wine consumption had tripled—just in time to soak up the increased capacity from the new Japanese vineyards. In 1883, domestic production had only accounted for 4 percent of domestic wine sales, but by 1887 Japanese production was meeting about a quarter of the greatly increased demand. The erstwhile marketing man, Kotaro Miyazaki, picking up the pieces from the collapse of

Iwaimura, quickly launched a new company. Although he always stayed loyal to the ideal of European winemaking, investing large sums in a state-of-the-art vineyard in Yamanashi, Miyazaki also carved out a large part of the sweetened and medicinal wine markets with his own Ebijirushi ("Prawn Brand") and Marunijirushi ("No. 2 Brand").

Denbei Kamiya moved in the other direction, starting his own vineyard in Ushiku, Ibaraki prefecture, around the turn of the century, with 6,000 seedlings imported from Bordeaux. In 1907, another major player arrived on the scene with the launch of the famous sweetened Akadama (赤玉) brand by Shinjiro Torii, the founder of the Suntory alcohol empire (they still sell Akadama, which is quite nice on ice). Torii had started out selling wine imported from Spain, but, like Kamiya and Miyazaki before him, discovered that the dry European taste was unpopular. In 1922, a poster campaign for Akadama featuring a head-and-shoulder portrait of an unclothed singer, one of the first "nudes" in Japanese advertising, caused a sensation and took sweetened wine sales to new heights.

Below Yamanashi prefecture, the home of Mount Fuji, is Japan's traditional winegrowing region. The Mercian wine brand (left), which uses grapes from Yamanashi, was launched in 1949.

Above, left to right Japanese wine production has matured into a sophisticated industry with distinct winegrowing regions. Mediterranean styles are produced in Kyushu in the south, French styles in the Japanese Alps, and northern European styles in Hokkaido. The mixture of Japanese technological efficiency and traditional methods is helping Japan develop its own unique terroir.
Facing page, bottom Yukusu wine bar in Fukuoka (see page 149) serves only Japanese wines.

The winemakers seem to have been a font of audacious marketing schemes. Miyazaki, maker of the Prawn Brand, even managed to hitch wine to the super-nationalist spirit of the times, arguing in a newspaper column in 1935:

> The ingredients for alcohol should never be the rice and grains that are our people's daily food. I am not saying sake is wrong or beer is wrong but . . . what country would waste the nation's staple for anything other than eating? . . . It would not be too difficult to replace sake with wine. . . . Grapes can be cultivated in places where the other crops cannot. . . . I hope you understand the national benefit of using fruit alcohol instead of grain and support us in our humble business. I will keep working hard at supplying a good, healthy national drink.

This prewar sweetened wine was hardly an exemplar of quality winemaking, but it did help establish a sturdy foundation for Japan's viticulture. In 1935, Yamanashi prefecture alone was producing 400,000 gallons (1.5 million liters) of wine and had more than 3,000 wineries. Most were family operations that would be aggressively rationalized

during the war, but the culture of wine had seeped deep into communities. In Yamanashi's wine capital, Katsunuma, they have the same Shinto ceremonies to bless the sites of newly built homes that they have all over the country, but they use wine for the ceremony, not sake. You see the same tobacco-puffing wizened "good ol' boys" there that you meet all over the Japanese countryside, but they shoot the breeze over a carton of cheap red wine rather than sake or shochu.

THE MODERN ERA

The Japanese palate has expanded massively in the postwar period and the country is now consuming wines in a range of styles that the prewar winemakers would never have dreamed of. A key early development came in 1949, with the launch of the Mercian (メルシャン) wine brand. It used grapes from Yamanashi cultivated on the traditional *tanajitate* vine canopies, but aimed for a style much closer to conventional European wine. It was specifically marketed to hotels and restaurants catering to a budding interest in European food, rather than to liquor shops selling directly to consumers. This marked the first time that wine was consistently presented in culinary contexts that approximated those for which it was designed.

Events like the Tokyo Olympics in 1964 and the Osaka World's Fair in 1970 boosted the number of Western-style hotels in the country, and the number of foreign restaurants increased rapidly after that. Hans Brinckmann, a writer who lived in Japan in the Showa era (1926–89), describes how early *yoshokuya* (Western food houses), with very limited

and Japanized menus, gave way to authentic eateries representing "virtually every one of the world's major and minor cuisines." Many of these new outlets demanded authentic wines, and as the caterers became more sophisticated, educating their consumers in the process, wine drinking went through the roof: from nearly 9 million gallons (33,000 kiloliters) in 1980 to over 100 million gallons (379,800 kiloliters) in 2016.

Unfortunately for Japanese vineyards, much of this demand, particularly at the higher end of the market, has been met by massive increases in imports. In 1970, it was virtually impossible to obtain foreign wine in Japan, but in the 1990s foreign- and Japanese-labeled wines were sharing the market about equally. Imports now account for about two-thirds of the market. Domestic production tends to go into very cheap wine, sometimes costing less than 500 yen ($4.50, £3.40, €3.80) per bottle (and tasting more like alcoholic grape juice than anything most people would recognize as wine, in many cases). The imported labels have also made aggressive inroads into this low-price sector. Very cheap South American, US, and French-labeled brands are now common in supermarkets. Even a "Made in Japan" label often conceals a largely foreign product: Japan's odd trading laws allow products containing 95 percent bulk-imported South American wine or grape juice to be designated Japanese. The government has made some efforts to ease the squeeze on domestic producers with localized relaxations of land laws that prevent wineries from owning more than experimental vineyards themselves,

thereby compelling them to subcontract to small farmers. Nevertheless, many in the Japanese wine trade see little long-term hope of competing on price and are instead aiming at a future in quality production.

Denis Gastin, a leading English-language writer on Asian wine, says of Japanese wine, "There have been substantial changes in the winemaking environment in Japan over the last decade—where the more adventurous operators have done a huge amount to create unique Japanese expressions in the bottle, sometimes despite very challenging viticultural conditions."

He considers the traditional grape variety, Koshu, to be the standard-bearer for Japanese wine, competing with domestically cultivated Chardonnays for the top white-wine medals at the prestigious Japan Wine Competition. In fact, in 2014, a 2013 Cuvee Misawa Akeno Koshu won gold internationally at the London-based Decanter World Wine Awards (and repeated the feat in 2016). As a result, says Gastin, "Koshu is increasingly being sold in international markets and gaining respect through these strong performances in international wine competitions." This newfound success for Koshu has been the direct result of a change in philosophy among Japanese producers. Previously, vintners had been trying to make Koshu something it was not—a rich, flavorful expression like a barrel-aged Chardonnay. Today, says Gastin, "There has been a very strong reversal in approach by the thinkers in the industry to present the intrinsic characteristics of this shy grape in a fresh and exciting way. The natural attraction of Koshu in Japan is that it complements Japanese food so well, and I think consumers are rediscovering this, too." Koshu can now be found as sparkling wine (e.g., Katsunuma no Awa Koshu Brut, Chateau Mercian), as a skin-fermented orange wine (Chateau Mars Koshu Orange Gris), and in blends with Mars Koshu–Viognier blend being an excellent example. Never content to rest, the Koshu grape and Malbec grapes have been bred to create the Bijou Noir style, which can be quite musty and dry relative to its progenitors.

This page Wine is extremely popular among Japanese, particularly women. With a growing number of wineries across the country you're very likely to discover something new wherever you travel in Japan. Unfortunately, very little Japanese wine exports at the moment. Wine bars that specialize in Japanese wine in the US are hard to find, but Bar B (center, see page 149) is a wine bar run by Japanese in New York City.

Left Mars Winery has opened a beautiful new tasting room in Yamanashi with stunning views of the vineyards below and Mt. Fuji in the distance. A master sommelier oversees a light pairing menu.

Another potential standout grape for the Japanese wine industry, according to Gastin, is the Muscat Bailey A (マスカット・ベリーA) variety, a hybrid of Muscat Hamburg and Labrusca Bailey grapes, developed by Zenbei Kawakami (1867–1944), who played a key role in building Suntory's wine operations before the war. The variety used to be associated with grape-juice-like sweeter wines, but has been extending its palette. Initially, high-quality Muscat Bailey A was expressed primarily in a rosé style, but now, says Gastin, "Further style definition has produced some outstanding examples in a Beaujolais style, and intense vineyard management and fine aging, plus some blending, has been producing some dark colored, more intense palate expressions." Evidence of its emerging prominence is the fact that at the 2017 Japan Wine Competition there were 102 Muscat Bailey A entries (40 of which were blends with Muscat Bailey A as the main variety). "It has great Japanese food matching potential. There is a lot of experimentation, including blends with other varieties, which is an exciting horizon," says Gastin. Oaking the Muscat Bailey A also results in a richer flavor profile. Taking matters a step further, Ajimu Winery in Oita prefecture has begun making port and brandy from Muscat Bailey A; both fit their categories extremely well.

"There are also a lot of interesting ideas being explored with the *yamabudo* (wild mountain grapes) and some of them are very good, especially among the hybrid versions and most particularly Yama-Sauvignon," Gastin notes. Ikeda winery's Yama-Sauvignon, using a cross of the indigenous wild mountain grape with Cabernet Sauvignon, offers "rich, almost Pinotage-like, aromas and flavors," says Gastin. Another interesting cross, Sawanobori Shokoshi, combining Japanese mountain grapes with Russian and Himalayan strains, is gaining converts with its intense flavors and rich colors not normally associated with yamabudo. Ajimu's Shokoshi release is stunning. The emergence of this category is part of a trend for experimentation clearly witnessed at the 2017 Japan Wine Competition, where 22 entries used a variety of approaches. Just three were pure yamabudo expressions, but ten were yamabudo hybrid single-varietal bottlings, and nine were blends using seven different yamabudo hybrids.

Perhaps this is where the Japanese wines hit a bit of a roadblock with foreign interest. Koshu, Muscat Bailey A, Bijou Noir, Shokoshi and other domestic varietals are meant to be appreciated on their own terms, but Westerners tasting them may be at a loss for vocabulary to describe these styles. The flavors and aromas can be unexpected or unfamiliar. Previously we described Bijou Noir as "musty," a term that is not usually associated with good wine, but it was not meant as a criticism; it's simply that we may lack the vocabulary to fully explain the flavor. The Albariño out of Ajimu Winery has a distinct "Christmas spice" on the palate, but when you

Hokkaido, the coldest wine-producing region on earth, is booming. In 2000 there were eight wineries; as of 2018 there were 33, including the largest Japanese wine producer, Hokkaido Wine, which holds 150 hectares (370 acres) of vineyards and contracts with 40 other independent grape growers. This contrasts with the average "large" winery elsewhere in Japan, which produces wines on about 10 hectares (25 acres). The Hokkaido region originally

mention this to the Japanese vintner he stares back blankly, because he, too, lacks the frame of reference (many Japanese believe Americans eat Kentucky Fried Chicken for Christmas dinner so "Christmas spice" is a step too far as a tasting note). But a deep dive into the Japanese varietals can be fascinating; you'll taste wines unlike anything you've experienced.

Production methods also differ. As mentioned earlier, the *tanajitate* vine cultivation method is uniquely Japanese. Not only does this greatly increase crop yield per vine, but it also protects the vines from Japan's inevitable heavy rains. They are often further covered with plastic sheeting overhead to protect the fruit while allowing the soil to soak up the rainwater. Vineyards that forgo the sheeting to allow more sunlight may use a tiny umbrella over each grape cluster. Crushed stone is also sometimes used around vines to facilitate efficient runoff so the vines don't gorge themselves.

Beyond the vine cultivation and water maintenance strategies, clay pots are sometimes used for aging wines. This is also done occasionally in Italy and Greece as an ode to the ancient Grecian wines. In Japan it harkens back to the country's heritage of earthenware and creates quite distinct styles when used in concert with their domestic varietals. Regional variation, of course, influences all of these production decisions related to humidity, temperature, precipitation and altitude.

focused on mainstream domestic grapes and yamabudo hybrids, but has now planted Kerner, Pinot Noir, Pinot Blanc, Muller Thurgau, Bacchus, Gewürztraminer, Zweilgeltrebe, Lemberger and Seibel. Vintners have also begun working with a few exotic varieties such as Regent (a Muller Thurgau–Sylvaner–Chambourcin hybrid) and Rondo (a Saperavi–St Laurent hybrid) to produce very attractive wines.

As Gastin notes, "Yamanashi is the spiritual headquarters of the industry in Japan, but in Nagano and, increasingly, Yamagata, wineries are also doing very good work with the conventional European varieties—especially Cabernet, Merlot and Chardonnay." In the south, wineries in Kyushu, especially in the mountains of Oita and Miyazaki, are putting out crisp Viognier, Albarino and Tempranillo. Tsuno Wines in nearly tropical Miyazaki prefecture has released what is believed to be the first Japanese expression of Syrah/Shiraz. Their sparkling Shiraz was produced by noted winemaker Seiji Akao, who early in his career produced a vintage at the famed Hardys Winery in McLaren Vale, South Australia.

This all aligns well with what the Japanese have long excelled at—taking a traditionally foreign product, perfecting it, and then improving on it. Japanese wine-growing regions are beginning to parse into similar regions, as in Europe and the US, with warm, temperate and cool climates differentiating their styles and creating wines unique to their terroir. Gastin enthuses, "It's very exciting. China is the largest producer in Asia by a long way and has ancient grape-growing and winemaking traditions, but Japan is indisputably, in my view, the quality leader." Most of the vines are still very young, but give them time.

WINE IN POPULAR CULTURE

The Japanese wine world has seen a revolution since 1995. Before then, wine in Japan was largely the preserve of businessmen with fat expense accounts and slick-haired wine waiters in unbearably snobbish French restaurants. It had no real connection with mainstream Japanese food and drink culture except as a vaguely understood symbol of foreign sophistication. As far as the international wine market was concerned, the country was a forgotten backwater—a place to hawk substandard bottles at inflated prices.

Then, in 1995, an obscure Japanese wine expert named Shinya Tasaki won the Best Sommelier in the World competition. His victory, in a competition that would merit only passing attention in most countries, had an electrifying effect in Japan. The idea that a Japanese person could know more about wine than the best the great wine cultures could offer seemed to open a world of possibilities. The mass-media interest was intense and sustained. For the first time in Japan, there was a genuinely popular interest in wine. The next year, "Sommelier," a manga about wine, was first published in *Oruman* magazine. (For the uninitiated, manga are a type of comic that sells more in Japan than any other type of publication. As mainstream as Hollywood, they have a comparable cultural influence.) A successor to "Sommelier" called "Kami no Shizuku" (The Drops of God) arrived in *Shukan Moningu* magazine in 2004 and led to an explosion in wine's popularity. By 2007, it had a readership of about half a million people. It

tells the story of a young hero called Shizuku Kanzaki, who is on an international quest to get the keys to his father's wine cellar. Like many manga of this sort, it really doubles as sort of textbook, featuring a real wine in every issue and stuffing its readers full of information about wine while they are entertained. It became a mover of the wine market not only in Japan, but also in many other parts of Asia, where manga enjoy wide popularity. When the Italian wine Colli di Conegliano Contrada di Concenigo appeared in one issue of "Kami no Shizuku," sales jumped 30 percent overnight. And after the manga compared Château Mont-Pérat to a Freddie Mercury rock concert, a Taiwanese importer reported selling 50 cases of that wine in two days.

The cumulative effect of Shinya Tasaki's success and the manga that emerged in his wake has been profound. There are now more manuals about wine than about sake in most Japanese bookshops. Wine is securely in the Japanese mainstream, even if their domestic products have yet to make inroads into overseas markets. As happened with their whisky and craft beer, it is likely only a matter of time before we see Koshu alongside Chardonnay, or Muscat Bailey A alongside Merlot, on wine lists in the West.

Below While Japanese wines are not widely available in the West, Japanese izakayas and bars such as Bar B in New York and Beige in Paris (see listings for both on page 149) have wine lists that complement their Japanese menus, which can give you an idea of the possibilities of pairing Japanese food with wine.

Japanese Cocktails

The World's Best Bartenders?

ORIGIN STORIES

As we've learned in the past few chapters, the Japanese are incredibly adept at mastering new crafts—whether it be whisky blending, beer-brewing or winemaking—in a relatively short timeframe. Cocktails are no different. To see the nation's journey from hermit island through wartime devastation to world-class cocktail destination, we should view it through the eyes of pioneer Tatsuro Yamazaki.

In 1945, Yamazaki was living with two younger sisters in a furnace boiler. Tokyo had been bombed flat. They had salvaged the boiler from a destroyed public bathhouse and furnished it with a rug, an improvised door and a single bare light bulb powered by electricity borrowed from a nearby pole. He was a bright and ambitious 25-year-old, but he had no parents, no proper home, no job and no prospects. He was not unusual in this. He was like millions of other Japanese people, struggling to survive in a country in which no fewer than 67 cities had been firebombed during the summer of 1945. The wooden architecture of prewar Japan burned like kindling in the Allied air raids.

Before the war, Yamazaki had taught himself English and dreamed of a career as a painter. The conflict had smashed those hopes, but he had applied himself so diligently to his work as an army medic that, in August 1945, a professor of medicine in Tokyo recommended him for transfer to Manchuria, where he might have trained as a doctor. Yamazaki remembers what happened on the day after he received the professor's recommendation: "I stood in front of Kashiwa Station

Below Frank Cisneros was the first foreigner to receive a work visa in Japan to tend bar. Watching the precision of his movements and his deft use of tools, you'd think he was Japanese rather than a US-raised Spaniard.

Left The father of Japanese bartending, Tatsuro Yamazaki, tended bar in Tokyo and then Sapporo for more than 70 years. He trained hundreds of the nation's barmen and his methods continue to be emulated throughout Japan.

and listened to the emperor's surrender broadcast, and the dream to become a medical doctor disappeared. Manchuria disappeared."

His big break after the surrender was getting a job cleaning toilets and mopping floors at the Tokyo Kaikan, a popular entertainment spot for the officers of the occupying forces. He worked his way into the bar at the Kaikan and then to the prestigious Mitsui Club, another favored location for the Americans. After nearly getting himself killed in a confrontation with a knife-wielding American sergeant who had been pestering a female colleague, he moved through a series of bars in Tokyo and Yokohama, each time in a more senior role, until, in 1953, his old boss asked if he would take a job in Hokkaido. A Tokyo bartender moving to Sapporo, Hokkaido is not unlike an LA bartender moving to Anchorage, Alaska. Nevertheless, Yamazaki moved north, intending to stay only for a year or so. He ended up spending the rest of his working life there.

His first job in Sapporo was in Susukino, Sapporo's legendary drinking district, at the Montana, a two-story wooden building with two barmen and more than a dozen hostesses. Susukino was a chaotic and lawless place in those days. Gangsters and pimps ran much of the quarter, and it had some of the most dangerous streets in Japan. The owner

of Montana and his wife just disappeared one day. He heard later that they had run off to Brazil. In 1957, Yamazaki opened his own bar, called Silo—or at least he thought he had. A woman who he will now only identify as "Lady H" helped him organize the opening. Later in the year, she, too, disappeared—with more than ¥200,000 of Yamazaki's savings, a very large sum in the 1950s. The extent of the betrayal only became apparent when it emerged that owners of the property actually regarded him as an employee, rather than an independent bar owner. They claimed Lady H had told them that Yamazaki was their bartender. He stuck it out for two months, still deeply in debt for the alcohol he had bought to start up Silo. Then, with the help of customers and a liquor shop, he set up the first Bar Yamazaki in 1958, recruiting 15 women as hostesses (bars always had hostesses in those days). He paid off his debts in two years, but more setbacks followed: his chief hostess left, taking half of his money and most of his hostesses with her; then, on December 15, 1975, the bar burned to the ground. One of his customers later told him the fire burned an extremely beautiful blue. The color was from the stock of distilled spirits Yamazaki had spent years building up.

Time and again Yamazaki seems to have been able to turn misfortune into new opportunity. At the suggestion of a friend, he took the brave step of reopening his bar without hostesses. The decision, which was well ahead of its time, presaged a change that has largely transformed Japan's drinking districts. "It was taken for granted that no bar could run without hostesses, but at the same time, they had given us so much trouble I thought that if we could do a bar without them, it would be great," Yamazaki recalls. "Contrary to perceived ideas, it was a great hit, probably because there were more young people who preferred to go out with people they liked to a bar with cheaper prices, just enjoying the alcohol together, rather than paying money to be served by women."

He said the decision also fundamentally changed his role as a bartender. "Before the fire, I did not have much contact with the customers. With no hostesses, I came into the spotlight and had far more opportunity to meet and talk to customers." This transition, from hostess bars to establishments in which the bar person is the center of the experience, explains a lot about contemporary Japanese drinking culture. In important ways, the hostesses shaped what we have now. For a start, they built the physical environment: hostessing generally requires small, intimate environments rather than the vast barn-like pubs that are typical in many other countries. With the decline of the hostesses, the drinking quarters left in Japan consisted of thousands of tiny bar units. Due to the determination of pioneers like Yamazaki, these bars have survived, and running a bar is now a rewarding career for sole proprietors throughout Japan.

Yamazaki was one of the first to realize that, while changing times and an increasing number of women drinkers were making the hostesses an anachronism, customers continue to expect a very personal experience from a bar. Of course, knowledgeable and engaging bar staff are a necessity in the best bars everywhere in the world, but nowhere is the expectation of conversation and interaction as ingrained as it is in Japan's small bars. In a sense, the man or woman tending the bar has replaced the hostess. Instead of flattering conversation (which, in most cases, was all that hostesses offered their customers), the bar offers a very intimate environment in which the customer can take his or her mind off the troubles of the day with a conversation at

the bar (always the most sought-after seats in Japan) and get an education in the glittering array of drinks behind it.

While the intimate environment can sometimes be jarring (and incredibly enchanting) to foreigners visiting Japanese bars, the other thing that really jumps out is the professionalism and sense of vocation of the people who run them. One might explore any numbers of theories as to why this is. One is simply the Japanese concept of hospitality, in which the customer is not only right, but is treated as downright royalty. In this culture, it doesn't matter if you're a CEO or a part-time late-night clerk at the local convenience store, you do your job well and you treat your customers with as much respect as possible. Another explanation might be that the relentless grind of the Japanese corporate world means that Japanese bars get more than their fair share of highly capable people unwilling to spend their lives on late-night spreadsheets. Certainly, you meet a lot of former salary men running Japanese bars. But, again, Yamazaki's generation put in the groundwork.

"[After the war] bartenders had a really bad image. Newspaper crime pages often carried the description 'ex-bartender' in them. Bartenders could not be proud," says Yamazaki.

One of the first things he did when he arrived in Sapporo was to help set up an association of barmen. By the late 1960s he had a bartenders' school, offering lectures from invited specialists and developing clear guidelines for professional conduct. There are now hundreds of bar owners across Japan trained by Yamazaki. "My dream used to be to visit all the bars that my employees opened after my retirement at 70. Unfortunately, many of my trainees have already retired, and at the age of 94 I have still not managed to do so," he says. Yamazaki, and others like him, made a career that was often forced on them by circumstance a respectable and rewarding one. He turned his career into the stuff of legend, culminating in 1993 with the Imperial Prize from the emperor of Japan, the first received by a bartender in the history of this very old country. He passed away at the age of 96 in November 2016 without ever quite retiring.

These days, professionally trained bartenders, many taught by Yamazaki himself, are working bars from Sapporo in Hokkaido to Fukuoka in Kyushu and seemingly everywhere in between. You can walk down a back alley in Japan's first capital city, Nara, and happen into a bar with a world-champion bartender in his early 30s. Or take an elevator to the top of the Mandarin Oriental in Ginza and have arguably the finest martini on earth.

THE GINZA LEGACY

When you ask Western bartenders where to find the best bartenders in the world, the answer is often, "Ginza." Not Tokyo—Ginza. A specific neighborhood in central Tokyo. Given that cocktails have a robust history since the 1800s in both Europe and the United States, you'd expect the answer to be Paris, New York, London or—perhaps due to its status as an unabashed world city—Hong Kong, but no. The answer is the Ginza district in Tokyo. In a neighborhood half a mile square there are no fewer than 364 bars, including dozens of the finest cocktail bars on earth.

Below Japanese cocktails are more than just a drink. Some of them are works of art, like this one created at the elegant Uchu in Manhattan (see page 145), the first bar to get a Michelin star in NYC.

The Ginza style of bartending has achieved legendary status for the precision of movement, the configuration of bar implements to minimize wasted energy and the fact that every single bartender in the place, no matter the size, will make each drink precisely the same way each and every time for each and every customer based on the exacting expectations of the head bartender. It's simply magical to watch. The fact that the bartenders are also extremely skilled conversationalists and provide a level of hospitality not found in most bars around the world only adds to the experience.

Spaniard Frank Cisneros, who now calls New York City home and has bartended at the elegant (and very expensive) Uchu (page 145) in the Lower East Side neighborhood of Manhattan, was the first foreigner to receive a work visa to bartend in Japan. He wasn't there to run a bar program; he was there to learn. He worked at the Mandarin Oriental in Ginza, and after a gaffe on his first night on the job he didn't make another drink for a customer for nearly three months, instead relegated to cutting fruit for the "real" bartenders. At the time, Cisneros wasn't a novice trying to break into the competitive New York bartending scene; he'd opened four

successful bars in Brooklyn, including Dram, a very popular Williamsburg cocktail bar. Yet when he went to Japan he was expected to learn the Japanese way from the bottom up. It was backbreaking and exhausting work. But he came back to New York a changed man. To watch him bartend today is to see the elegance of a Japanese bartender in a Western body. His precision and dedication to perfection are as present as those of any bartender in Japan. His transformation was total and complete.

Reversing Cisneros' journey are the bartenders who come from Japan to New York City to learn to bartend. They lend their Japanese precision to the creativity of the New York bar scene. Kenta Goto, who had moved to New York to study, became a salaryman, and eventually became interested in cocktails. He started picking up shifts at local bars around New York before answering an ad for a bartender. In 2007 he was hired for one shift a week at the famous Pegu Club. By 2011 he'd risen to head bartender and was selected US Bartender of the Year at Tales of the Cocktail. In 2015, he opened his own place, Bar Goto (page 151), down the street from Uchu.

Shingo (like the baseball legend Ichiro, he needs no last name) rose to international fame while bartending at the Japanese speakeasy Angel's Share (page 151), which is situated behind a heavy wooden door at the back of a dirty old East Village izakaya. Shingo won the Bacardi International Bartenders Competition in 2012, and has since become perhaps the world's most recognizable bartender with his signature pouring style and charming personality. A string of his Japanese protégés have gone on to win this competition and many others, leading him to open bars all over the world, including Shanghai, where his four-story Speak Low (page 152) has become legendary in just a couple years. His success hasn't changed him as a person. He's still as humble and friendly as ever, but he's certainly a lot busier. His trainees have also gone on to open their own places—perhaps most notably ROKC (Page 151) in Harlem.

Gen Yamamoto has had a particularly singular journey. He moved to New York in the early 2000s with no experience as a bartender. He learned from the best, eventually running bars in a series of Japanese restaurants in Manhattan before returning to Tokyo in 2013 to open Gen Yamamoto, an *omakase-* (tasting menu) only cocktail bar (see page 150). He's a bit of a renegade, not following in the path of Shingo Gokan and others in mastering the use of Western cocktail bases, but rather focusing almost exclusively on uniquely

Japanese spirits to make his unusual and delicious concoctions from fresh ingredients he sources from local markets daily. His bar is a zen experience in every way: calm, peaceful and singularly focused on the task at hand. In a sense, he has come full circle and returned to a completely innovative style of bartending not seen anywhere else in the world.

This blend of Japanese elegance with New York ingenuity has transformed the bartending scene worldwide. Shingo's smoked brandy cocktail, "Smoke Gets in Your Eyes," has inspired a profusion of smoky cocktails all over the world. Goto's use of Japanese shochu and sake in cocktails (recipes below) has led to experimentation with these bases across the globe. The elegant way jiggers are handled in Ginza is

copied in cocktail bars in Los Angeles and Madrid and Berlin. The elevation of Japanese bartenders to the world stage, which also unleashed them from the strictures of the hierarchical Japanese workplace, has bifurcated the Japanese bar scene in a big way in the past decade.

Much like Masataka Taketsuru, whose journey to Scotland to learn to make world-class whisky eventually led to Japan having some of the finest whisky in the world, these Japanese expats have further elevated Japanese cocktail culture. No longer are Ginza bartenders simply respected for their professionalism. Japanese cocktail makers both in Japan and overseas are revolutionizing the industry.

COCKTAIL RECIPES BY KENTA GOTO

SAKURA MARTINI

2½ oz (75 ml) sake
1 oz (30 ml) gin
¼ tsp Maraschino liqueur

Combine all ingredients in a mixing glass. Stir with ice. Strain into a martini glass and garnish with cherry blossom.

IMPROVED SHOCHU COCKTAIL

2 oz (60 ml) barley shochu
2 tsp bison-grass vodka
1½ tsp cane syrup
⅛ tsp Douglas-fir eau de vie

Combine all ingredients in a mixing glass. Stir with ice. Strain into a cypress *masu* box.

FAR EAST SIDE

2 oz (60 ml) sake
¾ oz (22.5 ml) elderflower liqueur
½ oz (15 ml) tequila blanco
¼ oz (7.5 ml) lemon juice
3 shiso leaves

Combine all ingredients in a mixing glass. Muddle the shiso leaves. Stir with ice, and then strain into a cocktail glass.

Bar
Guide

Nihonshu Stand Moto, Tokyo   Utsutsuyo, Osaka   Yoramu, Kyoto

Akaboshi to Kumagai, Tokyo

SAKE BARS

TOKYO

AKABOSHI TO KUMAGAI
赤星とくまがい

Situated on the third floor of an office building on a side street in the Azabu-Juban neighborhood of Tokyo, Akaboshi to Kumagai is a stunningly well-executed restaurant and bar. The space is dominated by the long bar where English-speaking Keita Akaboshi, a certified *kikizakeshi* (sake expert), serves as host and educator for those who seek his advice. The open kitchen at one end of the room serves both a seasonal course menu and a la carte options. The sake list is extensive, with more than 200 offerings listed at any given time. A handful of tables are available to cater to larger groups.

7F Coms Azabu-Juban, 3-3-9 Azabu-Juban, Minato-ku, Tokyo; akakuma-sake.com

NIHONSHU STAND MOTO
日本酒スタンド 酛

These sake-focused standing bars, in several locations around Tokyo are an excellent way to sample a variety of sake and small bites in a casual atmosphere without breaking the bank. The Shinjuku location (on the basement level of the building), is particularly lively, as the tipsy regulars are happy to practice their English and make recommendations. The sake list is always changing, and the food menu is posted on the wall (Japanese only). If you can't read the menu, point at what others are eating. The staff at this chain is always happy to help. It's often the other customers who are geeking out over the latest offerings, though, so sometimes it's best to see what others are drinking.

B1F Hakuho Bldg., 5-17-11 Shinjuku, Shinjuku-ku, Tokyo; fsknet.co.jp

OSAKA

UTSUTSUYO うつつよ

Doburoku sake (see pages 25 and 39) has been making a comeback. It's not easy to find, but if you do, it's worth ordering. Usually only served by the bottle since it's very temperamental, an excellent example can be had at Utsutsuyo, which is a restaurant first and bar second. On the second floor of a modern building, the space is dominated by a long bar that serves as an open kitchen with bar service executed at a tiny corner. Several tables accommodate larger parties. The seafood-heavy menu is seasonal and a la carte. The sake list is not as extensive as some of the other

Washu Bar Engawa, Ishikawa

Nihonshu Bar Katoya, Hiroshima

recommended spots, but what they do have is excellent. This is a favorite of the *toji* (master brewer) of Yucho Shuzo in Nara prefecture, who recommended it when he realized we were visiting Osaka. Very little English is spoken, but the staff is extremely accommodating.

2F, 3-2-1 Hon-machi, Chuo-ku, Osaka; ututuyo.com

KYOTO

YORAMU 酒BARよらむ

For foreign sake lovers, Yoramu has become a pilgrimage destination. Reservations are required at this small sake bar with an indoor zen-garden entrance. Proprietor Yoram Ofer is Israeli and has lived in Kyoto for over 30 years. He started his bar as a self-admitted novice, having discovered sake after moving to Japan. Over the past several decades he's gained more sake insight than just about any foreigner, possibly excepting *toji* Philip Harper. A word of warning: don't try to impress Yoram with your sake knowledge; he'll humiliate you with his. It won't even be intentional—he'll simply overwhelm you with facts you never knew. Best to go humble and expect to learn. While Yoram may have a gruff personality, he's very generous in sharing his passion, and never serves bad sake. He's been largely responsible for opening the eyes of even Japanese sake experts on the shelf life of *namazake* if properly cared for. Make sure you eat before you go, because you might find it difficult to fill up on his bar snacks, and you'll want to try so many of the sake offerings that going

on an empty stomach could have regrettable results.

35-1 Matsuya-cho, Nakagyo-ku, Kyoto; sakebar-yoramu.com/index_eng.html

ISHIKAWA

WASHU BAR ENGAWA
和酒BAR 縁がわ

The proprietor of this bar, Ishikawa native Yusuke Shimoki, fell in love with sake so deeply he gave up a steady job and moved to this onsen (hot-spring) village deep in the mountains—so deep, it's the last stop on the bus line from the nearest train station; the bar is another 15 minutes on foot—renovated a 100-year-old house, and opened Engawa. It's startling, in this humble onsen village in the mountains close to the Sea of Japan, to enter an old house to find a classic Japanese barman complete with tartan vest, but it completely works. It's also as much a classroom as it is a bar. Shimoki has a library behind the bar, which he is more than happy to break out for visual reference while explaining something about the sake he's likely recommended (you'd be silly not to follow his guidance). He's fond of walking you through the effects of both temperature and serving vessel, serving the same sake at different temperatures in the same vessel, or serving the same sake at the same temperature in different vessels, to show you just how much these small variations in service influence your experience. Not much food to speak of, just snacks, so stop by one of the local izakaya beforehand. Food and travel journalist Hannah

Kirshner, who spent two months as an apprentice at Engawa, recommends Kunyan, a ramen shop around the corner where you should definitely get the *kara-age* (唐揚げ) fried chicken.

82 Ro, Minami-machi, Yamanaka Onsen, Kaga-shi, Ishikawa; facebook.com/washubarengawa

HIROSHIMA

NIHONSHU BAR KATOYA
日本酒バル Katoya

Hiroshima's Saijo district is one of the most famous sake-brewing districts in Japan. Saijo sake dominates sake lists in nearly every bar, restaurant and izakaya in Hiroshima. And yet at tiny little Katoya, you won't find a single one; rather, you'll find beautiful expressions of sake from the rest of Japan. The owner decided that Hiroshima was too provincial in its sake preferences and wanted people to realize that there are amazing sake options from all over the country. He cooks, serves and recommends sake in a modern space on the first floor at the back of a nondescript building. A handful of bar seats and some small tables might hold 12 people on a busy night. Preferring to serve sake in stemmed glasses rather than traditional service vessels, he also skews his menu toward modern Japanese food. This is a great example of the little places you can stumble on throughout Japan if you're just willing to follow your nose.

2-10 Horikawa-cho, Naka-ku, Hiroshima; tel. 082-240-2017

Sakagura, New York

Hi-Collar, New York

Momi Nonmi, Boston

NEW YORK

SAKAGURA 酒蔵

The word *sakagura* refers to a building where sake is made, but it can also mean storage cellar. The second meaning is more relevant here. Sakagura, in mid-town Manhattan, in the basement of an office building, indisputably has the largest sake list of any place in the United States—around 250 brands at any given time. They could have easily called it a sake temple rather than a sake cellar and no one would have batted an eye. The staff is extremely knowledge-able; several former staff have gone onto careers as sake professionals after learning their craft at Sakagura—most notably Sake Samurai Chizuku Niikawa-Helton, who now travels the world preaching the sake gospel. The food is exceptional, and the staff is more than happy to recommend sake pairings or flights. One highlight is the brilliantly effervescent Kaze no Mori *namazake* from Yucho Shuzo in Nara. While Saka-gura could rightly be considered an izakaya, it's a fancy one, with fine fish and seasonal vegetable selections. Food pairings are a big part of the experience. Don't miss the sake-barrel restrooms.

211 E. 43rd Street B1, New York; sakagura.com

SAKE BAR SATSKO

If Sakagura is sake's American temple, Satsko is its shooting gallery. Situated east of Tompkins Square Park (which used to be called "needle park" in New York's bad old days), at Satsko you're as likely to encounter a sake brewer come to introduce his products as you are a local drunk wandering in with an offer to sweep the stoop for a drink. Fukuoka native Satsko Watanabe opened this place in the bad old days, and she's lived to tell the tale. The crowd is eclectic but friendly, like friends you haven't met yet. The food is izakaya style, made in a kitchen off the bar, and the sake list is surprisingly robust given the tiny space. Regulars drink whatever they like while sake-curious twenty-somethings stumble in and do sake bombs with the bartender. Sake aficionados may cringe at the very idea of a sake bomb, but it certainly adds energy to the place and gives novices a chance to experience sake in a casual setting. Those who graduate to finer styles will become fans—and those who don't? Well,

Satsko, New York

Satsko can keep her lights on. If all of this seems like a dive bar with sake on the menu, think again. Satsko's as likely to have a rare *bodaimoto* available as just about any other place in the city. You'll just see more tattoos here.

202 E. 7th Street, New York; satsko.com

HI-COLLAR ハイカラ

In Japanese, "high collar" refers to the white starched collar popular among fashionable young Japanese men during the rapidly modernizing Meiji era. A *kissaten* (喫茶店, coffee shop) by day, Hi-Collar serves excellent pour-over single-origin coffee in a Japanese style with a *teishoku* set-lunch menu. With sliding *shoji* screens behind the bar, at night the place transforms from a cof-fee shop to an elegant sake lounge where diners and drinkers linger at the long bar and enjoy carafes of premium sake. Hi-Collar has a hard liquor license, so the full drinks menu includes Japa-nese whisky, shochu and cocktails ex-pertly prepared by Japanese bartend-ers. The weekend brunch does a very brisk business, with lines out the door both Saturdays and Sundays. If this place is full or too high-collar for you, you're a very short walk from the leg-endary punk-rock sake bar Decibel (240 E. 9th Street), which has the rightful claim to the title of oldest continuously running sake bar in NYC (and the grungi-est—the men's toilet was missing its seat for several weeks at one point in 2016). Don't be surprised at who you might see lurking in a corner enjoying the energy and some sake.

214 E. 10th Street, New York; hi-collar.com

Sushi Kappo Tamura, Seattle   Shibumi, Los Angeles   Sakagura, London

BOSTON
MOMI NONMI

Not far from MIT and Harvard is a tiny place with all the charm you'd expect to find from a small mom-and-pop izakaya in Japan, but situated in a college neighborhood of Boston. The brainchild of owner-chef Chris Chung and his sake sommelier Stephen Connolly, the menu is proper izakaya style, with small dishes meant for sharing and a heavy focus on drinks. The sake selection is superb for the region while there is also shochu aplenty and a robust cocktail program. The most striking thing about Momi Nonmi may be that it manages to feel like a local neighborhood restaurant that could be serving any sort of farm-to-table seasonal menu and yet manages to exude completely Japanese *omotenashi* (hospitality) from these two Americans with a passion for their respective crafts. It's a very small place, so reservations are recommended, especially on weekends.

1128 Cambridge Ste Cambridge, MA; tel. (617) 945-7328; mominonmi.com

SEATTLE
SUSHI KAPPO TAMURA

Generally, the West Coast lacks the depth of authenticity in Japanese food and beverage culture of New York City, largely because West Coast Japanese have lived in the US for several generations, while the Japanese community in New York is much more recent. A great big exception to this is Sushi Kappo Tamura. What is a sushi restaurant doing in a sake guide? We'll get to that

in a minute. The food is stellar, as should be expected of any place bold enough to put *kappo* (割烹) in its name. Kappo is a style of counter dining where guests interact with the chef as the food is being prepared and is considered Japanese dining in one of its most sophisticated forms. At Tamura the menu is created by Chef Taichi Kitamura from Kyoto, who is usually at the sushi counter alongside former professional sumo wrestler turned sushi chef Bobby Suetsugu. They source local seafood, so you can try sockeye salmon, or geoduck if you're adventurous. But this is more than just a nice restaurant—you'll also get excellent pairing recommendations from their extensive sake list curated by bar manager Brad Smith, who is certified as both a sake and shochu adviser by the Sake School of America. They have approximately 60 sake offerings available at any one time, an extensive Japanese whisky list and enough shochu to keep you busy.

2968 Eastlake Ave E., Seattle, WA 98102; sushikappotamura.com

LOS ANGELES
SHIBUMI 渋み

Chef David Schlosser spent years training in Japan before opening his dream establishment, a *kappo*-style restaurant in downtown LA. He did much more than prepare as a chef. He brought a Japanese sensibility (*shibumi*) back with him. Every detail of the space is intended to evoke this sense: the bar of *hinoki* Japanese cypress, the light fixtures and, perhaps most of all, the ceramics, which

he sourced from Robert Yellin, an American who has spent a lifetime in the ceramics business in Kyoto. Each piece was designed to accentuate the food or drink for which it's used. Schlosser's food tends toward heavy use of fermentation, which makes it ideal for pairing with sake. The sake list is lean but extremely well chosen. The Japanese whisky list continues to grow. Shochu, umeshu, and Japanese beers are also available. The cocktail menu continues to evolve, with Japanese inspiration going into options like the Shibumi Negroni, or a cordial made with rice shochu and fermented melon. If you want to leave the drinking decisions in the hands of the chef, a beverage pairing is available for the tasting menu.

815 S. Hill Street, Los Angeles; shibumidtla.com

LONDON
SAKAGURA 蔵

Not to be confused with the New York establishment of the same name, the London location has neither the massive sake list nor the deep staff knowledge (apart from the manager), but it is owned and operated by the Japan Centre, which is the largest importer of Japanese goods to the United Kingdom. As such, the sake list is the largest you'll find anywhere in the country, and the staff is very adept at hospitality. The ground-floor bar allows you to peruse the drink selection, while the dining tables can double as stone grills for the restaurant's signature grilled steak. The basement is a *sumiyaki* (charcoal grilling)

Tokuri, Tokyo

Imozo, various locations in Japan

Ishizue, Kagoshima

kitchen with a dining bar, but the main floor is where the drinks all happen. Japanese whisky, sake, fruit liqueurs and beer are available in abundance. This is an excellent place to explore Japanese food and drink in London.

8 Heddon Street, Mayfair, London. sakaguralondon.com

SHOCHU BARS

TOKYO

TOKURI 焼酎蔵徳利

Tokuri, is a shochu-focused izakaya on the quiet side of Shinjuku (it's situated above a sake-focused izakaya owned by the same restaurant group). The first thing that strikes you about Tokuri is the line of large (and old) clay pots resting on the bar. These are being used for secondary aging of shochu and awamori, some of it in a *maewari* style (page 63). There is an extensive though not comprehensive selection of shochu that is always up to date with seasonal releases. On a recent visit, they had a 100-percent barley shochu from the Toyonaga distillery in Kumamoto that was bottled unfiltered days after distillation. There were globules of oil floating in the glass, and the smell and taste were sharp with esters since it was so new and raw. While you can find shochu almost everywhere in Tokyo, it's surprising how few people know anything about it. And that includes bar staff. Tokuri is a notable exception, run by a proprietor who knows his stuff as well as most anyone in Tokyo makes sure his

staff is equally on the ball. They have a standard izakaya food menu, but meats and vegetables grilled tableside are the most popular option.

1-14-4 Nishi-Shinjuku, Shinjuku-ku, Tokyo; tel. 03-3342-7889

NAGOYA

IMOZO 芋蔵

Imozo is a straight-up chain izakaya with 30 locations across the main island of Honshu. The reason it is listed here is that it's a place to find traditional Kyushu cuisine and a wide selection of shochu in many of the main tourist cities throughout Japan. This is a key consideration, because until the 1970s shochu was largely isolated to Kyushu alone, and even today places that serve a wide range of shochu can be hard to find outside Kyushu. There are no fewer than nine Imozo restaurants in Tokyo alone; you can also find branches in Yokohama, Kyoto, and Sendai as well in its original city, Nagoya (though the exact location where it started is no longer there). There are approximately 200 shochu brands to choose from and the staff is surprisingly knowledgeable, which is not always the case with chain izakaya in Japan.

3-6-35 Nishiki, Naka-ku, Nagoya; tel. 050-3490-9650. For other shop locations: j-groupholdings.com/free.html

KAGOSHIMA

ISHIZUE 本格 焼酎 バー 礎

If there is a shochu-makers' bar in Japan, it's Ishizue. With 120 active shochu distilleries in Kagoshima prefecture, there's a fair chance that there's an employee of at least one of those companies drinking at Ishizue every night of the week, every week of the year. Owner Yoichi Ikehata used to work at a distillery where he developed an encyclopedic knowledge of the spirit. There's probably no other bar in Japan where you'll get such a sommelier's guidance on taste and aroma preferences based on what you prefer. He has well over 1,000 brands, all from Kagoshima Prefecture, the undisputed "shochu kingdom." Ikehata has a helpful light-box map of Kagoshima to show where each distillery is located as you try their products. Even if you're a seasoned shochu drinker, if you're willing to let him guide you, you'll end up tasting things you never knew existed. Note: if Ishizue is full, he's opened a sister bar nearby called Roku (鹿), which also serves wine.

Tenmonkan Flower Building 4F, 6-1 Sennichi-cho, Kagoshima; honkakushochu-bar-ishizue.com

Izakaya Yokoban, Kagoshima

Glocal Bar Vibes, Kumamoto

Juban, New York

IZAKAYA YOKABAN 居酒屋よか晩

Yokaban is Kagoshima dialect for "a great night out with friends." When you say it to non-Kagoshima residents, they have no idea what it means. The owner of Izakaya Yokoban, Reina Mori, is a force of nature. This former elite soccer player runs her self-service shochu-focused izakaya with the same passion that led her to the top of her sport. She's stopped playing soccer, but she now captains the all-female Kagoshima city Ogionsa team that carries a portable shrine through the streets during the Gion Festival. She wanted to make Yokaban a place where everyone would feel welcome (and have a great night out), so when a deaf customer started to frequent her shop, she began learning sign language. Yokaban has now become a place where deaf people can come and socialize without risk of being alienated. Mori is enthusiastic in her broken English, though her sign language appears more fluent. She only serves shochu from distilleries she's personally visited, and there's a large map of Kyushu on the wall with photos of her at each distillery to verify her credentials. Drinks, which are entirely self-service, include draft beer and a side bar with ice, cold water, hot water, sparkling water and plenty of other options for mixing with shochu. The food menu is primarily tableside grilling; you can cook your own meat and vegetables on a slab of rock from the nearby Sakurajima volcano.

17-17 Higashisengoku-cho, Kagoshima; tel. 099-227-1010

KUMAMOTO

GLOCAL BAR VIBES

If ever there was a shochu evangelist, it's Glocal Bar Vibes proprietor Noriyuki "Nori" Yamashita. Born in Satsuma Sendai, a coastal city in Kagoshima, Yamashita visited the city of Kumamoto as a young man and realized that the denizens of this neighboring prefecture's capital knew next to nothing about *imo* (sweet-potato) shochu. He set a life goal of opening an imo shochu bar in Kumamoto and crowdfunded it into existence. Having lived in Australia in his 20s, he speaks English enthusiastically, and his bar has become a popular place for foreign tourists to interact with local Japanese eager to practice English. About once a month he hosts an "Absolutely No Japanese" night where guests are fined 100 yen if they speak Japanese. All fines go to a local nonprofit English-language program for children. Glocal Bar Vibes only carries shochu from distilleries Nori has personally visited. Nearly all are from Kagoshima, but he's bent to local realities and carries a handful of Kumamoto shochu as well, including Ike no Tsuruyu (池の露), a handmade sweet-potato shochu made by the Amakusa distillery on Amakusa Island. Nori serves light snacks, but it's probably best to eat something at one of the myriad izakaya nearby before venturing to his third floor bar. Note: if he calls you "dawg," you have a friend for life.

1-5-6 Shimotori, Chuo-ku, Kumamoto; vibes222.wixsite.com/glocalvibes

NEW YORK

JUBAN

This bar used to be known as Izakaya Ten, before a change of ownership resulted in a new name. Fortunately, the new owner was the manager of the old space, so other than a freshening of the décor, Izakaya Ten lives on in Juban (*juban* in Japanese means "number ten"). The menu is a nice mix of izakaya food and concession to the reality that Americans love their sushi rolls. Every Tuesday night shochu is $20 (£15, €18) off per bottle. The sake menu also has a nice "heat map" that helps you locate your flavor preferences and order from that section of the menu. Japanese whisky, beer and cocktails round out the bar selection. For a shochu-focused evening, the *buta kimchi* (thin-sliced pork belly and kimchi cooked on an iron skillet) is a flavor bomb that pairs really well with one of the sweet-potato offerings, like Satoh Kuro (佐藤黒), a black-koji sweet-potato shochu from Kagoshima, which is famous for its pork.

207 10th Avenue, New York; jubannyc.com

Uminoie, New York   Shochu + Tapas Aya, New York   Ippuku, San Francisco

UMINOIE うみのいえ

The first Japanese shochu was likely produced on Tsushima Island in modern-day Nagasaki prefecture. Japanese and Korean fishermen often traded when they met on the island; distillation technology appears to have been one of those trades. Uminoie ("beach house") proprietress Mutsumi Tanaka hails from nearby Goto Island in Nagasaki, and her father still makes (and sends over by mail) the Goto udon served at this izakaya where the emphasis is on shochu. The menu, by co-owner Mika Okui, is a mix of Nagasaki and Kyushu comfort food with a splash of Okinawa; all delicious. There are more than 40 shochu and awamori brands, and both women stand ready to make recommendations as needed. They helpfully offer flights to sample more varieties, and infuse shochu with *shiso* on site—an improvement on the Tantakatan shiso-infused shochu currently available in the US. Even with the surfboard and fishing net décor, there may be no spot in NYC that feels more like Japan when you walk in and sit down.

86 E. 3rd Street, #2, New York; tel. (646) 654-1122

SHOCHU + TAPAS AYA

The "snack" bars ubiquitous throughout Japan are nearly always run by women and nearly always frequented primarily by men who stop off on their way home from work. These hark back to the hostess bars of yesteryear (see page 129), but a "snack" (as the bars are called in Japanese) usually has some form of entertainment (a karaoke machine) and the proprietress becomes your female friend who is not your wife. These venues are often named after the owner. Aya Otaka is a bit of a celebrity in the New York shochu community. She was the first certified shochu adviser working in a bar in NYC as head bartender of the legendary Shochu Bar Hatchan (may it rest in peace). Hatchan had the reputation of being a "snack" for good reason: the bartenders were always female and always friendly. Aya left to open her own shop, an Italian-Spanish-Japanese fusion with an enormous selection of shochu as well as wine, whisky and just about anything else you'd like to drink. She brought the "snack" vibe with her, making it very popular with Japanese expat salarymen working in the midtown banking district. Happy hour specials include half-price shochu until 7pm, and she's always sure to have something special behind the bar, thanks to customers who bring her presents back from Japan.

247 E. 50th Street, New York; aya-nyc.com

SAN FRANCISCO
IPPUKU

Unlike the other shochu bars recommended here, Ippuku is actually most famous for its food, with arguably the best yakitori on the West Coast. Not technically in San Francisco, it is steps from the BART station in central Berkeley, and well worth the trip from anywhere in the Bay Area. Ippuku has 75 types of shochu to choose from; you're in good hands with Shuichi Washino behind the bar. The owner-chef, Chris-tian Giedemann, an American chef who learned to cook Japanese food in Japan, is a huge fan of Japanese food and drink. In fact, he travels to Japan every year to carry back domestic-market *isshobin* (1.8-liter [2-quart] bottles) of the shochu he carries at Ippuku to decorate his bar. This is also the only place in the US where *maewari* shochu (page 63) is served in a *kuro joka* black ceramic kettle over charcoal. Definitely worth a trip for those interested in shochu.

2130 Center Street, Berkeley; ippukuberkeley.com

CHICAGO
IZAKAYA MITA

If a local Chicago bar and an izakaya were to have a baby, it would be Izakaya Mita. Down to earth and cozy, this is the kind of place you could tuck into for an evening of filling comfort food and

Izakaya Mita, Chicago

Murasaki Lounge, Chicago

Urizun, Naha

Urizun, Tokyo

familiar drinks. The bar is a full-on proper neighborhood Chicago bar complete with stools, a television (invariably tuned to Chicago sports if anyone is playing), and a vast array of booze, including draft beer (both Japanese and local), sake, Japanese whisky, and what owner Brian Mita, a second-generation Japanese immigrant, claims is the largest shochu selection in the Midwest. The cocktail menu is full of Brian's own creations—he was a bartender before taking over the kitchen in his own restaurant. The food tends toward midwestern hearty rather than Japanese delicate, but that is exactly what it should be in a Chicago neighborhood bar.

1960 N Damen Ave, Chicago; tel. (773) 799-8677; izakayamita.com

MURASAKI SAKE LOUNGE

If Ippuku is food focused, Murasaki Sake Lounge is karaoke and anime focused. Anime runs on a continuous loop on several TVs, a DJ booth promises (but never seems to deliver) dance parties, and private karaoke rooms are available if you're so inclined. The shochu selection is eclectic, but well chosen. Sake and Japanese whisky are also prominent. The bar has low, comfortable chairs, and as at Aya in New York, a "snack" feeling pervades. The clientele is as eclectic as the space. You're as likely to be sitting next to a Japanese airline pilot on his turnaround as you are a karaoke queen or a local who happened to stumble in, drawn by the purple lighting and modern décor. Nevertheless, if you're looking for sho-

chu, sake, or Japanese whisky in downtown Chicago, Murasaki is the place to go. Don't let the purple lighting and DJ vibe throw you—it's well worth the visit.

211 E. Ontario Street, Chicago; murasakichicago.com

AWAMORI BARS

NAHA CITY, OKINAWA

URIZUN うりずん

When Saneyuki Tsuchiya opened Urizun in 1972 in Okinawa's capital city, the awamori scene was very different. The local drink had done poorly in competition with beer, cheap shochu and foreign spirits, and many makers were hoping for nothing more than to survive. A sort of unstated, mob-style code developed under which the distilleries did not try too actively to establish outlets on each other's turf, as long as their rivals stayed out of their areas. The awamori available in Naha tended to be made in Naha. But Tsuchiya shook all this up by touring the outlying islands in search of local spirits and badgering the makers to open up. His tireless championing of awamori from all parts of Okinawa at Urizun played an important part in ushering in the new era. Housed in an age-worn former domestic residence, the izakaya's dark wood interior, decorated with Okinawan musical instruments and dust-encrusted awamori bottles, is an atmospheric place to taste the local spirit. The food consists of delicious local Okinawan specialties you'd be hard pressed to find elsewhere

in Japan. For extra fun, try out Urizun's house *kusu* awamori (see page 74), unique blends from distilleries across the prefecture, aged in large clay pots.

388-5 Asato, Naha-shi, Okinawa; tel. 098-885-2178

TOKYO

URIZUN うりずん

If you can't get to Urizun's Naha location, the Tokyo branch is still an excellent place to explore awamori. A major bonus is the English menu. It is a bit more limited than the Japanese version (which itself has some very helpful photographs), but it covers most of the main points. The food includes all the usual *champuru* stir-fry, soba, and *rafute* braised pork belly that you would expect from Okinawan cuisine. The main attractions on Urizun's awamori list are the exclusive blends (created by the shop itself) of the products of various Okinawan distilleries. Those who want a name brand might try a carafe of Zuisen (瑞泉), the main brand from the Zuisen Distillery in the famed Sanka district of Naha. Having made awamori since 1887, Zuisen is now one of the most forward-looking distilleries, intent on producing very high-quality spirits and developing an export market. The aged awamori, which makes up the bulk of the distillery's output, comes in various styles, including quite complex spirits with honeyed, mustardy flavors as well as elegant, lighter-finishing *kusu*. Their cheaper unaged version is nice with ice on a sweaty summer day.

5F Shinmarunouchi Bldg., 1-5-1 Marunouchi, Chiyoda-ku, Tokyo; tel. 050-3464-9708

Yoshizaki Shokudo, Tokyo

Shugar Market, Tokyo

Yakushu Bar Sangenjaya, Tokyo

YOSHIZAKI SHOKUDO 吉崎食堂

For a more casual experience than can be had in an office building in Tokyo's business district, head to this basement Okinawan izakaya in the Ebisu neighborhood, a few blocks from Ebisu Station. The food is a mix of Okinawan favorites and Japanese izakaya fare. The friendly and enthusiastic staff is happy to make recommendations from the respectably sized awamori list. There is no bar area, but there is a counter around the open kitchen. These are great seats if you can get them—watch the cooks prepare the dishes and shout back and forth with the wait staff as orders come in. It has a very Okinawan feel despite being in the heart of Tokyo. Look out for Ikema (池間), a resolutely traditional *hinekoji* (page 73) awamori made by a one-armed *toji* head brewer who at last check was still going strong at 79 years of age. Japanese have the longest life expectancies of any country on earth, and Okinawans live longest among the Japanese. He may still be making awamori when he's 89 unless he decides to slow down.

B1F T Nakamura Bldg., 2-3-2 Ebisu-Minami, Shibuya-ku, Tokyo; tel. 03-5704-8867

FRUIT LIQUEUR BARS

TOKYO

SHUGAR MARKET

Don't let the misspelled name fool you. Shugar Market is a self-service bar that may be the best place in Japan to try the wide variety of *kajitsu-shu* fruit-based liqueurs produced in the country. Offerings range from banana to tomato (it's a fruit, too). You pay a flat ¥3,000 (US$27, £20.50, €23) fee at the entrance, take a glass and make your own drinks (you also wash your own glass, since you only get one). You can add ice, soda or even sour mix to your fruit liqueur, poured from 2-quart (1.8-liter) bottles stored in a fridge. At their Shinjuku location, for the single entry fee you can also visit their sister stores— Kurand for sake and Havespi for shochu (all three bars are on different floors of the same building). However, your table is only reserved on the floor where you pay your entry fee, so consider whether you'll be more likely to drink sake, shochu, or kajitsu-shu most often. Take note: the sake and kajitsu-shu floors typically have more customers during the day, particularly young women looking to indulge. Food is available for order as well, mainly drinking snacks.

5F Watase Tama Bldg., 3-9-9 Shinjuku, Shinjuku-ku, Tokyo; shugar.jp

YAKUSHU BAR SANGENJAYA 三茶の薬酒バー

Yakushu Bar Sangenjaya is not in many Tokyo guidebooks. Furthermore, even though it's a short walk from the station, finding the correct door in this rabbit warren of hard-angled back alleys can be a challenge. Look for the green light. Once you step inside the six-seat bar, you're struck immediately by the homemade infusions staring back at you (in some cases, quite literally). Barman Hikari helpfully explains, "There is *dobutsu-kei*, which is the snakes and iguanas and turtles and whatnot, and there's the *shokubutsu-kei*, which is just herbs and vegetables." Although some lizards do stare out at you from jars here, most of the drink actually consumed is made solely from herbs or vegetables by Hikari himself. The proprietor's single-word name gives a sense of the new-age feel of the place: they hold candle-making sessions in the second-floor tatami room. The music is mostly R&B, lounge and other smooth styles. "We get people coming after the clubs to chill out," says Hikari. He recommends a sweet *kukonomi yuzuwari* (wolfberry and citrus mix), which is supposed to be very good for mind and body. By the time you leave you'll be chill, though you may reflect on whether that's a result of Hikari's engaging laughter or the *yakushu*. If Sangenjaya is a step too far, sister bars have now popped up in Koenji and Asakusa as well, though the vibe is different. Koenji offers up live DJs, while Asakusa feels more like a classic bar.

2-13-20 Sangenjaya, Setagaya-ku, Tokyo yakusyu.net/sancha.html

Nanban, London   Bozu, Brooklyn   Hibiya Bar Whisky-S, Tokyo

LONDON

NANBAN なんばん

Nanban, which translates to "southern barbarian," was primarily used as a description of Portuguese priests and Dutch traders who came to Edo-era Japan from home ports in Southeast Asia. Inaugural *MasterChef* winner Tim Anderson, an American from Wisconsin who lived in Japan and moved to London to sell beer, may be as nanban as they come. His casual izakaya in the Brixton neighborhood of south London is a culinary delight, as he uses ethnic ingredients from the neighboring Brixton Market to bring flavors from the Caribbean, East Africa and elsewhere in the former British Empire into Japanese-style comfort food. His playfulness in the kitchen extends to his bar, where he has one of the largest selections of Japanese fruit liqueurs outside of Japan. Thanks to his hop-head background in craft beer, he's got an extensive beer list as well including his own brand, Kanpai, made in collaboration with the local Pressure Drop Brewery. His sake list is quite long, and a good selection of shochu, awamori and Japanese whisky can be found as well. Anderson originally intended Nanban to be a place to promote shochu in the UK, but quickly realized that the rich fruit-based liqueurs were enough to cut through some of the spiciness from his culinary adventures. If Brixton is out of your range, Chef Tim has now published not one, but two Japanese cookbooks.

426 Coldharbour Lane, Brixton, London; nanban.co.uk

BROOKLYN

BOZU

Bozu is perhaps the longest-lived izakaya in South Williamsburg, Brooklyn. The entryway to the horseshoe bar area is dominated by hanging eyeless red-and-white ball-shaped *daruma* dolls. There are several rooms, including a bilevel back garden—the only al fresco izakaya in the New York City area at the time of writing. While they have umeshu and a handful of other fruit liqueurs on their drinks menu, their real star is the house-made *kajitsu-shu* fruit liqueurs that line the bar. These home-style ferments incorporate just about any fruit you can imagine being reasonably delicious in a drink. The *mikan* (Satsuma orange) version is a standout. The menu is sushi and sushi-roll heavy, owing to the expectations of neighborhood diners who don't have a sense of what an izakaya is really supposed to be. However, if you're careful with your ordering, a solid izakaya experience can be had, perhaps topped off with some sushi rolls as a finisher.

296 Grand Street, Brooklyn; bozubrooklyn.com

JAPANESE WHISKY BARS

TOKYO

HIBIYA BAR WHISKY-S 日比谷

The Tokyo-based Hibiya chain of bars are owned and operated by Suntory, so you're only going to find Suntory whiskies. However, you're also going to pay much less for the age-statement bottlings, even if you're limited to one dram per customer per visit. Given that they will often have Hibiki, Hakushu and Yamazaki 12-, 17- and 21-year expressions, you're not going to be disappointed with only having one of each. They also have a wide variety of non–age-statement Suntory products and allow you to drink as many as you can reasonably stomach. The food menu is heavy on smoked meats and cheeses, which pair very well, particularly with the peated Hakushu line of whisky. The staff have great product knowledge, and at least one will speak very good English on any visit. The Hibiya bars are an elegant, authentic Tokyo bar experience that won't break the bank—not always the case in other bars, where vintage whiskies can add up fast.

3-3-9 Ginza, Chuo-ku, Tokyo; hibiya-bar.com/whisky-s

Nikka Blender's Bar, Tokyo   Malt Bar South Park, Tokyo   Bar K6, Kyoto

NIKKA BLENDER'S BAR

The Blender's Bar is owned by Nikka, and is limited to their products. That's not much of a limitation, though. They serve some phenomenal whiskies, and you could easily spend a week in here exploring their extensive range. It is a fairly large bar compared to the independent counter bars that are the norm in Japan. While this means you miss out on the cheek-by-jowl intimacy of the classic Tokyo drinking experience, there are advantages to the anonymity afforded, especially if you are not a great whisky buff and prone to feeling intimidated by small, connoisseur-driven locations. The Blender's Bar is definitely more geared to the non-expert than many of the private bars. There is a Malt and Coffey Grain Tasting Set which allows you to taste a range of Nikka's whiskies, from a highly sherried Yoichi to one of the well-regarded Nishinomiya single-grain whiskies. Note that the Blenders Bar shares its front door with "Usquebaugh", which is more of an eating establishment. Although also owned by Nikka, it is run as a totally separate enterprise. Bear left as you enter to get to the Blender's Bar.

B1F Nikka Whisky Bldg., 5-4-31 Minami-Aoyama, Minato-ku, Tokyo; nikka.com

MALT BAR SOUTH PARK
モルトバー サウスパーク

The first thing you notice about Malt Bar South Park is the nearly 300 Cadenhead bottlings lining the bar top. There isn't room for them on the shelves behind the bar due to the 2,000 other whiskies on display. The second thing you notice is the *South Park*–themed trash can in the restroom—and then you realize that the name is an ode to the owner's two favorite things: whisky and an irreverent American cartoon. His comedic tastes may be light, but his whisky list is dead serious, and some of them are quite dear. A half-dram of a Karuizawa single cask can put you back ¥8,000 ($72, £55, €61), and a 1970s vintage MacCallan even more. By Tokyo standards, however, most of his pours are relatively reasonable at ¥1,500 ($13.50, £10.25, €11.50) per dram, even for some pretty special stuff. He has a wide range of Owner's Cask releases from Suntory, which are almost impossible to find elsewhere (prices vary based on how many bottles were produced). While most of the bars in Japan listed in this guide were chosen for both quality and convenience, this is an exception. It's a hike from the station, and it's not in a neighborhood tourists usually go, but it's certainly worth the trek if you're seeking out rare whiskies. Sadly, the original owner passed away suddenly in early 2018, though his bar—and his collection—carry on.

B1F Miyazono Co-op, 2-1-2 Nakano, Tokyo; tel. 03-3229-6133

KYOTO

BAR K6

Bar K6 could easily fit into the cocktail chapter, as it's a classic Ginza-style cocktail bar in many ways, but it stands out enormously in Kyoto due to the massive whisky selection (about 600 Scottish single malts). Word has it the cleaning of the bar's more than 1,300 bottles is performed on a biweekly schedule and essentially never ends. While they have some Japanese whisky—some of which can be quite hard to find elsewhere—they really excel in their private labels. The head barman, Minoru Nishida, a legend in the Japanese whisky world, has obtained private editions of a number of rare bottlings. On a recent visit they were pouring a 19-year-old Benrinnes and a 21-year-old Ben Nevis. The 19-year-old was a single-cask-strength bottling, which meant that particular whisky was simply not available anywhere else in the world. Given how much of the history of Japanese whisky is tied up in Scotland, it only makes sense to recommend a whisky bar with huge Scotch selection. This is actually true of most whisky bars in Japan since there simply aren't enough Japanese expressions available at the moment to keep a whisky bar fully stocked with age statements. If you're sitting at the bar (and where else would you really want to sit when in a bar in Japan?), order a whisky highball. The resulting tea-ceremony-like artistry of the preparation, complete with recessed lighting (in the bar!), is fun to watch, and the drink itself is extremely refreshing, especially on a hot summer evening. *Oyuwari* (mixed with hot water) whisky is served during the winter for the complete tea-ceremony-like experience.

2F Vals Bldg., 481 Higashi-Ikesucho, Nagakyo-ku, Kyoto; ksix.jp

Old Course, Osaka   Bar Kitchen, Fukuoka   Bar Leichardt, Fukuoka   Uchu, New York

OSAKA

OLD COURSE オールドコース

The name is a reference to St. Andrews, golf course in Scotland, though the whisky selection comes from far and wide around the world. The barman knows his whisky and makes cocktails of any description. The Japanese whisky selection is eclectic, usually including rare bottlings from some of the less well-known distilleries. Given the frenetic energy of this drinking district in Osaka, Old Course is a welcome quiet oasis of fine drinks and sophisticated conversation. You're likely to rub shoulders with business executives, university professors and the occasional salaryman who enjoys a fine dram in a refined setting. If all of this sounds a bit spendy, it can be, so order judiciously and don't be shy about asking the price before deciding to make a purchase. The barman loves Glenmorangie 18 as a highball, which is a beautifully crafted drink, but it will also cost more than some dinners in Japan.

1F Arusu Bldg., 1-14-15 Higashi-Shinsaibashi, Chuo-ku, Osaka; bar-old-course.com

FUKUOKA

BAR KITCHEN

Don't let the name fool you: Bar Kitchen has no kitchen, so don't go if you're feeling hungry. Fortunately, it's also in Fukuoka, which has more restaurants per capita than any other city in Japan. So eat at one of the hundreds of nearby restaurants and then step into Bar Kitchen for a nightcap. While it can end up costing you a small fortune to sample rare bottlings at other whisky bars in Japan, Bar Kitchen's owner, Tomoyuki Oka, sells nearly everything in his 3,000-bottle collection for ¥1,000 ($9.00, £6.80, €7.65) per pour. If it's very rare or no longer available, he'll apologetically charge you more. On a recent visit he had the 2017 Chichibu Matsuri Single Cask bottle, which won the best single cask of the year at the World Whisky Awards in Scotland. He grimaced when he said it would be ¥1,500 ($13.50, £10.25, €11.50). One of the final bottlings from Karuizawa before the distillery closed—and was therefore lost to history—went for the same price.

107 Grand Park Tenjin, 1-8-26 Maizuru, Chuo-ku, Fukuoka; tel. 092-791-5189

BAR LEICHARDT

It may seem odd to recommend two whisky bars in Fukuoka when Fukuoka is not whisky country, no whisky is currently made there, and it's not on most tourist itineraries. It is, however, a vibrant city and the capital of Kyushu, the southernmost of Japan's four main islands. It's recently become a tech hub in Japan and has long been a thriving port city. There's a lot of money here, and some of those well-heeled residents like a good dram. Bar Leichardt fills that role with aplomb, designed like a traditional Japanese cocktail bar, but with a focus on whisky. The tuxedo-clad barman, Yu Sumiyoshi, is one of the brightest young whisky experts in Japan—so well regarded, in fact, that he was responsible for translating Stefan Van Eycken's *Whisky Rising* from English to Japanese. He's a mainstay at Whisky Talks Fukuoka, an annual whisky festival that brings enthusiasts from all over Japan. If you want to go to his bar, don't go that weekend, because it'll be almost impossible to get in. Go on any other weekend to have a relaxed drink in a refined atmosphere and try some amazing whiskies from Japan and beyond.

5F Nishimura Bldg., 2-2-1 Watanabe-dori, Chuo-ku, Fukuoka; leichhardtcafe.blog73.fc2.com

NEW YORK

UCHU

Uchu is the first Japanese bar to get a Michelin Star. Let that sink in: this is a bar with a Michelin star for dining. The tasting menu is sublime, and the drink pairings are flawlessly prepared. But we're placing Uchu in the whisky section, because as amazing as the cocktails are—and they are amazing—Uchu also has the largest selection of Japanese whisky in New York City. It also likely has the most expensive selection of Japanese whisky in United States. A 1-ounce (30 ml) pour of some of the rarer expressions can set you back several hundred dollars, and a double could cost you a cool $1,500 (¥167,000, £1,142, €1,278).

217 Eldridge Street, New York; uchu.nyc

Bar Moga, New York   Canon, Seattle   Y.Y.G. Brewery & Beer Kitchen, Tokyo   Popeye, Tokyo

BAR MOGA

Bar Moga is a curious little place on a prominent corner of Houston Street in lower Manhattan. Tucked just between Soho and Greenwich Village, the area teems with bars and bistros. *Moga*, short for "modern girl," is reference to the Showa-era woman who scorned traditional Japanese gender roles and began working, and drinking, and paying her own bills. The décor features dark wood, leather, a tin ceiling and Showa-era advertisements. There's a lounge area as well as a back room. The food menu is firmly *yoshoku* (Japanese interpretations of Western dishes) such as *omu-rice*—rice wrapped in an omelet and topped with brown sauce or ketchup. The broad drinks menu has plenty of sake and shochu, but the whisky list is where Bar Moga really shines. This fits the theme as well, since modern girls in Japan began going out to drink just as whisky became a popular alcohol. There are a good two dozen Japanese whiskies available, and they even have a rotating whisky highball on tap. For the full experience, look out for "Coco's Spirits," a weekly happy hour featuring Kayoko "Coco" Seo, a Japanese expat who dresses up as a Showa-era moga and plays hostess in the bar area.

128 W. Houston Street, New York; barmoga.com

SEATTLE

CANON

There's nothing Japanese about Canon except for the whiskies on its six-page Japanese whisky list, which includes bottlings from as far back as the 1950s, Karuizawa releases, and a handful of Suntory Owner's Casks (nearly impossible to find even in Japan). The most expensive dram is $1,199 (¥133,500, £913, €1,022) for a Yamazaki 25, so don't expect to find a bargain, but if you're looking for a particular Japanese whisky and don't want to go to Japan, this may be the best place in North America to find it. Canon is well known in Seattle, and in the spirits world more generally, for having the largest spirits collection in North America: 4,000 bottles and counting.

928 12th Ave, Seattle; canonseattle.com

JAPANESE BEER BARS

Many of the best beer bars in Japan change their beer menus on a weekly basis, which poses a problem for the authors of a drinking guide. For information on specific beers and which bars carry them, we recommend Joe Robson and Rob Bright's website, beertengoku. com. Overseas, Japanese beers tend to be carried in craft-beer bars rather than in Japan-specific places, so we don't have much to recommend on where to drink Japanese craft beer outside of Japan. A few brands, such as Coedo and Hitachino Nest, do seem to be popping up all over the place, however.

TOKYO

POPEYE ポパイ

Any guide to Japanese beer bars should rightly start with Popeye. It is a sort of Lourdes for beer drinkers, except the cures are so much more immediate and hedonistic. Everyone who writes about the place slips into hyperbole, so here goes: it has by far the largest range of beer in Japan and the greatest range of Japanese beer in the world. Proprietor Tatsuo Aoki has 70 beers on tap and three hand pumps. You won't find every good beer in Japan here, but the selection verges on being comprehensive. The menu is largely in English, so it's easy to pick and choose. Aoki has now gone so far as to open his own microbrewery to make his own beers if those available from other Japanese brewers don't strike his fancy. Be sure to check out the "hopulator," a homemade machine that allows Aoki to add extra hops to any beer he chooses! No smoking.

2-18-7 Ryogoku, Sumida-ku, Tokyo; lares.dti.ne.jp/~ppy

TOWA

Towa is a curious place at the top of some stairs on the second floor under the elevated train tracks just south of Ueno Station. By all accounts it's a soba shop, and that's what draws most of the tourists who visit for a bowl of noodles before or after a stroll in nearby Ueno Park. However, it's so much more than a simple noodle shop. It's got a fine selection of rotating craft beers from all over Japan. Extra care is taken with the brews, with specific Towa-branded glassware that differs based on the type of beer being served. With 12 taps and plenty of bottles, there's a lot to choose from—though it's not as epic as Popeye, it's still a lot more interesting than your average train-station soba shop. They also have sake, shochu,

Towa, Tokyo   Hitachino Brewing Lab, Tokyo   Ginza Lion, Tokyo

whisky and an izakaya menu that can make a visit to Towa more like a night out for drinks than a quick stop for noodles.

6-11-12 Ueno, Taito-ku, Tokyo; tel. 03-5816-3934

HITACHINO BREWING LAB
常陸野ブルーイング・ラボ

With three locations around Tokyo, Hitachino is finally making its presence felt domestically in Japan. The original Akihabara location has brewing equipment for actual experimentation (thus the "brewing lab" name) while the Tokyo Station and Shinagawa outposts serve more as post-work beer bars for the local office workers. The food menu offers eclectic Japanese takes on Western bar food, and the rotating taps serve up delicious Hitachino Nest standards along with seasonal brews. If you visit the Akihabara location, be sure to step around the corner to the standing bar that doubles as a sake shop selling parent company Kiuchi's line of premium sake. Ask the staff for details.

N-1 Maach Ecute Kanda Manseibashi, 1-25-4 Kandasudacho, Chiyoda-ku, Tokyo; hitachino.cc/brewing-lab

Y.Y.G. BREWERY & BEER KITCHEN

Microbreweries have taken off in Japan, and one of the finest is Y.Y.G. Brewery (the initials are a play on nearby Yoyogi Park). The taproom on the first floor serves up their own beers along with other craft beers they like, whether they be Japanese or foreign. Their own brews run the spectrum from pilsners to easy-drinking IPAs to sour porters. The brewery equipment is in full view be-

hind the bar, and more often than not someone is in there making beer. The taproom only serves up a few simple bar snacks, but the Y.Y.G. Beer Kitchen on the top floor of the same building has a full food menu with lots of Western-style comfort dishes and ample beer options. You'll want to make reservations for the beer kitchen, but the tap room is a casual walk-in space.

1F & 7F Ohchu Daiichi Bldg., 2-18-3 Yoyogi, Shibuya-ku, Tokyo; yygbrewery.com/en

GINZA LION 銀座ライオン

One of Japan's largest brewers, Sapporo, runs the Ginza Lion chain of beer restaurants through its Sapporo Lion subsidiary. They serve standard Sapporo lagers in big glasses and lots of sausages. That's about all that can be said about them, but this particular Ginza Lion (don't confuse it with the branches down the street) is special. It is a direct descendent of Japan's first proper beer hall, the Yebisu Beer Hall, established a bit to the south of here in 1899. Back then, a 1½ pint (500-ml) beer cost a tenth of a yen, about a quarter of a industrial worker's daily wage. Nowadays, a pint of beer here will cost you closer to ¥700 ($6.30, £4.80, €5.40). But the real reason to come to this cavernous beer hall is to stare slack-jawed at Eizo Sugawara's marble and tile Art Deco interior, or, if that's not your thing, at the large mosaic of scantily clad maidens at the head of the room. This successor to the original Yebisu Beer Hall opened in 1934, on the ground floor of the Dai Nippon Beer company's headquarters. The beer hall has been left pretty much untouched

since then. Take a trip to the toilets to understand how untouched: when the time came to add a toilet for women, they simply chopped the men's toilet in two because they didn't want to harm the building's fabric. The result? A cavernous beer hall serving beer by the kiloliter with a privy fit for a rural train station.

1F Ginza Lion Bldg., 7-9-20 Ginza, Chuo-ku, Tokyo; ginzalion.net/ginza7

NAKAMEGURO TAPROOM
中目黒タップルーム

The Nakameguro Taproom is one of a chain of pubs run by Baird Brewing, a craft brewery that started in Numazu on the southern slopes of Mount Fuji. All of the beer is by Baird, which is no bad thing; they are commonly acknowledged as one of the best craft breweries in Japan. While you are sipping their delicious pints, take note of the beer names. There is usually a pun or a historical reference or a family joke in there somewhere. Baird opened this Nakameguro outlet in 2008. They also have a taproom in Harajuku, a *kushi-age* fried-skewer izakaya in Takadanobaba near Shinjuku, a barbecue joint in Yokohama (Bashamichi

Nakameguro Taproom, Tokyo

Thrash Zone, Yokohama   Before9, Kyoto   Marca, Osaka

Taproom), a beer garden at their new brewery in Shizuoka prefecture (Brewery Gardens Shuzenji), and a delightful place on the dockside in Numazu itself (Fish-market Taproom). There's also Hakuba Pub on a ski slope in Nagano (site of the 1998 Winter Olympics) and the Harajuku Taproom in Los Angeles (4410 Sepulveda Blvd, Culver City, CA). More are planned in the future. American Bryan Baird, who runs the brewery with his wife Sayuri, decided to leave his job in Tokyo in 1996 and take himself back to California to learn his trade in what was then estab-lishing itself as one of the most creative craft-beer industries in the world. A year later, he was back in Japan, having com-pleted the American Brewers' Guild apprenticeship, and began turning out beer in 8-gallon (30-liter) batches. "Actu-ally, the only reason we survived was that we started small," says Bryan. "We were selling it all ourselves at the start. What we learned was that Numazu was a great place to brew beer, but the local people we had thought we might sell to were very conservative. The Tokyo taprooms and the wider distribution are vital, because it's in the city that we find peo-ple who know about beer and want to drink our stuff."

2F Nakameguro GT Plaza Bldg. C, 2-1-3 Kamimeguro, Meguro-ku, Tokyo; bairdbeer.com/taprooms

YOKOHAMA
THRASH ZONE

The name itself should probably clue you in to the fact that this is not a genteel, refined drinking establishment. Rather,

Thrash Zone (and its sister bar, Thrash-zone Meatballs) is a death metal bar where the craft beers are every bit an assault on the senses as the roaring guitar riffs and hummingbird drum beats. The owner, not content with just trying to get his hands on the hoppiest IPAs and the tartest sours the world has to offer, has now started brewing his own beers with a focus on challenging the senses. Fortunately for our mental health, the music actually isn't very loud and the beers end up being quite inter-esting. The original bar has no food menu and is a bit removed from the tourist area of Yokahama, Japan's second largest city, but Thrashzone Meatballs—complete with delicious meatballs made on a takoyaki grill—is in the heart of the city's drinking area. There is a helpful big-screen TV displaying the artist infor-mation for each song, which is a must if you're not a death metal aficionado.

Thrash Zone, Tamura Bldg, 2-10-7 Tsuruyacho, Kanagawa Ward, Yokohama. Thrashzone Meatballs, 2-15-1 Tokiwacho, Naka-ku, Yokohama.

KYOTO
BEFORE9

Before9 would not be out of place in Brooklyn or Portland—an older Kyoto building reclaimed and reimagined as a two-story casual drinks spot. The second floor is more of a mezzanine over the kitchen and bar, which leaves the dining area on the first floor open to soaring ceilings. Their focus is on craft beer from around Japan, usually featuring eight draft products from a

single brewery at a time. They also feature local craft sake. Drinks and food are ordered at a counter at the front entrance and seating is first come, first serve. Their open kitchen serves mod-ern Japanese cuisine that always smells amazing as soon as you walk in. Mean-while, black-and-white samurai movies play silently high up on the wall oppo-site the mezzanine, but the real fun comes from people-watching out the large picture windows at the front as locals and tourists mill past on the busy avenue. Be sure to check out their sister bars, Hachi (meaning "eight"), also in Kyoto, and Another8 (Meguro, Tokyo).

545 Nijodencho, Karasumaoike-agaru, Nakagyo-ku, Kyoto; sakahachi.jp

OSAKA
MARCA

Minoh Brewery, in a residential neighbor-hood of northern Osaka, has developed a reputation as one of Japan's top craft breweries. Not surprisingly, many Japa-nese craft brewers train at Minoh before opening their own shops. Perhaps the most interesting of these is Marca, whose female brewmaster, Mizuki Ka-miya, learned her craft at Minoh and then set up her own microbrewery in the back of her industrial-chic café. Situated in a lesser-known part of central Osaka, Marca tends to get crowded with locals looking for a night out. Kamiya rarely brews the same style of beer twice, so it's impossible to make specific recom-mendations. Her beers tend toward refreshing styles, though she's always experimenting. The small food menu at

Daikaya Izakaya, Washington, DC   Yushima 6Vin Stand, Tokyo   Yukusu, Fukuoka

the café is simple, but tasty. The regular menu is in English, but daily specials are usually only in Japanese. It's nonsmoking and there's free wifi, if those are deciding factors.

3-7-28 Kitahorie, Nishi-ku, Osaka; beermarca.com

WASHINGTON, DC

DAIKAYA IZAKAYA

Across the street from the professional basketball and hockey arena in downtown DC, you enter a door simply marked "izakaya," make your way to the second floor above a ramen shop, and find yourself in a warm, comfortable space peppered with hidden odes to anime. It's surprising how simultaneously Japanese and Brooklyn the space manages to be. The food and drink menus cater to the realities of Japanese food expectations in a city like Washington, DC, but that doesn't mean it suffers. The food is creative and extremely well prepared, while the bar program shines with a finely curated lineup of shochu, sake, Japanese whisky and house-created cocktails. The beer menu stands out not only because so few American izakaya focus on Japanese craft beer, but also because a number of local craft beers are on tap as well. Diners can try beer pairings with Japanese food, which is uncommon, considering 98 percent of Japanese beer is adjunct lager. The happy-hour scene is vibrant and the dining room is full from open to close most nights. Casual and fun.

705 6th Street NW, 2nd floor, Washington, DC; daikaya.com

JAPANESE WINE BARS

TOKYO

YUSHIMA 6VIN STAND
湯島6vinスタンド

Wine is huge in Tokyo. There are wine bars everywhere, specializing in everything—Spanish, French, Italian, American, South American, Australian . . . you name it. Some of the finest collections of Bordeaux outside of France reside in Ginza. Cosmopolitan Tokyo residents have been slower to embrace domestic Japanese wines, but a few spots around town do exist. Many of them either offer Japanese wines alongside others or pair Japanese wine and sake. Yushima is that rare shop that is resolutely Japanese wine only. Even better, unlike most wine bars in Tokyo, which pair their wines with European fare, Yushima pairs its wine with dishes from around Japan and source meats and vegetables from winemaking regions. The menu offers beef and vegetables from Yamanashi (the birthplace of Japanese wine) and cheese from Hokkaido (now the largest wine-growing region in Japan).

Kawanami Building, 1-7-3 Ueno, Taito-ku, Tokyo; tel. 050-3461-6927

FUKUOKA

YUKUSU ユクス

In most wine bars in Japan, you'd be hard pressed to find more than one or two token Japanese wines from the largest producers. At Yukusu you find nothing but Japanese wines, curated by the proprietress Kimiko Iwahashi, who

opened this wine bar in 2013 when she discovered the beauty of Japanese wine and realized its unheralded reputation in its own country. Her collection (hard to call it a selection, since it's impeccably curated) is vast and ever changing. She has eight bottles open at once, and they rotate throughout the evening. Usually this includes one sparkling, one rosé or orange, three whites and three reds. Once you've sat down, she gives you the rundown of each bottle—the prefecture, grape varietal, production notes (e.g., barrel aging, skin contact duration) and a simple taste description. If a bottle is emptied during your visit, it is replaced with a new wine, and she'll introduce it when you're ready to order your next glass. In some ways it's the luck of the draw. You might be drinking a rare vintage from a famous producer in one glass and a delicious newcomer with a screw-top and artsy label in the next. Whatever you end up with, though, you'll know it was chosen carefully. The food menu focuses on seasonal ingredients, with an unchanging smoked *otsumami* (おつまみ, snack) selection that ranges from smoked cheese to spam. She offers a *moriawase* (盛り合わせ, chef's selection) of these smoked appetizers that is well worth ordering. Everything else is delicious, though it's impossible to make recommendations, since the food menu is ever-changing.

2-4-26 Yakuin, Chuo-ku, Fukuoka; tel. 092-791-1247

Beige, Paris   Bar B, New York   Gen Yamamoto, Tokyo   Bar Bunkyu, Kyoto

PARIS

BEIGE ベージュ

It should come as no surprise that the izakaya with the largest wine list in the world is in the heart of Paris. Steps from the oppressively touristy Latin Quarter, Beige (formerly Lengue) is run by a Japanese chef with a clear sense of izakaya food and French tastes. His wine list is extensive, but his cellar contains more than 500 expressions, most of which are not on the menu. It never hurts to ask if you're looking for a specific style, but you'd best speak French or Japanese, as the staff are all from Japan. The food runs the spectrum of Japanese izakaya fare, but with a nod toward French tastes, so expect more cheese and roux than you'd find in a typical izakaya in Japan. While Japanese wines are not usually available, you should get a very clear sense of the possibilities of pairing Japanese food with wine.

31 Rue de la Parcheminerie, Paris; tel. 01 46 33 75 10

NEW YORK

BAR B

Japanese wine has not yet made it to the US in any meaningful quantities, so this is a wine bar run by Japanese in New York City. Started by the owners of Basta Pasta, a long-running Japanese-owned Italian restaurant, this is also the only proper *tachinomi* (standing bar) in NYC. Customers stand along a counter that runs the length of the narrow shop and nibble on Italian-inspired food prepared by a Japanese chef. From

charcuterie to scallop sashimi to personal-sized pizzas, these snacks are accentuated by the two dozen or so wines available at any given time. A single sake and a single umeshu sit on a low shelf, grudgingly acknowledging the Japanese ownership. Draft (Peroni, of course) and bottled beer are also available. Both the menu and wines change regularly.

84 7th Ave, New York; barbnyc.com

JAPANESE COCKTAIL BARS

TOKYO

LITTLE SMITH

There are certainly more classic cocktail bars in Ginza than Little Smith, but there's something about this subterranean space that's absolutely mesmerizing. Perhaps part of the allure is just how difficult it is to find in the rabbit warren of Ginza's multilevel bar buildings. The oval-shaped bar of 24 seats is manned by six tuxedoed bartenders – that's a maximum of four customers per barman, so you're never wanting for attention. The oval is cut in half by the bottle wall, so despite the shape there's surprising

Little Smith, Tokyo

sense of privacy for each guest. There's no cocktail menu, just a few questions about what you like to drink and don't. If you're willing to let them decide, you probably won't be disappointed. Otherwise, feel free to make requests and see what they come up with. All this while you enjoy the comfort of a ¥400,000 ($3,590, £2,733, €3,060) Japanese handmade wooden chair that's so comfortable you'll never want to leave—at least not until you've had enough to drink.

B2F KN Bldg., 6-4-12 Ginza, Chuo-ku, Tokyo; .net

GEN YAMAMOTO

If ever there were a bar that deserved the recognition of Michelin, it is Gen Yamamoto. His cocktail *omakase* (chef's— or in this case, bartender's—choice) demonstrates deep respect for seasonality. Japan considers the year to have 24 seasons, not four, and since he relies on seasonal ingredients, the omakase changes every week or two. He works with Japanese spirits and ingredients nearly exclusively. The ingredients might range from Kyoto green tea to Hokkaido milk to Miyazaki citrus to daikon radishes from his home town. For one cocktail he made on a winter visit, a Le Lectier pear from Niigata, aged for 90 days after harvest, was muddled with an eau de vie from Kagoshima shochu and spirits producer Bunise. The resulting drink was so creamy and lush it was nearly like a pear gazpacho. To get the full experience, we recommend getting an early reservation, because if you're his first customer, he'll start with whole pieces of fruit and break them down almost like you'd expect from

Bar K-Ya, Kyoto   Angel's Share, New York   Bar Goto, New York

a sushi master with a piece of fish. Later customers may get some of the remaining fruit, but yours will be fresh that day, usually found at market that morning.

1F Anniversary Bldg., 1-6-4 Azabu-Juban, Minato-ku, Tokyo; genyamamoto.jp/bar_tokyo/English

KYOTO

BAR BUNKYU 文久

Kyoto has an interesting relationship with its historical architecture. As one of the only major Japanese cities that was spared bombing in World War II, it has a great deal of prewar architecture still in existence. This has led to a lot of preservation efforts—while Tokyo seems to be completely rebuilt every 30 years, Kyoto has 200-year-old wooden houses. While Bar Bunkyu is not in a 200-year-old house, it has that feeling. The architect who designed the space, Katsumi Yasuda, attempts to maintain old Kyoto materials in modern spaces. In this case, the bar is tucked in a small alley behind a coffee shop. The bar itself has a small courtyard before the entrance and is a single room with just nine seats. The name refers to the era in the late Edo and early Meiji periods when the owner's family opened their flower shop, which specialized in flower arrangements for *ryokan* inns and tea houses. The barman, Naoyuki Sakauchi, was a seaweed farmer and video producer before moving to Kyoto in 2000 to become a bartender. He has no menu, works with a handful of spirits, and can make you just about any classic cocktail you'd like. He attempts to do all of this in a style that pays homage

to the tea-ceremony culture that infuses the aura of Kyoto so deeply.

Kawaramachi-sanjo, Nakagyo-ku, Kyoto; barbunkyu.jimdo.com/english

BAR K-YA

Kyoto is seemingly full of bars like Bar K-ya, but K-ya stands out in that it's not hard to find, has ample seating, and does a great job with cocktails and whisky. When you enter the bar, it's a long walk into the main bar area; the back wall is a picture window looking on to a Japanese garden. Further on into the garden are private drinking rooms where larger parties can gather and enjoy an evening. The bar area itself is reserved for solo drinkers and couples, with a few small tables on the opposite wall for parties of up to four. The tuxedoed barmen make classic cocktails in the Japanese style, and the whisky selection, while it doesn't rival Bar K6 (page 144), does hold its own if you're looking for a dram. Don't be surprised to see a maiko (apprentice geisha) drinking with a gentleman who frequents her tea house. Try not to stare.

103 Yaoyacho, Rokkaku-dori Goko-machi Nishi-iru, Nakagyo-ku, Kyoto; tel. 075-241-0489

NEW YORK

ANGEL'S SHARE

The epitome of Japanese bartending in NYC, Angel's Share is a speakeasy situated behind a heavy wooden door on the second floor of a divey New York University–area izakaya called Village Yokocho. Angel's Share is not exactly

unknown, but you'll still occasionally meet Village Yokocho regulars who never noticed that the people waiting at the top of the stairs weren't queuing for a table at the izakaya. Stepping into Angel's Share is a shock after the lively, casual environment outside the door. Quiet, reserved. No standing, no parties of more than four people. The barmen are in shirt and tie, and a massive angel mural dominates the area over the bar. The cocktail menu is extensive and the drinks are elegantly prepared with very fine ingredients. The mood lighting and music make it quite romantic, so if you're looking for a date spot, it's an excellent choice. Pro tip: there's an annex open only on weekends situated on the second floor of the Japanese restaurant next door. This is where you're likely to find former Angel's Share head bartender Shingo Gokan making a surprise appearance whenever he's in New York.

8 Stuyvesant Street, New York; tel. 212 777-5415

BAR GOTO

The eponymous bar of former Pegu Club head bartender Kenta Goto is a great place for Japanese cocktails in NYC. The space is small but well apportioned, with a dozen bar seats and several tables along one wall. There's a rail to stand by the large picture window, which can be opened to let in a cool evening breeze, but stays closed most of the time since Eldridge Street has several less sophisticated bars (with the resulting revelry). The bar is actually an ode to Goto's family in several ways.

ROKC, New York   Karasu, Brooklyn   Speak Low, Shanghai

The lone piece of art along the wall above the tables is the fabric from one of his grandmother's kimonos. His mother's *okonomiyaki* (savory pancake) restaurant in Chiba is memorialized in the food menu. Bottles from his father's home bar line the top of the bar here. Goto's cocktails are extremely creative, beautifully blending both Japanese ingredients (see recipes, page 133) and Western spirits. He expertly tweaks classic cocktails to make his own variations. You can also order the classics, and his whisky selection continues to grow. Goto himself is not often behind the bar—he's usually playing host to make sure that those who have to wait for a seat feel welcome despite the delay. He's so humble in this role that if you don't recognize him, you'd think he's just a member of the staff.

245 Eldridge Street, New York; bargoto.com

ROKC

Short for "Ramen, Oysters, Kitchen, Cocktails" ROKC is the brainchild of three alumni from the bar Angel's Share (Shigefumi Kabashima, Tetsuo Hasegawa and Joji Watanabe) who decided to open up their own place in Harlem. The food menu is simple: ramen, raw bar and appetizers. The cocktails are incredibly creative. A spin on the Bloody Mary is served in a conch shell. Another drink is served in—yes—a light bulb. But these aren't just gimmicks, they are elegantly crafted cocktails, the original creations of very talented bartenders who are pushing the limits of what cocktails can be, all in a casual environment. They don't take reservations and

there's virtually always a wait, but it's well worth it. Go hungry.

3452 Broadway, New York; rokcnyc.com

BROOKLYN
KARASU

Because New York City can't have just one Japanese speakeasy, Karasu was opened in the Fort Greene neighborhood of Brooklyn, at the back of Walter Foods, a hipster neighborhood American restaurant. This elegant cocktail-focused bar has a full menu by Prune Restaurant alumna Yael Peet and her partner Elena Yamamoto, served out of a kitchen smaller than that of the average Manhattan apartment. Yael is fast becoming a celebrity chef in the Brooklyn restaurant scene; to her credit, she always shares accolades with Elena. The food and drink are worth the trip in equal measure and a nice sake, shochu and whisky selection means that Karasu could have been placed in any number of sections in this guide. They take reservations, and it's best to make one, as they rarely have room for walk-ins without a wait.

166 Dekalb Ave, Brooklyn; karasubk.com

SHANGHAI
SPEAK LOW

When Shingo Gokan won the 2012 Bacardi Legacy Global Cocktail Competition, his life was irrevocably changed. He went from manager of the Angel's Share bar to bar owner virtually overnight. His signature pouring style is a sight to behold, but his bar concepts have proven

even more clever. His first bar, Speak Low in Shanghai, made the World's 50 Best Bars list almost immediately, and in 2017 was ranked #10 by Drinks International. The speakeasy faces the street as a bar supply store—you can shop for muddlers, strainers, cocktail books, etc. Tell the clerk behind the counter that you're thirsty and he'll pull aside the bookshelf to let you in. Follow a narrow brick corridor to a staircase and climb to the second floor for the main bar. Once there, grab a drink and request a seat at the third-floor bar. There may be a wait, as it is seated only (you can, and will, stand on the second floor unless you have the great good luck to grab a seat). If you become a regular, you may be invited to the fourth floor, where favored customers have bottle lockers and can drink from Shingo's private whisky stash. So successful was Speak Low that Shingo opened Sober Company nearby (99 Yandang Road), which is a Brooklyn-style café on the first floor; upstairs there are two doors, one marked Hungry and the other marked Thirsty. You can imagine what happens from there. When in Shanghai, both are worth a visit.

579 Fuxing Middle Road, Huangpu Qu, Shanghai; tel. 021 6416 0133

Buyer's Guide

INTRODUCTION

This chapter is intended to give you some insight into how to pick a brand or style that you're going to be satisfied with even if you've never tried it before. Unfortunately, we're not able to be definitive, as the nuances of liquor laws around the world means that our recommendations will not apply to everything everywhere. Further, given the proliferation of online retailers and the sheer number of liquor stores around the world, these recommendations barely scratch the surface.

BUYING TIPS

All of these tips are meant as general rules of thumb; given the diversity of the available products, there are exceptions in virtually every category. You'll need to explore on your own and discover your own preferences, but that's the fun, isn't it?

SAKE

Buying sake overseas can be very tricky. There's plenty of it available, but much of what is most easy to find is not very good. *Futsushu*, the table wine of sake, appears on liquor-store shelves with a great deal of regularity, often the Ozeki or Gekkeikan brands. These are not bad sake per se, but they are not the best. And if the liquor shop doesn't care for the sake properly, it can end up being less than it should be. A lot of very good sake is left on liquor-store shelves at room temperature. You wouldn't do that with a fine white wine, so why would you do it with sake? To find the good stuff you'll often need to dig a little bit deeper and seek out liquor shops that refrigerate their sake. Even better, find one of the growing number of sake specialty shops that are starting to appear. They'll usually have the most interesting and diverse selection, as well as the most knowledgeable staff.

Helpful Numbers

Sake labels can be mystifying, so it's useful to refer to the sake chapter in this book for a refresher on the styles. There are several key points to keep in mind. First, all premium sake is labeled either *honjozo* or *junmai*. Honjozo has a small amount of brewers' alcohol added before pressing, while junmai does not. In order for sake makers to sell their product as either of these premium styles, they must print on the label the rate at which the rice has been polished. There is no minimum polishing rate for junmai, but the rice used to make honjozo must be polished to a minimum of 70 percent. *Ginjo* sake is polished to 60 percent; *daiginjo* sake to 50 percent, but polishing rates can often go much lower. Dassai 23, polished until just 23 percent of the rice grain remains, proves to be a very light, refreshing drink. You'll sometimes also see the word *tokubetsu* on labels, which means that the rice used has been polished to at least 60 percent.

Also note that sake is required to have the bottling date printed on the label. While these are sometimes in the Japanese calendar (defined by emperor's reign), export bottles usually adhere to a Gregorian calendar. Sake is typically meant to be consumed soon after bottling, much like white wine, so unless you see *koshu* or *jukuseishu* (meaning "aged") on the label, you may want to think twice about buying a bottle that has been sitting on a shelf for long. Anything more than two or three years old may have missed its peak. Then again, if you're an adventurous type,

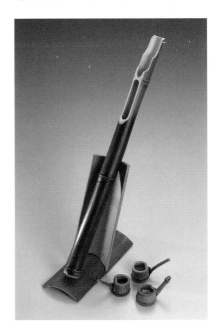

you could play around with making your own aged sake.

Two other figures often found on labels may help you understand better what you are buying: the *nihonshudo* (日本酒度), sometimes called the sake meter value or SMV, which is usually between -4 and +15 but can range much more widely. Put very simply, this figure shows whether a sake is dry or sweet: −3 is sweet, 0 is sweetish and anything above +4 is getting dry. Of course, other taste components influence the perception of sweetness and dryness, so the nihonshudo is not always a reliable guide.

The acidity (*sando* 酸度) of a sake also affects its flavor, and labels often carry measurements of this tanginess (typically from a lowish acidity of 1.0 to highs in excess of 2.0). They will sometimes also measure amino acids (*amino sando* アミノ酸度), high levels of which can give the sake a feeling of body (again, 1.0 to 2.0 is a normal range). But all these figures can be very confusing. The sake industry was undoubtedly trying to provide more information to consumers, but these measurements are so technical and lacking in context for most drinkers that they're probably more confusing than helpful. It might be best to just glance at the nihonshudo and decide the rest with your tongue.

Recommended Reading

We recommend John Gauntner, who is easily the top English-language sake writer and educator. His books are must-reads for the sake-curious, and his print magazine *Sake Today* and website sake-today.com are an invaluable resource. For a slightly different perspective, we're very fortunate that master brewer Philip Harper has written a book, *The Insider's Guide to Sake*.

More sake buying information can be found on other popular sake websites. Sake Samurai (his official title) Timothy Sullivan's sake guide has reviews of more than 900 brands: urbansake.com. John Puma's sake guide is a beautiful website with a lot of useful information: thesakenotes.com. There's even an app for sake, Sakenomy, available for both iPhone and Android: sakenomy.net.

SHOCHU

Shochu, as a distilled spirit, is much more shelf stable than sake. However, there are still key buying tips that will help you maximize your enjoyment. First, stick with *honkaku* shochu (本格焼酎). This will always be clearly printed on the label. There are some rare exceptions of non-honkaku shochu that are worth trying, like the popular Tantakatan *shiso* shochu (鍛高譚), though we can assure you from experience that honkaku shiso shochu is still much more interesting.

It's best to stick with regional specialties: sweet potato shochu from Kagoshima and Miyazaki in southern Kyushu, rice shochu from Kumamoto, barley shochu from northern Kyushu (particularly Iki Island where they make shochu with a 2:1 barley/koji rice blend, or Oita where they make 100% barley shochu), soba (buckwheat) shochu from Miyazaki or Nagano, and *kokuto* (black sugar) shochu, which is exclusively made in the Amami Islands. *Kasutori* shochu from sake lees is made all over Japan; some sake makers from outside Kyushu make very nice examples, though they can be hard to find since they are made in limited quantities. To give a sense of how regional the shochu styles are, Kagoshima and Kumamoto border one another, and in fact both used to be part of the Satsuma domain. They're separated by the Kirishima Mountains, but you can get from Kumamoto city to Kagoshima city in 45 minutes by bullet train. Nevertheless, if you mention rice shochu to people from Kagoshima, they say, "You mean sake?" To them, shochu is sweet-potato based.

The type of koji mold used in shochu production matters quite a bit, though it's not always clearly marked on the label. Shochu made with white koji is the most popular; it's usually mild and easy drinking. Shochu from black koji is rich and earthy, and yellow koji is generally more floral and fruity. The Hozan brand of shochu actually lets you try all three with the same base ingredient (sweet potatoes) made in the same distillery. Satsuma Hozan has white koji, Kiccho Hozan black, and Tomino Hozan yellow. When the koji is not clearly defined on the ingredients list, it can sometimes be

divined. Look for the word *kuro* (黒、くろ、black) in the product name, as those are virtually always made with black koji. Also, if you find multiple products from the same producer with different colored labels (white, black, yellow), this can sometimes be a key. Some producers will put black-koji shochu in black or brown bottles and white-koji shochu in clear or white-frosted bottles. None of this is ironclad, but can give you a hint.

A key consideration when shopping for shochu is whether you want something light and easy drinking or a liquor with more punch. Honkaku shochu is most often bottled at 20 or 25 percent alcohol for the Japanese market, but is often 24 percent in the US (to comply with an absurd California liquor law). (The 24 percent shochu is the 25 percent with 1 percent more water.) To further confuse the situation, the same law requires the word *soju* (a low-proof Korean spirit with a similar name but a very different production method) to appear on the label. Look for "Japanese shochu" or "honkaku shochu" on those labels. Otherwise, avoid.

Shochu can legally be bottled at up to 45 percent alcohol, so pay attention to the label. Some very nice *genshu* (undiluted) shochu exist in foreign markets, which makes them much closer in proof to Western spirits. Some are even barrel-aged, such as Mugon (無言), a 40 percent ABV rice shochu aged for 10 years. Shochu aged at least three years qualifies for the *koshu* (古酒, aged) designation, but not all put it on the label for export brands. Typically, if shochu is stored in wood or clay, it's been aged for a minimum of three years.

A final tip is to try to find whether a shochu is made with a vacuum or atmospheric still. Vacuum-distilled shochu tends to be light, clean and easy drinking, while atmospheric-distilled shochu tends to be full bodied. This is rarely clearly written on the label, but some tasting experience should help you figure it out pretty quickly.

The definitive English-language resource for shochu is the website kanpai.us edited by Christopher Pellegrini, author of *The Shochu Handbook*, and Stephen Lyman.

AWAMORI

Okinawan awamori is not nearly as commonly available outside of Japan as sake or shochu. This is partly because there are fewer than 50 awamori producers, and also because they tend to be much smaller companies. Since all awamori is made with Thai rice and black koji mold, the real differentiation tends to come from the proof and the aging. Awamori tends to be bottled at higher proofs, usually 30–35 percent ABV. (In Yonaguni, a far-flung island outpost of the Okinawan archipelago, they make awamori that's up to 65 percent ABV. That'll put hair on your chest!) Once awamori is aged at least three years it is labeled *kusu* and demands a premium, though "premium" is relative. A five-year-old kusu might sell for around ¥1,800 ($16.20, £12.30, €13.80) in Japan compared to about ¥800 for the main brand from the same distillery. They get more expensive once they export, with eight- or ten-year-old expressions going for several times that price.

Again, the definitive English-language resource for awamori is the kanpai.us website.

UMESHU AND OTHER FRUIT LIQUEURS

Umeshu is by far the most popular fruit-based liqueur in Japan. The key differentiator for many umeshu is what the base alcohol is made from. Umeshu made with *korui* shochu (basically grain ethanol) is less interesting than umeshu made with sake, honkaku shochu or awamori. You'll also have to decide if you want something relatively clear and liqueur-like, or if you'd prefer some pulp left in the bottle. The pulp results in a more flavorful drink, but reduces shelf-stability. A final decision point is whether you'd like it to be sparkling or not—the same decision that has to be made for other types of fruit liqueur.

While there is currently no dedicated website for umeshu or *kajitsu-shu* fruit-based liqueurs, the Australian website sakeguide.com.au has some good information about brands and styles.

WHISKY

There have been a good half-dozen books written about Japanese whisky just in the past few years. Those that stand out as worth reading are Stefan VanEyken's *Whisky Rising*, which is such a definitive guide to Japanese whisky that it's been translated back into Japanese (by the bartender of Bar Leichardt in Fukuoka [page 145]), and *The Way of Whisky* by David Bloom, which reads more as memoir or travel guide than a whisky guide. The most recent addition to this crop is the comprehensive *Japanese Whisky* by Brian Ashcraft.

A liquor-shop owner overseas would have to be living under a rock to be unaware of the value of age-statement Japanese whiskies, but if you can find any for a reasonable price, pick them up. In New York City, older age statements such as Hibiki 21 or Yamazaki 18 can sometimes be found, but they're going for Wall Street prices. Don't be afraid of the non-age statement versions of the same brands. While they are lighter than their age-statement older siblings, they are still genuine reflections of the styles. When in Japan, any well-known whisky shop will be picked clean long before you get there, so it's often better to explore smaller liquor shops in residential neighborhoods. You may stumble across a gem.

There is an English-language Japanese website that sells Japanese whisky, but you need to be sure that you live in an area that allows for the postal delivery of alcohol. The website, dekanta.com, has a lot of very rare whiskies for sale, though the prices are high.

For those lucky enough to live in countries that have a whisky resale market for collectors or speculators, consider yourselves fortunate. You can find some extremely rare bottlings from secondary retailers or at auction. This is an excellent way to pick up some rare Japanese whiskies if you're willing to spend the money.

A word of caution. Several shochu makers from Kumamoto have begun selling their barrel-aged shochu as whisky in the US market. While these products comply with the letter of US whiskey laws, they are made with koji mold rather than malt—not necessarily a bad thing, considering that Professor Takamine (see page 87) patented that malt-less whisky process in the 1890s—koji whisky was a thing at least for a short time. What's unfortunate is that these products are being produced by rice shochu makers who have no whisky-making experience. This could potentially affect the reputations of other Japanese whisky makers (even those who also make shochu, such as Mars, Komasa, or Eigashima). It's probably best to stick with the whisky distillers mentioned in the whisky chapter of this book, at least for the time being.

And when shopping for aged whisky, please don't waste your money on "Japanese" whisky bearing the Matsui label, which is not what it seems (see page 98). Buy a decent Scotch instead.

BEER

Exported Japanese beer is a conundrum. With the exception of Orion and large-format Asahi (17–fluid ounce [500-ml] and 2-quart [2-liter] cans), all major Japanese brands sold in the United States and Canada are produced in those countries. Therefore, unlike all Japanese beer, they are pasteurized. The telltale sign is that the kanji that appears on all Japanese domestic market cans (生, *nama*, raw) is missing or replaced with different kanji (Asahi cleverly replaces 生 with 辛口, which means "dry taste," on its Super Dry cans so as not to disrupt their iconic design). Also look for "bottled by Molson" or "bottled in Boulder, Colorado."

Japanese craft beers are starting to show up in the US market. The most common is Hitachino Nest, but many others are appearing too. Unlike the majors, these craft beers are all produced in Japan. The definitive online guide to Japanese craft beer is beertengoku.com from Rob Bright and Joe Robson. While it has a wealth of information about Japanese craft beers, it's focused on drinking them in Japan, so you'll have to do a little deeper research to find out what's available overseas. Fortunately, the Japanese beers that are exported are listed on beer-rating apps such as Untappd.

WINE

Japanese wine is still very hard to find overseas. A few styles from major vineyards (owned by Suntory, Hombo-Mars, etc.) have started to appear, but they have very high price points relative to those from more established wine regions. Koshu (native Japanese white wine) has started to appear in Europe after scoring high in international wine competitions, but most other Japanese wines have not yet begun to export.

The website Dekanta (dekanta.com/cellar) has a wine cellar service that delivers Japanese wine, if you're in a region where you can have alcohol delivered via post.

The best English-language resource for Japanese wines at the moment is the online guide asianwinereview.com, though a few brands have started to appear on major wine websites and apps such as Delectable.

WHERE TO BUY

JAPAN
Here we recommend one or two major stores for each style of alcohol.

DEPARTMENT STORES Most cities in Japan have large premium department stores. Most of these have a basement food hall, with sprawling food courts and a sake shop. Sometimes the sake shop will be on a higher floor, so consult the floor maps for confirmation. You'll pay a premium at these sake shops, but you'll also get excellent service.

DON QUIJOTE & BIC CAMERA All across Japan, these discount stores have large alcohol selections. Due to their market reach, they often receive nice allocations of otherwise hard-to-find sake, shochu and whisky. They also have reasonable prices due to their discount branding. Another bonus: they have very easy to use duty free facilities which can save you even more on purchases over ¥5,000 ($45, £34.30, €38.60).
Don Quijote: donki.com/en
Bic Camera: biccamera.co.jp.e.lj.hp.transer.com/shoplist/index

Tokyo
ANTENNA SHOPS Every prefecture in Japan sells its regional specialties at an "antenna shop" in Tokyo (some have more than one), and nearly every prefecture in Japan makes interesting local alcohols. Like sake from a specific region? Visit their antenna shop. Shochu? Check out the Kyushu prefectural antenna shops. Awamori? The Okinawa antenna shop. Wine? Yamanashi. Umeshu? Wakayama. If you're looking for something specific, these are a safe bet, or at least worth exploring. Find more information at city-cost.com/blogs/City-Cost/MvKrz-shopping_tokyo

JAPAN SAKE AND SHOCHU INFORMATION CENTER One recommended stop is the information center for the Japanese Sake and Shochu Maker's Association. This small shop has informational materials, displays, and a tasting bar. They offer very affordable tasting samples of more than 60 types of sake and 30 types of shochu and awamori. Their concierge can also recommend places to buy shochu, sake and awamori around Tokyo.
1-6-15 Nishi-Shinbashi, Minato-ku, Tokyo
japansake.or.jp/sake/english/goto/jssic.html
Monday–Friday, 9 am–5:30 pm (closed weekends and holidays)

HASEGAWA SAKETEN This shop has one of the best selections of Japanese sake and shochu of any supplier you are likely to find in Tokyo, and unlike most liquor stores in the city, they also carry some Japanese wine. They have several locations around town, but their Azabu-Juban location has English-speaking staff. Some locations have tasting counters as well. You can find information about their other shop locations on their website at the address below.
Azabu-Juban 2-3-3, Minato-ku, Tokyo
hasegawasaketen.com
Open daily 11 am–8 pm

SHOCHU AUTHORITY This is the largest shochu shop in Tokyo, and perhaps Japan, with between 2,500 and 3,500

types of shochu available at any given time. They also have a large selection of awamori and some sake and wine.
Higashi-Shinbashi 1-8-2, Minato-ku, Tokyo
rakuten.ne.jp/gold/s-authority/
Monday–Saturday 11 am–10 pm
Sunday 11 am–9 pm

LIQUORS HASEGAWA A very interesting shop where you can sample select whiskies before trying them. You're only allowed two samples, and they're priced relative to what you're considering buying, but it can help you choose. This is a very popular shop so it may be hard to find rare bottlings as they'll sell out quickly.
2-1-4 Yaesu, Chuo-ku, Tokyo (located in Idea Seventh Sense); liquors-hasegawa.com
Open daily 10 am–8 pm

DEGUCHIYA This shop sells just about everything, but they have a nice selection of Japanese craft beer and you can drink on premises if you like.
2-3-3 Higashiyama, Meguro-ku, Tokyo
deguchiya.com
Monday–Saturday 11 am–10 pm (closed Sundays)

WINESHOP & DINER FUJIMARU This wine store and diner is heavily devoted to Japanese wine. You can buy bottles to go, or stay and enjoy a meal with recommendations from the staff. They also have a shop in Osaka.
Tokyo: 2F S Bldg., 2-27-19 Higashi-Nihonbashi, Chuo-ku
Wednesday–Monday 1 pm–11 pm (closed Tuesdays)
Osaka: 14-1 Kuzuha Hanazono-cho, Hirakata
Daily 10 am–11 pm
papilles.net

Osaka
SHIMADA SHOTEN A liquor store with a surprise basement tasting room where you can explore rare sake from all over Japan. You pay for your basement tastings on an honor system, telling the cashier how many glasses you sampled. The owner of this 60-year-old shop has visited more than 250 sake breweries. His son speaks English.

3-5-1 Itachibori, Nishi-ku, Osaka
sake-shimada.co.jp
Monday–Friday 9 am–7 pm
Saturday 9 am–6 pm; closed Sundays

Fukuoka

TODOROKI SAKETEN No liquor shop in Fukuoka is more famous than Todoroki, but their main shop is fair distance from downtown. It's worth a visit if you're a shochu fan or are interested in older Japanese architecture, but if you don't want to travel, they've now helpfully opened a standing bar in downtown Fukuoka which also has a small liquor shop attached.

todoroki-saketen.com
Main shop: 2-2-31 Sanchiku, Hakata-ku, Fukuoka; 092-571-6304
Tuesday–Saturday 10 am –7 pm
Sunday 10 am–6 pm; closed Mondays

Standing Bar/Shop: 3-7-30 Yakuin, Chuo-ku, Fukuoka; tel. 092-753-8311
Liquor shop hours 12 pm–9 pm
Standing bar hours 4 pm–9 pm
Closed Fridays, Sundays, holidays, and the last Monday of every month

Kagoshima

SHOCHU ISHINKAN Kagoshima residents are shochu-obsessed, and this shop may help you understand why. More than 1,500 kinds of shochu are on offer from Kagoshima alone, as well as 50 to 100 brands to taste. Limited-release bottles almost always come here as well. It's in the basement of the department store at the bullet-train station, so there's almost no excuse not to visit if you make it this far south.

1-1 Chuo-cho, Kagoshima (in the basement of Amu Plaza Kagoshima) shochuishinkan.jp
Open daily 10 am–9 pm

Okinawa

AWAMORI KAN Not just a liquor shop, but a shrine to all things awamori. With more than 1,000 different awamori and exclusive bottlings of *kusu* (aged) awamori, this is a must-see shop when in Okinawa. The owner, Akiyoshi Miyagi, has helped lead a resurgence in awamori's popularity throughout Japan.

Shochu Authority, Tokyo

1-81 Shurisamukawacho, Naha; awamori.co.jp
Wednesday–Monday 10 am–6:30 pm (closed Tuesdays)

JAPAN online

If you're visiting Japan, you can have bottles delivered to your hotel. Even Amazon (and Japanese rival Rakuten) deliver alcohol. Dekanta is a Japanese online alcohol store that delivers overseas.

dekanta.com
amazon.co.jp
rakuten.co.jp

USA

Oakland

UMAMI MART This cute shop started as a Japanese kitchen-supply store selling food and kitchenware, but has now expanded to alcohol, with offerings of Japanese sake, shochu, whisky and beer. They do in-store events if you happen to be in the Oakland area, and also sell online throughout California.

815 Broadway, Oakland; umamimart.com
Monday–Saturday 12 pm–7 pm
Sunday 11 am–5 pm

San Francisco

TRUE SAKE The first dedicated sake store in the US, this remains the largest sake-focused liquor store nationwide. They carry everything from *futsushu* to seasonal *namazake* and have an online store if you are can receive alcohol delivery by post.

560 Hayes Street, San Francisco; truesake.com
Monday–Thursday 12 pm–7 pm
Saturday 11 am–7 pm; Sunday 11 pm–6 pm

Chicago

CHINA PLACE LIQUOR CITY Situated in a strip mall in Chicago's Chinatown, this shop has a surprisingly large selection of Japanese sake, shochu and umeshu. It's a bit of a hike from downtown, so it's probably best to drive.

2105 South China Place, Chicago
tel. 312 225-8118
Daily 11 am–7:45 pm

Boston

RELIABLE MARKET When in provincial cities like Boston, go to where the immigrants live. In Boston, you'll have to head out to Somerville to find the city's best sake selection at this Korean-Japanese super market. They also have craft beer and ramen events (not always together).

45 Union Square, Somerville
facebook.com/Reliable-Market-129263773805615
Daily 9:30 am–9 pm

New York

AMBASSADOR WINES Ambassador has made a strong commitment to Japanese alcohol with the installation of a walk-in sake cooler and an entire wall for shochu and awamori. They also carry Japanese whiskies and sometimes have rare bottlings.

1020 2nd Avenue, New York
theambassadorsofwine.com
Monday–Thursday 9 am–10 pm
Friday 9 am–12 am; Saturday 10 am–12 am
Sunday 12 pm–8 pm

ASTOR WINES & SPIRITS Astor is the largest liquor store in Manhattan and carries a wide selection of Japanese alcohol. They also have a dedicated classroom and host frequent classes for the public and bar professionals. Astor also has an online store if you can receive booze by mail.
399 Lafayette Street, New York
astorwines.com
Monday–Saturday 9 am–9 pm
Sunday 12 pm–6 pm

LANDMARK WINE & SPIRITS Landmark carries the widest selection of Japanese shochu in the United States with between 80 and 100 brands available at any given time. The back wall of the shop is completely dedicated to Japanese alcohol. The only giveaway that this isn't your usual neighborhood liquor shop are the sake barrels in the window.
167 W. 23rd Street, New York
wineon23.com
Monday–Saturday 11 am–10 pm
Sunday 12 pm–8 pm

SAKAYA Rick Smith and Hiroko Furukawa run this dedicated sake shop (*sakaya* means "sake shop") with a small selection of shochu and fruit liqueurs, but with a very large selection of highly curated sake. They hold frequent in-store tastings to introduce sake to their neighborhood. Rick and Hiroko have also developed very good relationships with many sake brewers thanks to trips to Japan when they close the shop for a couple weeks for the annual pilgrimage.
324 E. 9th Street, New York; sakayanyc.com

Seattle
SAKE NOMI This small sake shop is a labor of love for the owners, Johnnie and Taiko Stroud, who have gained a strong reputation in the Pacific Northwest for their sake knowledge and outstanding selection.
76 S. Washington Street, Seattle
sakenomi.us
Tuesday–Saturday 2 pm–10 pm
Sunday 2 pm–6 pm

Other US locations
MITSUWA Mitsuwa is a large Japanese supermarket chain with 11 locations across the US. Seven stores are in California, while the others are in Plano, TX; Chicago, IL; Fort Lee, NJ; and Waikiki, HI. They carry a variety of sake, shochu, chu-hai, plum wine and Japanese beer. Some locations carry Japanese whisky, depending on local laws. They usually have dine-in food courts serving a variety of Japanese food, though drinking is usually not permitted on premises. Hours vary by location. mitsuwa.com

UWAJIMAYA Uwajimaya is a Washington State–based Japanese supermarket with locations in Seattle, Bellevue and Renton in Washington as well as Beaverton, OR. They carry sake, shochu, Japanese beer, umeshu and some Japanese whisky (where permitted). Hours vary by location. uwajimaya.com

USA online
astorwines.com (New York)
mmsake.com (California)
sakayanyc.com (New York)
sake.nu (California)
sakesocial.com
truesake.com (California)
umamimart.com (California)

UK

London
HEDONISM WINES Situated in the ultra-posh Mayfair neighborhood, this is a place for absolute debauchery. With one of the largest wine selections in London, they also carry a dizzying array of Japanese whisky and a healthy selection of sake, as well as the occasional shochu, awamori, umeshu and Japanese wine. UK residents, you're in luck: they have an online store.
3-7 Davies Street, Mayfair, London
hedonism.co.uk
Monday–Saturday 10 am–9 pm
Sunday 12 pm–6 pm

JAPAN CENTRE Japan Centre, operated by the UK's largest importer of Japanese goods, has their flagship store in central London and recently opened the Ichiba Marketplace, the largest Japanese food hall in Europe.
35b Panton Street, London; japancentre.com
Monday–Saturday 10:30 am–9:30 pm
Sunday 11 am–8 pm

ICHIBA MARKETPLACE
Unit 0220, Relay Square, Westfield, London ichibalondon.com
Monday–Saturday 10 am–11 pm
Sunday 12 pm–6 pm

UK online
japancentre.com
hedonism.co.uk
amazon.co.uk/beer-wine-spirits
thewhiskyexchange.com

GERMANY

GINZA BERLIN While German bars or retail shops were beyond the scope of this English language guide, Ginza Berlin's online store has an English language page and an impressive selection of Japanese alcohol available for sale throughout the EU.
ginza-berlin.com/?lang=en

AUSTRALIA

TOKYO MART/ FUJI MART The Jun Pacific Group has a chain of Japanese grocery stores with robust selections of sake, plum wine, beer, whisky and a splash of shochu. Their shop is called Tokyo Mart in Sydney and Fuji Mart elsewhere in Australia (Melbourne, Perth, Brisbane, and Gold Coast).
junpacific.com/tokyomart/

Australia online
sakeonline.com.au
sakejapan.com.au

Back endpaper Ginza Lion, Tokyo (see page 147)

Photo Credits

All jacket photography Stephen Lyman
Front endpaper Chris Bunting
Page 1 PD-US-Expired. Kitagawa Utamaro, from Wikimedia Commons. Public Domain.
Page 2, page 3 Stephen Lyman.
Page 6 Chris Bunting
Page 8 Tatsuo Yamashita 2014, flckr Creative Commons
Page 9 ©2009 Stefano Bassetti
Page 10 PD-US-Expired. Toyohara Chikanobu, from Wikimedia Commons. Public Domain.
Page 12 Chris Bunting
Page 13 top Prasit Rodphan, Dreamstime.com
Page 13 bottom Stephen Lyman
Page 14 Joshua Davenport, Shutterstock.com
Page 15 Chris Bunting
Page 16 top Andres Garcia Martin, Dreamstime.com; **Page 16 bottom** Eiji Ienaga, flckr Creative Commons
Page 17 LMspencer, Shutterstock.com
Pages 18–19, top row, left to right ©Q. Sawami/JNTO; ©John Puma; Washu Bar Engawa PR; Stephen Lyman; Provided by and ©Waseda University Library; Stephen Lyman
Page 18 bottom row, bottom left photo Stephen Lyman; **page 18 bottom half: top, center and left** Chris Bunting
Page 19 bottom row, left ©Todd Van Horne; **right** ©Adam Staffa
Page 20 ©Ysbrand Rogge
Page 21 PD-US-Expired. Utagawa Kuniyoshi, from Wikimedia Commons. Public Domain.
Page 22 left Teow Cek Chuan, Shutterstock.com; **Page 22 right** Stephen Lyman
Page 23 tamu1500, Shutterstock.com
Page 24 ©Q. Sawami/JNTO
Page 25 Courtesy of the American Friends of the British Museum. Photo ©The Trustees of the British Museum
Page 26 left ©Tony McNicol; **page 26 right** Chris Bunting
Page 28–29 Stephen Lyman
Page 30 left Chris Bunting; **page 30 right** ©Tokyofoodcast.com
Page 31 Stephen Lyman
Page 32, 33 Chris Bunting
Page 34–35, 36, 37 left Stephen Lyman
Page 37 right Chris Bunting
Page 38 left ©John Puma
Page 38 right, page 39, page 40 right Stephen Lyman
Page 40 left maxpixel.net/Nature-Mountain-Snow-Frost-Frozen-Cold-Winter-3082076
Page 41 ©Anthony Rose
Page 42 bottom Chris Bunting, **top** Stephen Lyman
Page 43 left PHGCOM, Wikimedia Commons
Page 43 right, page 44, 45 Chris Bunting
Page 46, page 47 top right, bottom right ©Joseph Overbey

Page 47 left Stephen Lyman
Page 48 ©Joseph Overbey
Page 49 courtesy Shirakane distillery
Page 50 left ©Joseph Overbey
Page 50 right Stephen Lyman
Page 51, page 52 top Chris Bunting
Page 51 bottom Stephen Lyman
Page 54 ©Joseph Overbey
Page 55 bottom Chris Bunting
Page 56 top Stephen Lyman
Page 57 bonchan, Shutterstock.com
Page 58 greanggai hommalai, Shutterstock.com
Page 59 ©Joseph Overbey
Page 60 top ©Matt Bruck; **page 60 middle** Stephen Lyman
Page 60–61 bottom ©Joseph Overbey
Page 62, page 63 top right; left Stephen Lyman
Page 63 bottom right Chris Bunting
Page 64, 65 Stephen Lyman
Page 66 © Nathan A. Keirn
Page 67 top Chris Bunting; **page 67 bottom** Stephen Lyman
Page 68 Chris Bunting
Page 70 Stephen Lyman
Page 71 Chris Bunting
Page 72, page 73 top Stephen Lyman
Page 73 middle and bottom Chris Bunting
Page 74 top ©459i, flckr; **page 74 bottom** Chris Bunting
Page 75 Stephen Lyman
Page 76 top Chris Bunting
Page 76 bottom, page 77 bottom Stephen Lyman
Page 77 top sunabesyou, Shutterstock.com
Page 78 bottom pheeby, Shutterstock.com
Page 78–79 top Stephen Lyman
Page 79 inset ©Todd Van Horne
Page 80 ©Nancy Singleton Hachisu
Page 81, page 82–83 top ©Todd Van Horne
Page 82 bottom Stephen Lyman
Page 83–84, top row left to right 1 and 2 ©Suntory Holdings Ltd; 3 and 4 Chris Bunting; 5 ©Suntory Holdings Ltd
Page 83 bottom left Stephen Lyman; **insert and bottom right** Chris Bunting
Page 84 center and bottom Chris Bunting
Page 86 bottom PD-US-Expired. Gasshukoku suishi teitoku kōjōgaki (Oral statement by the American Navy admiral), artist unknown. Library of Congress digital ID cph.3g10708. Accessed through Wikimedia Commons. Public Domain.
Page 86 top, page 87 Stephen Lyman
Page 88 Chris Bunting
Page 89 left Per Bjorkdahl, Dreamstime.com
Page 89 right Stephen Lyman
Page 89 bottom, page 90 ©Suntory Holdings Ltd
Page 91 top PD-US-Expired. From Wikimedia Commons. Public Domain.
Page 91 bottom, page 92, page 93 left Chris Bunting
Page 93 right ©Suntory Holdings Ltd
Page 94–95 Chris Bunting
Page 96 Stephen Lyman
Page 97, 98 Chris Bunting
Page 99 left Stephen Lyman; **page 99 top right, bottom right,** Chris Bunting
Page 100–105 Stephen Lyman
Page 106 Geiko Miharu of Japanexpertna.se 2014
Page 107, page 108 bottom Chris Bunting
Page 108 top ©Coedo

Page 109 bottom right provided by Sapporo Lion
Page 109 top left, top right; page 110 Chris Bunting
Page 111 top left Chris Bunting; **page 111 bottom left, top right** Stephen Lyman; **page 111** ©Jeff Cioletti
Page 112 top left Chris Bunting; **page 112 top right, bottom right** Stephen Lyman; **page 112 bottom left** urbanbuzz, Shutterstock.com
Page 113 top Stephen Lyman; **page 113 bottom** Yangxiong, Shutterstock.com
Page 114 Chris Bunting
Page 115 top ©Coedo; **page 115 bottom** Stephen Lyman
Page 116 ©Suntory Holdings Ltd
Page 117 top Stephen Lyman
Page 118 bottom, page 118 ©Takaharu Mori
Page 119 courtesy Shiroyama Hotel
Page 120 ©Suntory Holdings Ltd
Page 121 Chris Bunting
Page 122 left and center Chris Bunting; **page 122 right, page 123 left** Stephen Lyman
Page 123 right Chris Bunting; **page 123 bottom** Stephen Lyman
Page 124 top Chris Bunting; **page 124 center** Stephen Lyman; **page 124 right** Ng Zheng Hui, Shutterstock.com; **page 124 bottom** Takashi Images, Shutterstock.com
Page 125 Stephen Lyman
Page 126 Chris Bunting
Page 127 Evgeny Starkov, Shutterstock.com
Page 128 Stephen Lyman
Page 129 Chris Bunting
Page 130 PD-US-Expired. Kobayakawa Kiyoshi, from Wikimedia Commons. Public Domain.
Page 131 Stephen Lyman
Page 132 top Courtesy Park Hyatt; **page 132 bottom and right, page 133** Stephen Lyman
Page 134 top left ©John Puma; **page 134 top center and right, bottom left** Stephen Lyman
Page 135 top left courtesy Washu Bar Engawa
Page 136 top right, page 136 top left; bottom Stephen Lyman; **page 136 top center** ©John Puma; **page 136 top right** ©Adam Staffa
Page 137 left Stephen Lyman
Page 138 right Courtesy Shibumi
Page 138–139, page 140 top left and center, bottom Stephen Lyman
Page 140 top right ©Ivan Munoz
Page 140 bottom © Tobin Geidemann
Page 141 left and center Chris Bunting; **page 141 right, page 142 left and center** Stephen Lyman
Page 142 right Chris Bunting
Page 143 left and center Stephen Lyman; **page 143 right, page 144 left and right** Chris Bunting
Page 144 center, page 145, page 146 left Stephen Lyman
Page 146 center Courtesy Canon; **page 146 right** Stephen Lyman
Page 147 left, right, bottom Chris Bunting; **page 147** Towa and Hitachino, Stephen Lyman **page 148 left and center** Stephen Lyman
Page 148 right ©Jeff Cioletti
Page 149, page 150–151, page 152 left and right Stephen Lyman
Page 152 center Courtesy Speak Low
Page 153 Chris Bunting
Page 157 Stephen Lyman
Back endpaper Chris Bunting

Published by Tuttle Publishing, an imprint of Periplus Editions (HK) Ltd

www.tuttlepublishing.com

ISBN: 978-4-8053-1495-1

Distributed by

North America, Latin America & Europe
Tuttle Publishing
364 Innovation Drive, North Clarendon, VT 05759-9436 U.S.A.
Tel: 1 (802) 773-8930, Fax: 1 (802) 773-6993
info@tuttlepublishing.com, www.tuttlepublishing.com

Japan
Tuttle Publishing
Yaekari Building 3rd Floor, 5-4-12 Osaki, Shinagawa-ku, Tokyo 141-0032
Tel: (81) 3 5437-0171, Fax: (81) 3 5437-0755
sales@tuttle.co.jp, www.tuttle.co.jp

Asia Pacific
Berkeley Books Pte. Ltd.,
3 Kallang Sector #04-01, Singapore 349278
Tel: (65) 67412178; Fax: (65) 67412179
inquiries@periplus.com.sg; www.tuttlepublishing.com

22 21 20   10 9 8 7 6 5 4 3 2

Printed in Hong Kong   2003EP

TUTTLE PUBLISHING® is a registered trademark of Tuttle Publishing, a division of Periplus Editions (HK) Ltd

The Tuttle Story "Books to Span the East and West"

Our core mission at Tuttle Publishing is to create books which bring people together one page at a time. Tuttle was founded in 1832 in the small New England town of Rutland, Vermont (USA). Our fundamental values remain as strong today as they were then—to publish best-in-class books informing the English-speaking world about the countries and peoples of Asia. The world has become a smaller place today and Asia's economic, cultural and political influence has expanded, yet the need for meaningful dialogue and information about this diverse region has never been greater. Since 1948, Tuttle has been a leader in publishing books on the cultures, arts, cuisines, languages and literatures of Asia. Our authors and photographers have won numerous awards and Tuttle has published thousands of books on subjects ranging from martial arts to paper crafts. We welcome you to explore the wealth of information available on Asia at **www.tuttlepublishing.com.**

A Special Thanks

A very special thanks to our wives who put up with this obsession with Japanese booze. Rumi Takaki, from Oita in Kyushu, is not much of a shochu drinker, but she does like her wine. Ayako Yoshino hails from Kanagawa near Tokyo and likes to drink everything. Also thanks to Chris & Ayako's boys, George and Dan, who fed Stephen on a visit to the UK.

We would also like to thank those who have helped us along the way. A book like this is not a one (or two) man effort. The project could not have happened without the support of Tuttle publisher Eric Oey who agreed to take a chance on us. Editor Cathy Layne was incredibly patient and supportive throughout the editorial process. This was Stephen's first book and he couldn't have done it without the guidance and support of professional writers and friends Jeff Cioletti, Jamie Feldmar, Hannah Kirshner, and Matt Gross. We are indebted to all of the alcohol producers who opened their doors to us and were extremely generous with their knowledge and passion for their craft: Toshiro Manzen and his sons Naoyuki & Hiroyuki, Bryan & Sayumi Baird, Brandon Doughan, Naoya Honbo, Kohtaroh Kinoshita, Kazuhiro Kinoshita, Yoshitsugu Komasa, Shinya Nakamura, Brian Polen, Masahiko Shimoda, Michiaki Shinozaki, Takuya Sunagawa, Tekkan Wakamatsu, Yoshihiko Yamamoto, and Kentaro Yagi.

Along the way we've also received massive education from our sake sensei John Gauntner, Jamie Graves, Oliver Hilton Johnson, Chris Johnson, Jessica Joly, John McCarthy, Chizuko Niikawa-Helton, John Puma, Andrew Richardson, Monica Samuels, Timothy Sullivan, Masahiro Takeda; shochu & awamori sensei Justin Elliott Cobb, Jesse Falowitz, Bill Gunther, Taeko Ichioka, Akiko Kadota, Mai Kumagami, Chuck Malone, Tetsuro Miyazaki, Aaron Neal, Aya Otake, Christopher Pellegrini, Kenji Tomozoe, Ryo Uchida, Toshio Ueno, Shinichi Washino; umeshu sensei Nancy Singleton Hachisu, Todd VanHorne; whisky sensei Stefan VanEycken, Joseph Overbey, Yuno Hayashi, Eric Swanson; beer sensei Rob Bright, Garrett DeOrio, Joe Robson; wine sensei Denis Gastin; cocktail sensei Joshin Atone, Frank Cisneros, Shingo Gokan, Kenta Goto, Eric Konon, Joji Watanabe; Tokyo Sensei Ben Johnson, and our actual sensei Professor Takaharu Mori (wine), Professor Koichi "Raku" Sakaguchi (shochu), Professor Shuichi Matsuda (Kyoto bars), and Professor Norimasa Nakamura (Osaka bars).

We are further indebted to those who helped us with bar research throughout the world: Miho Arai, Bret Larson, Soki Li, Sachiko Miyagi, Tomoko Miyata, Hitomi Shibata, Brad Smith, Sayaka Takahashi, Mimi Takizawa, Markus Tschuschnig and those who helped us with acquiring photographs: Fuko Chubachi, Tobin Giedemann, Kenji Mori, Ivan Munoz, Adam Staffa, Jun Takanarita, Yoko Uchida, and Justin Wilson. Very special thanks also to Dean and Janet Weston and their little monsters, Casper and Miles, for providing shelter when in Tokyo for bar research.